T0374738

Modern China and Opium

Modern China and Opium
A Reader

ALAN BAUMLER
Editor

Ann Arbor

THE UNIVERSITY OF MICHIGAN PRESS

Copyright © by the University of Michigan 2001
Published in the United States of America by
The University of Michigan Press
Manufactured in the United States of America
♾ Printed on acid-free paper

2004   2003   2002   2001   4   3   2   1

A CIP catalog record for this book is available from the British Library.

Library of Congress Cataloging-in-Publication Data

Modern china and opium : a reader / Alan Baumler, editor.
        p.   cm.
    ISBN 0-472-09768-7 (alk. paper) — ISBN 0-472-06768-0 (pbk. : alk. paper)
    1. Opium habit—China.   I. Title.
HV5816 .B38   2002
394.1'4—dc21   2001003727

Acknowledgments

I would like to thank some of the many people who have assisted me in producing this book. Curtis Bradford, Tim Brook, Garvin Davenport, Ingrid Erickson, and Marcia LaBrenz gave inspiration and assistance in selecting and editing the readings. The anonymous readers provided helpful comments about both the scope and the details of the project. Students, especially Daniel Seals and Evereth Aldana, provided suggestions on earlier versions of some of the readings. Robert Wilson of the Spatial Sciences Research Center at Indiana University of Pennsylvania created the map of Guangxi. Jason and Rachel provided innumerable insights about all sorts of things. My wife, Shari, provided invaluable assistance in assembling this book, which is only one of the many things for which I am grateful to her.

Contents

U S S R

MONGOLIA

HEILUNGKIANG

KIRIN

CHAHAR

JEHOL

FENGTIEN

SUIYUAN

Kalgan   Jehol
Yellow R. Tatung   Liao R. •Mukden
                              Antung Yalu R.
                    PEKING   LIAOTUNG
                    Hai-ho
            Paoting○ Tientsin   Dairen
                    HOPEI   Yellow R.
Yenan   Taiyuan   Chefoo
        SHANSI
Lanchow   Hua   ▲Tsinan   Tsingtao
        Shan   Tai Shan   Kiaochow Bay
Wei R. SHENSI   SHANTUNG
Chialing R. Sian▲ Loyang Sung Kaifeng   Yellow R.
                    Shan   (1938-46)
Hanchung   HONAN ANHWEI   KIANGSU
                    Nanking   Yangchow
        Hsiang-yang   Chinkiang
SZECHWAN Han R.   JAPAN
        HUPEI   Ho-fei Wu-hu T'ai L.
        Wuhan   Shanghai
O-mei Chengtu Ichang   Anking Soochow
Shan Chungking Yangtze R. Yochow Hangchow Ningpo
                Lu-Shan Ching-te-
        Tungting L. Poyang chen CHEKIANG
                L. Nanchang
        Changsha   Wenchow
        Hsiang-t'an Heng Shan▲
KWEICHOW HUNAN   KIANGSI
        Hsiang R. Kan R. Min R.
Kunming Kweiyang   Foochow
        Kweilin○   FUKIEN
YUNNAN   Ch'üan-chou Taipei Keelung
        KWANGSI   Amoy TAIWAN
Mengtze Wuchow KWANGTUNG   Tainan
Nanning West R. Canton Waichow Swatow
Hanoi   Hong Kong
        Pakhoi Macao
FRENCH   Kwangchouwan
INDO-CHINA

Hainan I.

SIAM

Provinces of China under the Republic
--- Province boundaries
○ Province capitals
• Other cities
▲ Famous mountains

0   500   1000 km
0   500 miles

Reprinted with the permission of Cambridge University Press.

Introduction

China and opium have been synonymous for non-Chinese throughout the nineteenth and twentieth centuries. In Western caricatures the decadent Chinaman was always portrayed with an opium pipe. This connection between opium and China's troubles was also evident to Chinese. Modern Chinese textbooks begin the modern period of Chinese history with the Opium Wars, and opium itself is connected to all of the major pathologies that beset China in the disastrous century that followed. Opium had come to China with the British, and Chinese could and did draw the natural conclusion that opium was a tool of foreign imperialism, deliberately intended to weaken the Chinese people. This supposed *duhua zhengce* (policy of poisoning) was talked about less frequently as the British withdrew from the trade in the early twentieth century, but it returned to the forefront as the Japanese began selling opium, morphine, and heroin in China in the 1920s. Opium was also connected, again accurately, to warlordism. The regional militarists, who were the most notable feature of Chinese politics under the Republic, all profited from the opium trade, and many could not have existed without it. China's economic backwardness was partially explained by opium's drain on the nation's finances, and China's overall status as the "Sick Man of Asia" was linked to the effects of opium on the health of the people. Strong political leadership was seen as necessary to overcome these problems, and all Chinese governments of the twentieth century have been judged, both at home and abroad, in part on their ability to deal with the opium problem. When the Chinese Communists attacked the opium trade after 1949 they portrayed it as a holdover from the old Warlord/semicolonial period and viewed their triumph over it as a victory of a new, modern, communist China over the forces of darkness, both foreign and domestic.

The story of opium and modern China is more complex than this rousing narrative would have it. The Qing reformer Kang Youwei attacked both opium smoking and foot binding as evil customs that would hold back the development of a new Chinese nation and citizenry. Foot binding proved to be a far less resilient custom than opium smoking, however. Opium created a powerful set of economic and political interests that assured that it could not be simply set aside. Opium was not just a foreign poison being used for the destruction of the Chinese people. The English and later the Japanese did not push drugs on the Chinese people; it was Chinese desire to smoke opium that drew it in and Chinese demand that encouraged Chinese to produce it. Opium production, use, and sale became important parts of China's society and economy, and opium taxes became a vital part of state revenue. Poppies could bring a Chinese peasant ten times the income wheat could, and especially in remote regions of West China it became a crucial part of Chinese agriculture. Opium was also a trade good, both wholesale and retail. Merchants could make enormous profits, and officials and the state itself could profit from protecting them. Opium played an important role in China's nineteenth-century commercial expansion both as a way of accumulating capital and as a form of capital. Opium was a high-value trade good that could be taxed with minimal state investment, leading countless Chinese governments, from the county level through the national, to make steady efforts to control and tax the trade in opium. The Qing, the Communists, the Guomindang under both Sun Yat-sen and Chiang Kai-shek, Wang Jingwei, and all the warlords sold opium while claiming that their ultimate goal was elimination of the trade.

All this opium moved around China for two reasons: people wanted to make money from it, and they wanted to smoke it. As a result of both of these motivations, opium sank deep into Chinese society. Merchants who dealt in opium may or may not have been disreputable, but they were not criminals. Opium smoking was widespread in all strata of Chinese society. R. K. Newman estimates that 70 percent of Chinese men and 50 percent of Chinese women in the Late Qing used opium at least occasionally.[1] Opium was offered to guests in homes and was smoked in all sorts of public and private spaces. Opium dens (*yan guan*) were places to socialize and interact as well as smoke opium. In parts of West China the opium harvest was a major festival, and fathers would encourage their children's first breath of a puff of opium smoke. Although the blame for bringing opium to China might be laid on the foreigners, it was very much a domestic problem by 1900.

Calling opium use a "problem" is to adopt modern terminology. Current statistics about drug use make it seem that China had a serious drug problem in the nineteenth and twentieth centuries. Yet, identifying opium use as a drug problem was possible only after a long process of intellectual development. The first Chinese campaigns against opium, in the 1840s, were aimed as much at controlling China's coasts and preventing the outflow of silver as they were at eliminating opium use. Opium use was seen as potentially dangerous, but neither the modern idea of addiction nor the idea that opium addiction was an imminent danger to the entire society was present. These positions were being developed in the West and would be imported to China by missionaries.[2] It was only at the very end of the nineteenth century, just as Chinese began to believe that there was an international struggle for dominance going on and that they were losing, that modern ideas about drugs first began to take hold in China. Emerging Western discourses on drugs claimed that drug use was progressive and an individual's drug use would inevitably increase until it destroyed the individual. Under the influence of the germ model of disease it was also assumed that addiction would spread throughout the nation and destroy the entire society. Opium was thus a threat to the individual and the nation, and no person or nation could be considered truly modern until they had flushed this poison from their system.

In the decade before the Revolution of 1911 the Qing court presided over a series of far-reaching reforms that laid the foundation for China's modern state, while at the same time Chinese society, especially in the cities, began to change rapidly. Although some of the New Policies reforms were drastic, such as abolition of the exam system in 1905, most of them were elite centered, asking ordinary Chinese to do little more than pay higher taxes to support new institutions. Opium suppression was one of the most successful reforms and one of the few that tried to change the lives of ordinary people. The Chinese state had traditionally had little contact with the day-to-day lives of the people; now all Chinese modernizers would be faced with the task of finding ways to mobilize and control people's behavior at a level that had never been attempted before.

The Qing and Republican governments had considerable success in reducing the amount of opium produced and smoked in China and convinced the British to end legal imports of Indian opium. After 1916, however, opium began to return. This was in part due to the collapse of order that came with the Warlord period; the state was no longer able to impose its will on society. More important, however, the state was no longer sure what its will was. The financial lure of opium was still there, and all Chinese states succumbed to it. Reformers denounced this as treason and in return got false promises from governments that they would not make a single cent of profit from opium. In practice this promise was impossible to keep. Opium was a crucial source of the money that made the warlord system work, and to denounce it was simply to leave the profits to rivals. No Chinese state had the power to entirely ban opium, and for most the solution was some sort of state opium sales system aimed at eventual prohibition. Of course, in the short run such a system would be indistinguishable from a system aimed at profit. States had to find ways to both control the trade in this slippery substance and convince critics that their motives were pure.

Chinese people proved less willing than reformers would have liked to abandon the pleasures and profits of opium. As local governments relaxed suppression and even encouraged poppy growing in the 1920s, production returned to old levels. Opium smoking does not seem to have been as socially acceptable as it had been before the New Policies reforms, but it was still ubiquitous. Chinese states and Chinese citizens clearly did not accept official positions on the dangers of opium and their own roles as a modern state and modern citizens. In different contexts both new and old ideas about opium were applied. For example, a grandfather's opium smoking might have been seen as a relatively harmless personal failing. On the other hand, Japanese opium and heroin smugglers clearly fit the model of imperialist attempts to corrupt China and her people. That Chinese people felt free to apply different sets of ideas to the use of opium in different contexts is not surprising, since the ideas of the anti-opium crusaders themselves were less than coherent. Was the root of the problem the weak will of the individual user, or was it the mere presence of opium that could corrupt anyone? Were opium smokers and growers victims or criminals? Policy would vary drastically as different ways of understanding opium and drugs were emphasized.

The Guomindang state went further than any before it in coming to grips with the opium trade. Its core policy was to take control of the Yangzi River opium route and gradually expand its control from there. This policy served to restrict the independence of the local powerholders on both ends who produced and distributed the opium and brought revenue to the central government while denying it to rivals. All of these achievements supported the Nationalists' state-building goals but could easily be portrayed as more efficient versions of the warlords' opium-related depredations of the Chinese people. The Nationalists' control of the opium trade led to concrete measures to eliminate opium use, however. Distribution channels, as well as production, were reduced. Opium merchants were put under tight state control to try to eliminate smuggling. Most important, opium users were registered and were encouraged and eventually forced to give up opium smoking. These two successes fed off of each other: the state's control over the opium trade made suppression possible, and the state's actions to suppress the trade legitimated its control over opium, giving the state solutions to both its state-building and nation-building problems.

The final solution to China's opium problem was provided by the Communists. Like other governments, the Communists had traded in opium, although less than many other governments. Also like other governments the

Communists had proclaimed sweeping plans to rid the nation of opium. After 1949 they had considerable success at this, in part because of the many techniques they borrowed by the Nationalists but also because of the tremendous effectiveness of Communist methods of controlling individual behavior. Presently, although opium and drug use has returned to China due to the relaxation of social control since the death of Mao, it has returned in the form of a social vice, not as a fundamental part of China's political and economic system.

Opium touches on most of the themes that were important in modern Chinese history. Imperialism in both the nineteenth and twentieth centuries, China's international position, local versus central control, state attempts to regulate individual behavior and inculcate new ideas of citizenship, attempts of private individuals and the public sphere to control the behavior of the state, and attempts at modern economic development were all tied to the opium trade, thus making opium an excellent way to examine the complexities behind these abstractions.

NOTES

1. R. K. Newman, "Opium Smoking in Late Imperial China: A Reconsideration," *Modern Asian Studies* 29, no. 4 (1995): 765–94.

2. Virginia Berridge and Griffith Edwards, *Opium and the People: Opiate Use in Nineteenth-Century England* (New Haven, CT: Yale University Press, 1987).

The Debate on the Legalization of Opium, 1836

These documents relate to the debate that took place in the Qing court in 1836 on the topic of legalizing opium. Although opium could no longer be legally imported into Canton, it was widely smuggled up and down the coast. Opium imports and silver exports had been increasing rapidly, and the government seemed to be losing control of the coast.

Both sides in the debate reflect the limited knowledge that the Qing court had of the outside world and the limits of its powers, both in controlling the foreigners and in controlling its own people. The participants in the debate saw the problem much differently than did the leaders of the twentieth-century anti-opium campaigns, as both the prohibitionists and the legalizers assessed the threat of opium very differently than would later writers. Even Zhu Zun makes a number of statements that would have been attacked in the twentieth century, and it is hard to imagine anyone after 1900 taking many of the positions Xu Naiji takes. The debate was decided by the emperor in favor of prohibition. Lin Zexu was sent to Canton to deal with the matter, and the First Opium War resulted.

Memorial to the Emperor, Proposing to Legalize
Its Importation

Xu Naiji, vice president of the sacrificial court, presents the following memorial in regard to opium, to show that the more severe the interdicts against it are made, the more widely do the evils arising therefrom spread; and that it is right urgently to request that a change be made in the arrangements respecting it, to which end he earnestly entreats his sacred majesty to cast a glance hereon and to issue secret orders for a faithful investigation of the subject.

I would humbly represent that opium was originally ranked among medicines; its qualities are stimulant; it also checks excessive secretions and prevents the evil effects of noxious vapors. When anyone is long habituated to inhaling it, it becomes necessary to resort to it at regular intervals, and the habit of using it, being inveterate, is destructive of time, injurious to property, and yet dear to one even as life. Of those who use it to great excess, the breath becomes feeble, the body wasted, the face sallow, the teeth black: the individuals themselves clearly see the evil effects of it yet cannot refrain from it. It is indeed indispensably necessary to enact severe prohibitions in order to eradicate so vile a practice.

On inquiry I find that there are three kinds of opium: one is called company's; the outer covering of it is black, and hence it is also called "black earth"; it comes from Bengal; a second kind is called "white-skin" and comes from Bombay; the third kind is called "red-skin"and comes from Madras.[1] These are places that belong to England.

In Qianlong's reign, as well as previously, opium was inserted in the tariff of Canton as a medicine, subject to a duty of three taels per hundred catties, with an additional charge of two taels, four mace, and five candareens under the name of charge per package. After this, it was prohibited. In the first year of Jiaqing, those found guilty of smoking opium were subject only to the punishment of the pillory and bamboo. Now they have, in the course of time, become liable to the severest penalties, transportation in various degrees, and death after the ordinary continuance in prison. Yet the smokers of the drug have increased in number, and the practice has spread throughout almost the whole empire. In Qianlong's and the previous reigns, when opium passed through the customhouse and paid a duty, it was given into the hands of the hong merchants in exchange for tea and other goods. But at the present time, the prohibitions of government being most strict against it, none dare openly to exchange goods for it; all secretly purchase it with money. In the reign of Jiaqing there arrived, it may be, some hundred chests annually. The number has now increased to upward of 20,000 chests, containing each a hundred catties. The "black earth," which is the best, sells for about 800 dollars, foreign money, per chest; the "white-skin," which is next in quality, for about 600 dollars; and the last, or "red-skin," for about 400 dollars. The total quantity sold during the year amounts in value to ten and some odd million dollars, so that, in reckoning the dollar at seven mace, standard weight of silver, the annual waste of money somewhat exceeds ten million taels. Formerly, the barbarian merchants brought foreign money to China, which, being paid in exchange for goods, was a source of pecuniary advantage to the people of all the seaboard provinces. But latterly, the barbarian merchants have clandestinely sold opium for money; which has rendered it unnecessary for them to import foreign silver. Thus foreign money has been going out of the country, while none comes into it.

During two centuries, the government has now maintained peace and, by fostering the people, has greatly promoted the increase of wealth and opulence among them. With joy we witness the economical rule of our august sovereign, an example to the whole empire. Right it is that yellow gold be common as the dust.

Always in times past, a tael of pure silver exchanged for nearly about 1,000 coined cash, but of late years the same sum has borne the value of 1,200 or 1,300 cash: thus the price of silver rises but does not fall. In the salt agency, the price of salt is paid in cash, while the duties are paid in silver: now the salt merchants have all become involved, and the existing state of the salt trade in every province is abject in the extreme. How is this occasioned but by the unnoticed oozing out of silver?[2] If the easily exhaustible stores of the central spring go to fill up the wide and fathomless gulf of the outer seas, gradually pouring themselves out from day to day, and from month to month, we shall shortly be reduced to a state of which I cannot bear to speak.

Is it proposed entirely to cut off the foreign trade and turn to remove the root to dam up the source of the evil? The celestial dynasty would not, indeed, hesitate to relinquish the few millions of duties arising therefrom. But all the nations of the West have had a general market open to their ships for upward of a thousand years; while the dealers in opium are the English alone, it would be wrong, for the sake of cutting off the English trade, to cut off that of all the other nations. Besides, the hundreds of thousands of people living on the seacoast depend wholly on trade for their livelihood, and how are they to be disposed of? Moreover, the barbarian ships, being on the high seas, can repair to any island that may be selected as an entrepot, and the native seagoing vessels can meet them there; it is then impossible to cut off the trade. Of late years, the foreign vessels have visited all the ports of Fujian, Zhejiang Jiangnan, Shandong, even to Tianjin and Manchuria, for the purpose of selling opium. And although at once expelled by the local authorities, yet it is reported that the quantity sold by them was not small. Thus it appears that, though the commerce of Canton should be cut off, yet it will not be possible to prevent the clandestine introduction of merchandise.

It is said that the daily increase of opium is owing to the negligence of officers in enforcing the interdicts? The laws and enactments are the means that extortionate underlings and worthless vagrants employ to benefit themselves; and the more complete the laws are, the greater and more numerous are the bribes paid to the extortionate underlings, and the more subtle are the schemes of such worthless vagrants. In the first year of Daoguang, the governor of Guangdong and Guangxi, Yuan, proceeded with all the rigor of the law against the head of the opium establishment, then at Macao. The consequence was that foreigners having no one with whom to place their opium proceeded to Lintin to sell it. This place is within the precincts of the provincial government and has a free communication by water on all sides. Here are constantly anchored seven or eight large ships, in which the opium is kept, and which are therefore called "receiving ships." At Canton there are brokers of the drug, who are called "melters." These pay the price of the drug into the hands of the resident foreigners, who give them orders for the delivery of the opium from the receiving ships. There are carrying boats plying up and down the river; and these are vulgarly called "fast-crabs" and "scrambling-dragons." They are well armed with guns and other weapons and are manned with some scores of desperadoes, who ply their oars as if they were wings to fly with. All the customhouses and military posts that they pass are largely bribed. If they happen to encounter any of the armed cruising boats, they are so audacious as to resist, and slaughter and carnage ensue. The late governor Lu, on one occasion, having directed the commodore Zun Yuchang to cooperate with the district magistrate of Xiangshan, they captured a boat containing opium to the amount of 14,000 catties. The number of men killed and taken prisoners amounted to several scores. He likewise inflicted the penalty of the laws on the criminals Yaouhow(?) and Owkwan(?) (both of them being brokers) and confiscated their property. This shows that faithfulness in the enforcement of the laws is not wanting; and yet the practice cannot be checked. The dread of the laws is not so great on the part of the common people, as is the anxious desire of gain, which incites them to all manner of crafty devices, so that sometimes, indeed, the law is rendered wholly ineffective.

There are also, both on the rivers and at sea, banditti, who, with pretense of acting under the order of the government, and of being sent to search after and prevent the smuggling of opium, seek opportunities for plundering. When I was lately placed in the service of your majesty as acting judicial commissioner at Canton, cases of this nature were very frequently reported. Out of these arose a still greater number of cases in which money was extorted for the ransom of plundered property. Thus a countless number of innocent people were involved in suffering. All these widespread evils have arisen since the interdicts against opium were published.

It will be found on examination that the smokers of opium are idle, lazy vagrants, having no useful purpose before them, and are unworthy of regard, or even of contempt. And though there are smokers to be found who have overstepped the threshold of age, yet they do not attain to the long life of other men. But new births are daily increasing the population of the empire; and there is no cause to apprehend a diminution therein; while, on the other hand, we cannot adopt, too great, or too early, precautions against the annual waste that is taking place in the resources, the very substance, of China.

Since, then, it will not answer to close our ports against [all trade], and since the laws issued against opium are quite inoperative, the only method left is to revert to the former system, to permit the barbarian merchants to import opium, paying duty thereon as a medicine, and to require that, after having passed the customhouse, it shall be delivered to the hong merchants only in exchange for merchandise, and that no money be paid for it. The barbarians, finding that the amount of duties to be paid on it is less than what is now spent in bribes, will also gladly comply therein. Foreign money should be placed on the same footing with sycee silver, and the exportation of it should be equally prohibited. Offenders when caught should be punished by the entire destruction of the opium they may have and the confiscation of the money that be found with them. With regard to officers, civil and military, and to the scholars and common soldiers, the first are called on to fulfill the duties of their rank and attend to the public good; the others, to cultivate their talents and become fit for public usefulness. None of these, therefore, must be permitted to contract a practice so bad or to walk in a path that will lead only to the utter waste of their time and destruction of their property. If, however, the laws enacted against the practice be made too severe, the result will be mutual connivance. It becomes my duty, then, to request that it be enacted that any officer, scholar, or soldier found guilty of secretly smoking opium shall be immediately dismissed from public employ, without being made liable to any other penalty. In this way, lenity will become in fact severity toward them. And further, that, if any superior or general officer be found guilty of knowingly and willfully conniving at the practice among his subordinates, such officer shall be subjected to a court of inquiry. Lastly, that no regard be paid to the purchase and use of opium on the part of the people generally.

Does any suggest a doubt that to remove the existing prohibitions will derogate from the dignity of government? I would ask if he is ignorant that the pleasure of the table and of the nuptial couch may also be indulged in to the injury of health? Nor are the invigorating drugs *footsze(?)* and *wootow(?)* devoid of poisonous qualities: yet it has never been heard that any one of these has been interdicted. Besides, the removal of the prohibitions refers only to the vulgar and common people, those who have no official duties to perform. So long as the officers of government, the scholars, and the military are not included, I see no detriment to the dignity of government. And by allowing the proposed importation and exchange of the drug for other commodities, more than ten millions of money will annually be prevented from flowing out of the central land. On which side then is the gain, on which the loss? It is evident at a glance. But if we still idly look back and delay to retrace our steps, foolishly paying regard to a matter of mere empty dignity, I humbly apprehend that when eventually it is proved impossible to stop the importation of opium, it will then be found that we have waited too long, that the people are impoverished, and their wealth departed. Should we then begin to turn round, we shall find that reform comes too late.

Though but a servant of no value, I have by your majesty's condescending favor been raised from a subordinate censorship to various official stations, both at court and in the provinces, and filled on one occasion the chief judicial office in the region south of the great mountains (Guangdong). Ten years spent in endeavors to make some return have produced no fruit, and I find myself overwhelmed with shame and remorse. But with regard to the great advantages, or great evils, of any place where I have been, I have never failed to make particular inquiries. Seeing that the prohibitions now in force against opium serve but to increase the prevalence of the evil, and that there is none found to represent the facts directly to your majesty, and feeling assured that I am myself thoroughly acquainted with the real state of things, I dare no longer forbear to let them reach your majesty's ear. Prostrate I beg my august sovereign to give secret directions to the governor and lieutenant governor of Guangdong, together with the superintendent of maritime customs, that they faithfully investigate the character of the above statements and that, if they find them really correct, they speedily prepare a list of regulations adapted to a change in the system and present the same for your majesty's final decision. Perchance this may be found adequate to stop further oozing out of money and to replenish the national resources. With inexpressible awe and trembling fear I reverently present this memorial and await your majesty's commands.

Report of the Governor and Lieutenant Governor.
Sept. 7th, 1836

We have, in obedience to the imperial will, jointly deliberated on the subject of repealing the regulation now in force in regard to the importation of opium and of permitting it to be sold in barter for other commodities; and we herein present a draft of regulations, which we have sketched, comprising nine sections, on which we humbly illicit your sacred majesty to cast a glance. . . .

We are humbly of opinion that in framing regulations it is of the first importance to suit them to the circumstances of the times and that, to govern well, it is essential in the first place to remove existing evils. But if in removing one evil, an evil of greater extent is produced, it then becomes the more imperative to make a speedy change suited to the circumstances of the occasion.

We, your majesty's ministers, having examined the original memorial and considered the details therein contained respecting the evils to be removed, regard the whole as true and accurate. The request for a repeal of the prohibitions and change in the system, and a return to the former plan of laying a duty on opium, is also such as the circumstances of the times render necessary; and it is our duty to solicit your majesty's sanction thereof. In case of such sanction, any foreigner, who in the course of trade may bring opium, must be permitted to import and pass it at the customhouse, paying the duty on it as fixed by the maritime tariff of Qianlong, and must deliver it to the hong merchants, in the same manner as long-ells, camlets, and other goods bartered for native commodities, but on no account may he sell it clandestinely for money.

If this plan be faithfully and vigorously carried into effect, the tens of millions of precious money that now annually go out of the empire will be saved, the source of the stream will be putrid, and the stream itself may be eventually stayed. The amount of duties being less onerous than what is now paid in bribes, transgressions of the revenue laws will cease of themselves; the present evil practices of transporting contraband goods by deceit and violence will be suppressed without effort; the numberless quarrels and litigation now arising therefrom at Canton, together with the crimes of worthless vagrants, will be diminished. Moreover, if the governmental officers, the literati, and the military be still restrained by regulations and not be suffered to inhale the drug, and if offenders among these classes be immediately dismissed from the public service, while those of the people who purchase the drug and smoke it are not interfered with, all will plainly see that those who indulge their depraved appetites are the victims of their own self-sacrificing fully, persons who are incapable of ranking among the capped and belted men of distinction and learning. And if in this way shame be once aroused, strenuous exertion and self-improvement will be the result—for the principles of reform are founded in shame and remorse. Nor, as is truly said in the original memorial, will the dignity of government be at all lowered by the proposed measure. Should your majesty sanction the repeal, it will in truth be attended with advantage both to the arrangements of the governments and the well-being of the people. . . .

    1. The whole amount of opium imported should be paid for in merchandise: in this there must be no deception. The object in repealing the interdict on opium is to prevent the loss of specie occasioned by the sale of the drug for money. When opium is brought

in foreign vessels, therefore, the security and senior merchants should be held responsible for the following arrangements being carried into effect: the value of the opium to be correctly fixed; an amount of native commodities of equal value to be apportioned; and the two amounts to be exchanged in full: no purchase to be made for money payments. . . .

2. The naval cruising vessels, and all the officers and men of the customhouse stations, should be required diligently to watch the entrances and passages of rivers but at the same time to confine their search to such entrances and passages; they should not be allowed to go out to seaward and under cover thereof to cause annoyance. . . . If the soldiers, or vagabonds feigning to be soldiers, frame pretexts for cruising about in search of them [opium smugglers], not only can they effect no good, but they may also give occasion to disturbances, attended with evil consequences of no trivial character. They should, therefore, be strictly prohibited so doing.

3. [skipped]

4. [skipped]

5. This amount of duties should be continued the same as formerly, no increase is called for; and all extortionate demands and illegal fees should be interdicted. . . . Perspicuous and strict proclamations should therefore be issued, making it generally known that, beyond the real duty, not the smallest fraction is to be exacted and that offenders shall be answerable to the law against extortionate underlings receiving money under false pretexts.

6. No price should be fixed on the drug. It is a settled principle of commerce that, when prices are very low, there is a tendency to rise, and when high, a tendency to fall. Prices then depend on the supply that is procurable of any article, and the demand that exists for it in the market they cannot be limited by enactments to any fixed rate. Now, though the prohibition of opium be repealed, it will not be a possible thing to force men who buy at a high price to sell at a cheap one. Besides, it is common to men to prize things of high value and to underrate those of less worth. When therefore opium was severely interdicted, and classed among rarities, everyone had an opportunity to indulge in overreaching desires of gain; but when once the interdicts are withdrawn, and opium universally admitted, it will become a common medicinal drug, easily to be obtained.

"The gem, when in the casket, prized,
When common, is despised!"

So the price of opium, if left to itself, will fall from day to day; whereas if rated at a fixed value, great difficulty will be found in procuring it at the price at which it is rated. It is reasonable and right, therefore, to leave the price to fluctuate, according to the circumstances of the times, and not to fix any rate.

7. [skipped]

8. The strict prohibitions existing against the cultivation of the poppy, among the people, may be in some measure relaxed. Opium possesses soothing properties but is powerful in its effects. Its soothing properties render it a luxury, greatly esteemed; but its powerful effects are such as readily to induce disease. The accounts given of the manner in which it is prepared among the foreigners are various; but in all probability it is not unmixed with things of poisonous quality. It is said that of late years, opium has been clandestinely prepared by natives, by boiling down the juicy matter from the poppy; and that thus prepared, it possesses milder properties and is less injurious, without losing its soothing influence. To shut out the importation of it by foreigners, there is no better plan than to sanction the cultivation and preparation of it in the empire. It would seem right, therefore, to relax, in some means, the existing severe prohibitions and to dispense with the close scrutiny now called for to hinder its cultivation. If it be apprehended that the simple people may leave the stem and stay of life to amuse themselves with the twigs and branches, thereby injuring the interest of agriculture, it is only necessary to issue perspicuous orders, requiring them to confine the cultivation of the poppy to the tops of hills and mounds, and other unoccupied spots of ground, and on no account to introduce it into their grainfields, to the injury of that on which their subsistence depends.

9. All officers, scholars, and soldiers should be strictly prohibited and disallowed the smoking of opium. . . . With regard to officers, civil and military, and to the scholars and common soldiers, the first are called on to fulfill the duties of their rank and attend to the public good; the others, to cultivate their talents and become fit for public usefulness. None of these, therefore, must be permitted to contract a practice so bad or to walk in a path that will lead only to the utter waste of their time and destruction of their property.

If the laws be rendered overly strict, then offenders, in order to escape the penalty, will be tempted to screen one another. This, assuredly, is not then so good a plan as to relax the prohibitions and to act upon men's feelings of shame and self-condemnation. In the latter case, gradual reformation may be expected as the result of convection. Hence the original memorial also alludes to a reformation noiselessly effected. The suggestions therein contained are worthy of regard and of adoption. Hereafter no attention should be paid to the purchase and use of opium among the people. But if officers, civil and military, scholars, or common soldiers secretly purchase and smoke the drug they should be immediately degraded and dismissed, as standing warnings to all who will not arouse and renovate themselves. Orders to this effect should be promulgated in all the provinces, and strictly enjoined in every civil and military office, by the superiors on their subordinates, to be faithfully obeyed by everyone. And all who, paying apparent obedience, secretly transgress this interdict should be delivered over by the high provincial authorities to the Civil or Military Board, to be subjected to severe investigation.

Memorial in Favor of Banning Opium

Zhu Zun, member of the council and of the Board of Rites, kneeling, presents the following memorial, wherein he suggests the propriety of increasing the severity of certain prohibitory enactments, with a view to maintain the dignity of the laws and to remove a great evil from among the people: to this end he respectfully states his views on the subject and earnestly entreats his sacred majesty to cast a glance thereon.

I would humbly point out that wherever an evil exists it should be at once removed and that the laws should never be suffered to fall into desuetude. Our government, having received from heaven the gift of peace, has transmitted it for two centuries: this has afforded opportunity for the removal of evils from among the people. For governing the central nation, and for holding in submission all the surrounding barbarians, rules exist perfect in their nature and well fitted to attain their end. And in regard to opium, special enactments were passed for the prohibitions of its use in the first year of Jiaqing [1796]; and since then, memorials presented at various successive periods have given rise to additional prohibitions, all of which have been inserted in the code and the several tariffs. The laws, then, relating thereto are not wanting in severity; but there are those in office who, for want of energy, fail to carry them into execution.

Hence the people's minds gradually become callous; and base desires, springing up among them, increase day by day and month by month, till their rank luxuriance has spread over the whole empire. These noisome weeds, having been long neglected, have become impossible to eradicate. And those to whom this duty is entrusted are, as if hand bound, wholly at a loss what to do.

When the foreign ships convey opium to the coast, it is impossible for them to sell it by retail. Hence there are at Canton, in the provincial city, brokers, named "melters." These engage money changers to arrange the price with the foreigners and to obtain orders for them, with which orders they proceed to the receiving ships, and there the vile drug is delivered to them. This part of the transaction is notorious, and the actors in it are easily discoverable. The boats that carry the drug and that are called "fast-crabs" and "scrambling-dragons" are all well furnished with guns and other weapons and ply their oars as swiftly as though they were wings. Their crews have all the overbearing assumption and audacity of pirates. Shall such men be suffered to navigate the surrounding seas according to their own will? And shall such conduct be passed over without investigation? . . .

It is said that the opium should be admitted, subject to a duty, the importers being required to give it into the hands of the hong merchants in barter only for merchandise, without being allowed to sell it for money. And this is proposed as a means of preventing money from secretly oozing out of the country. But the English, by whom opium is sold, have been driven out to Lintin (a small island in the Pearl River estuary) so long since as the first year of Daoguang (1821), when the then governor of Guangdong and Guangxi discovered and punished the warehousers of opium: so long have they been expelled, nor have they ever since imported it into Macao. Having once suppressed the trade and driven them away, shall we now again call upon them and invite them to return? This would be, indeed, a derogation from the true dignity of government. As to the proposition to give tea in exchange, and entirely to prohibit the exportation of even *foreign* silver, I apprehend that, if the tea should not be found sufficient, money will still be given in exchange for the drug. Besides, if it is in our power to prevent the extortion of dollars, why not also to prevent the importation of opium? And if we can but prevent the importation of opium, the exportation of dollars will then cease of itself, and the two offenses will both at once be stopped. Moreover, is it not better, by continuing the old enactments, to find even a partial remedy for the evil than by a change of the laws to increase the importation still further? As to levying a duty of opium, the thing sounds so awkwardly, and reads so unbeseemingly, that such a duty ought surely not to be levied.

Again, it is said that the prohibitions against the planting of the poppy by natives should be relaxed and that the direct consequences will be daily diminution of the profits of foreigners and in course of time the entire cessation of the trade without the aid of prohibitions. Is it, then, forgotten that it is natural to the common people to prize things heard of only by the ear and to undervalue those that are before their eyes—to pass by those things that are near at hand and to seek after those that are afar off—and, though they have a thing in their own land, yet to esteem more highly such as comes to them from beyond the seas? Thus, in Jiangsu, Zhejiang, Fujian, and Guangdong, they will quietly be guided by the laws of the empire, but must needs make use of foreign money; and this foreign money, though of an inferior standard, is nevertheless exchanged by them at a higher rate than the native sycee silver, which is pure. And although money is cast in China after exactly the same pattern, under names of Jiangsu pieces, Fujian pieces, and native or Canton pieces, yet this money has not been able to gain currency among the people. Thus, also, silk and cotton goods of China are not insufficient in quantity; and yet broadcloths, and camlets, and cotton goods of the barbarians from beyond the place of the empire are in constant request. Taking men generally, the minds of all are equally unenlightened in this respect, so that all men prize what is strange and undervalue whatever is in ordinary use.

From Fujian, Guangdong, Zhejiang, Shandong, Yunnan, and Guizhou, memorials have been presented by the censors, and other officers request that prohibitions should be enacted against the cultivation of the poppy and against the preparation of opium; but while nominally prohibited, the cultivation of it has not been really stopped in those places. Of any of those provinces, except Yunnan, I do not presume to speak; but of that portion of the country I have it in any power to say that the poppy is cultivated all over the hills and the open campaign and that the quantity of opium annually produced there cannot be less than several thousand chests. And yet we do not see any diminution in the quantity of silver exported as compared with any previous period, while, on the other hand, the lack of the metal in Yunnan is double in degree to what it formerly was. To what cause is this to be ascribed? To what but that the consumers of the drug are very many and that those who are choice and dainty, with regard to its quality, prefer always the foreign article?

Those of your majesty's advisers who compare the drug to the dried leaf of the tobacco plant are in error. The tobacco leaf does not destroy the human constitution. The profit too arising from the sale of tobacco is small, while that arising from opium is large. Besides, tobacco may be cultivated on bare and barren ground, while the poppy needs a rich and fertile soil. If all the rich and fertile ground be used for planting the poppy, and if the people, hoping for a large profit therefrom, madly engage in its cultivation, where will flax and the mulberry tree be cultivated or wheat and rye be planted? To draw off in this way the waters of the great fountain, requisite for the production of goods and raiment, and to lavish them upon the root whence calamity and disaster spring forth, is an error that may be compared to that of a physician who, when treating a mere external disease, should drive it inward to the heart and center of the body. It may in such a case be found impossible even to preserve *life*. And shall the fine fields of Guangdong, which produce their three crops every year, be given up for the cultivation of this noxious weed—those fields in comparison with which the unequal soil of all other parts of the empire is not even to be mentioned?

To sum up the matter—the widespreading and baneful influence of opium, when regarded simply as injurious to property, is of inferior importance; but when regarded as hurtful to the people, it demands most anxious considera-tion: for in the *people* lies the very foundation of the empire. Property, it is true, is that on which the subsistence of the people depends. Yet a deficiency of it may be supplied, and an impoverished people improved; whereas it is beyond the power of any artificial means to save a people enervated by luxury. In the history of Formosa we find the following passage: "Opium was first produced in Kaoutsinne[?], which by some is said to be the same as Kalapa (or Batavia). The natives of this place were at the first sprightly and active, and being good soldiers, were always successful in battle. But the people called Hongmao [*Red-hairs*, a term originally applied to the Dutch] came thither, and having manu-factured opium, seduced some of the natives into the habit of smoking it; from this the mania for it rapidly spread throughout the whole nation, so that in process of time, the natives became feeble and enervated, submitted to the for-eign rule, and ultimately were completely subjugated." Now the English are of the race of foreigners called Hongmao. In introducing opium into this country, their purpose has been to weaken and enfeeble the central empire. If not early aroused to a sense of our danger, we shall find ourselves, ere long, on the last step toward ruin. . . .

Since your majesty's accession to the throne, the maxim of your illustrious house that horsemanship and archery are the foundations of its existence has ever been carefully remembered. And hence the governors, the lieutenant gov-ernors, the commanders of the forces, and their subordinates have again and again been acted to pay the strictest attention to the discipline and exercise of the troops, and of the naval forces, and have been urged and required to create by their exertions strong and powerful legions. With admiration I contemplate my sacred sovereign's anxious care for imparting a military as well as a civil education, prompted as this anxiety is by desire to establish on a firm basis the foundations of the empire and to hold in awe the barbarians on every side. But while the stream of importation of opium is not turned aside, it is impossible to attain any certainty that none within the camp do ever secretly inhale the drug. And if the camp be once contaminated by it, the baneful influence will work its way, and the habit will be contracted, beyond the power of reform. When the periodical times of desire for it come round, how can the victims—their legs tottering, their hands trembling, their eyes flowing with childlike tears—be able in any way to attend to their proper exercises? Or how can such men form strong and powerful legions? Under these circumstances, the military will become alike unfit to advance to the fight or in a retreat to defend their posts. Of this there is clear proof in the instance of the campaign against the Yao rebels in the twelfth year of our sovereign's reign [1832]. In the army sent to Yongzhou [Hunan], on that occasion, great numbers of the soldiers were opium smokers, so that although their numerical force was large, there was hardly any strength to be found among them. . . .

At the present moment, throughout the empire, the minds of men are in imminent danger; the more foolish, being seduced by teachers of false doctrines, are sunk in vain superstitions and cannot be aroused; and the more intelligent, being intoxicated by opium, are carried away as by a whirlpool and are beyond recovery. Most thoughtfully have I sought for some plan by which to arouse and awaken all but in vain. While, however, the empire preserves and maintains its laws, the plain and honest rustic will see what he has to fear and will be deterred from evil; and the man of intelligence and cultivated habits will learn what is wrong in himself and will refrain from it. And thus, though the laws be declared by some to be but wastepaper, yet these their unseen effects will be of no trifling nature. If, on the other hand, the prohibitions be suddenly repealed, and the action that was a crime be no longer counted such by the government, how shall the dull clown and the mean among the people know that the action is still in itself wrong? In open day and with unblushing front, they will continue to use opium till they shall become so accustomed to it that eventually they will find it as indispensable as their daily meat and drink and will inhale the noxious drug with perfect indifference. When shame shall thus be entirely destroyed, and fear removed wholly out of the way, the evil consequences that will result to morality and to the minds of men will assuredly be neither few nor unimportant. As your majesty's minister, I know that the laws of the empire, being in their existing state well fitted to effect their end, will not for any slight cause be changed. But the proposal to alter the law on this subject having been made and discussed in the provinces, the instant effect has been that crafty thieves and villains have on all hands begun to raise their heads and open their eyes, gazing about and pointing their finger, under the notion that, when once these prohibitions are repealed thenceforth and forever, they may regard themselves free from every restraint and from every cause of fear.

Though possessing very poor abilities I have nevertheless had the happiness to enjoy the favor of your sacred majesty and have, within a space of but few years, been raised through the several grades of the censorate, and the presidency of various courts in the metropolis, to the high elevation of a seat in the Inner Council. I have been copiously imbued with the rich dew of favors yet have been unable to offer the feeblest token of gratitude; but if there is aught within the compass of my knowledge, I dare not to pass it by unnoticed. I feel in my duty to request that your majesty's commands may be proclaimed to the governors and lieutenant governors of all the provinces, requiring them to direct the local officers to redouble their efforts for the enforcement of the existing prohibitions against opium and to impress on everyone, in the plainest and strictest manner, that all who are already contaminated by the vile habit must return and become new men—that if any continue to walk in their former courses, strangers to repentance and to reformation, they shall assuredly be subjected to the full penalty of the law and shall not meet with the least indulgence—and that any found guilty of storing up or selling opium to the amount of 1,000 catties or upward, the most severe punishment shall be inflicted. Thus happily the minds of men may be impressed with fear, and the report thereof, spreading over the seas (among foreigners), may even there produce reformation. Submitting to my sovereign my feeble and obscure views, I prostrate implore your sacred majesty to cast a glance on this my respectful memorial.

Imperial Edict, September 1836

The councilor Zhu Zun has presented a memorial, requesting that the severity of the prohibitory enactments against opium may be increased. The subcensor Xu Qiu also has laid before us a respectful representation of his views and, in a supplementary statement, a recommendation to punish severely Chinese traitors.

Opium, coming from the distant regions of barbarians, has pervaded the country with its baneful influence and has been made a subject of very severe prohibitory enactments. But, of late, there has been a diversity of opinion in regard to it, some requesting a change in the policy hitherto adopted and others recommending the continuance of the severe prohibitions. It is highly important to consider the subject carefully in all its bearings, surveying at once the whole field of action, so that such measures may be adopted as shall continue forever in force, free from all failures.

Let Deng [Deng Tingzhen, the governor-general of Guangdong and Guangxi] and his colleagues anxiously and carefully consult together upon the recommendation to search for, and with utmost strictness apprehend, all those traitorous natives who sell the drug, the hong merchants who arrange the transactions in actions in it, the brokers who purchase it by wholesale, the boatmen who are engaged in transporting it, and the naval militia who receive bribes; and having determined on the steps to be taken in order to stop up the source of the evil, let them present a true and faithful report. Let them also carefully ascertain and report whether the circumstances stated by Xu Qiu in his supplementary document, in reference to the foreigners from beyond the seas, be true or not, whether such things as are mentioned therein have or have not taken place. Copies of the several documents are to be herewith sent to those officers for perusal; and this edict is to be made known to Deng and Ke, who are to enjoin it also on Wan, the superintendent of maritime customs. Respect this.

NOTES

John Slade, *A Narrative of the Late Proceedings and Events in China* (Canton: Canton Register, 1839).

    1. The author means Turkey.

    2. This was also a serious issue for peasants, since they normally used copper cash but had to pay taxes in silver. It is not clear that the rise in the price of silver was entirely due to the opium trade.

The Qing State and Opium Suppression

Although opium remained illegal after the Treaty of Tianjin the trade spread rapidly as both imported opium and Chinese opium found ready markets. Opium use became widespread in China between 1860 and 1906. Chinese opium was significantly cheaper than Indian or Persian opium, although not considered to be of as high quality, and thus it made the drug affordable to ordinary Chinese. Improved distribution meant that opium became available to consumers all over China. Chinese production and distribution of opium meant that a far larger range of Chinese came to have an economic stake in the opium trade and probably also made opium a less exotic and more socially acceptable substance.

Some Chinese officials made attempts to eliminate opium from Chinese society. This is an account of one such attempt. Like most of the attempts at reform during this period, it was the brainchild of a single energetic official and was likely to lose steam if that official was transferred. The reading also reflects the limited methods available to energetic officials who wanted to suppress opium.

The most successful attempt to check the consumption of opium is thus described by Mr. W. D. Spence, who is attached to the Consulate at Shanghai:

The closing of the opium divans by the officials throughout the province of Jiangsu has been mainly the work of one man, Tan Zhunpei, the present acting governor. He came to the province in 1874 as prefect of Changzhou and was soon impressed with the evils attendant on the system of public opium-smoking divans. Regarding them as nurseries of crime and immorality and having also a keen sense of the evils that opium smoking entails on those who indulge in it, in 1875 he issued orders for all the opium dens to be shut up. In the city of Changzhou itself, and in the districts round it, coming under his own personal observation, these orders were in the course of a few months effectively carried out, but in the outlying parts of the prefecture the same strictness was not observed.

In 1876 Shen Baochen became governor-general of Jiangsu and Zhejiang, and hearing of Tan Zhunpei's successful crusade, he instructed the prefect of Nanjing to shut up the divans in that city and issued orders to the whole body of provincial officials to shut up the opium divans in their respective districts. With the exception of Yangzhou Zhenjiang prefectures, in the first of which prefectures the instructions were, strictly, and in the second partially, carried out, the governor-general's orders were not paid much attention to. His proclamation on the subject in fact was regarded by his subordinates as one of those solemn enunciations of moral platitudes with which provincial officials of whatever rank usually commence their career.

In 1878 Tan Zhunpei was transferred to Suzhou, the most important prefecture of the province, where he initiated a lively series of reforms among his people. The most important of these was the shutting up of the opium divans, which he did in the most vigorous manner, giving the proprietors a few days' grace to wind up their business in, and actually pulling down and demolishing, all divans not shut up within the prescribed period. However, in a short time Tan was promoted to be *daotai* of Xuzhou, a circuit in the extreme northwest of the province and bordering on the province of Henan. This section of China, *i.e.* the Xuzhou circuit, and the parts of Henan conterminous with it, constituted, before the famine of 1877–78, one of the most important of the poppy-growing parts of the country and presented an admirable field for the new *daotai*'s peculiar energies. He proceeded at once to pull up the poppy crops that he found his country covered with and in a short time found himself involved in unfortunate relations with his people. Riots resulted, and he had to send for reinforcements to put down the disorders that his rigorous crusade against opium had evoked. A regiment of cavalry was sent to him, and with its aid, and I fear also the aid of famine, the poppy crops were destroyed and the opium dens shut up.

In the meantime his administrative talents in other respects had attracted the attention of the governor-general at Nanjing and of the central government at Beijing, and he was appointed provincial treasurer of Jiangsu. He proceeded to Beijing to thank the emperor for the appointment, and on his return from Court last winter, he assumed office in his new appointment at Suzhou. He found that the reform he had effected a year before as prefect had been to a great extent set aside and that divans were flourishing in secret. He at once sent for the subordinate officials and told them that the opium divans must be shut up and reinforced his staff of detectives by several scores of men, to see that his orders in this respect were carried out. About the 1st January 1880 he issued a code of regulations enforcing his reform in which he states:

"When I formerly was prefect of Such, I interdicted certain established usages that, in my opinion, had an evil effect on public morality. My intention was to extirpate them thoroughly. By the people generally my commands were obeyed, but after a year passed they were disregarded by the criminal and vagabond classes, and much harm to peaceful citizens resulted. I have to notify that I shall see for myself that my orders are properly carried out, and I have given orders to the prefect and magistrate to arrest those who disobey them."

In a few days after his becoming provincial treasurer, Shen Baochen died, and Wu Yuanping, the governor of Jiangsu, became acting governor-general. The acting governorship of the province was conferred on Tan, who now for the first time had scope and powers to give his reforms full effect throughout the province. This he lost no time in doing. On the 15th March he issued the following proclamation.

"Tan, acting governor of the province of Jiangsu, issues a proclamation. The opening of opium dens by the people is a frightful calamity, and in my previous posts as *daotai* and prefect I have done everything in my power to put a stop to it with the best effect. In Changzhou, for example, the amount of opium sold by the wholesale houses fell off after my closing the divans $500 daily, which was a saving to the people in this place alone of $170,000 to $180,000 per annum, and the saving in places where these divans were more common than in Yangzhou was incalculable. At a time like the present, when men's means are straightened, a small saving of this nature helps to bring back the prosperity of other days. The evil tendencies of these dens, especially to young people, are more than I dare speak about. Officials, however, are apt to regard them as everyday necessities of existence, and traders, in the hopes of gain, open more and more of them, without fear of the consequences. If I do not put them down with a strong hand, where will this *evil* end? I have drawn up a code of rules to be put in force by every prefect and district magistrate throughout the province, in order that these opium-smoking houses may be thoroughly suppressed, and I have given secret instructions to the police to watch that proper effect is given thereto. In now publishing these rules, I hereby proclaim to all people in this province, of what degree soever, that, from after the date this notice, householders are forbidden to open opium divans and must take to some more respectable line of business. If my orders are disobeyed or evaded, *I* will send my officers to arrest the offenders, and if their guilt or complicity be established I shall visit them with the punishment named in the rules. Officials who are unable to carry out these rules I shall denounce and request the emperor to dismiss them from the public service. My orders must be carried out. Exception must be made in favor of nobody. A special proclamation."

With the proclamation were circulated throughout the province the following rules:

1st. Whenever it is discovered that an opium divan is being opened, the keeper thereof shall be put in the cangue,[1] the divan furniture shall be destroyed, and the house and land shall be confiscated, no matter whether held in fee or in lease, and sold by the authorities for the benefit of public charities.

2nd. Whenever it is reported to the authorities that an opium divan is being kept, the divan shall be shut up and the keeper brought to the Yamen. In the event of a conviction, the informer shall be rewarded with 10,000 cash. The informer must give the name and address of the offender with the sign of the divan, to facilitate his arrest and the shutting up of the establishment. Those who give wrong information shall not be liable to a penalty.

3rd. In the suburbs of cities, and in market towns, the local authorities shall empower two or three impartial and respectable citizens, by warrant, to investigate cases where it is suspected that divans exist and to make secret reports.

4th. If, after an opium den has been once shut up, a single opium lamp is lit therein, or an opium couch spread, and the owner thereof pretends that these are for his own delectation, and if on two or three visits different persons are found smoking there, this shall be held to be a divan within the purview of these rules.

5th. Whenever the owner of any house, the *dibao*,[2] and the neighbors report that the lessee is keeping a divan therein, confiscation in this case shall not follow, and the owner shall be deemed entitled to the informer's reward. If the owner is aware of the offense of the lessee and condemns it, and it comes to the ear of the authorities, the house shall be at once confiscated, the *dibao* punished, and the neighbors on either side shall be fined. If the *dibao* neglects his duties on three occasions in this manner, his own house shall also be confiscated.

The acting governor also addressed two circular letters of instruction to all the local officials throughout the province. One of these orders them to dismiss from the public service every officer who refuses to give up opium smoking within two months from the date of being warned of the penalty attaching to the practice or who may be in any way interested in the sale of the drug. The other letter orders the classification, on an ancient plan, of the householders in each district into groups of ten, a hundred, and a thousand houses.[3] Each group has to choose its headman, and these headmen are to be responsible for the carrying out of the reforms that the acting governor has instituted.

During the past three months reports from the various prefectures in the province have been published in the Chinese newspapers, and they all testify to the thorough manner in which the governor's commands have been obeyed, and, I believe, I am safe in saying that, with the exception of the foreign settlements of Shanghai, there are no public opium-smoking divans now in this province. The question of the power of the Chinese authorities to shut them up in the settlements has not yet come before the consular body, but it is not likely that the Chinese will seek to take action in the matter, except with the consent of the consuls of the treaty powers. There are a great many licensed divans in the settlement that yield to the two municipalities concerned a sum of something like seventeen thousand taels per annum.[4]

Concurrently with the shutting up of the divans by Governor Tan, great pressure has been brought to bear on the literary classes of this province to compel them to give up the smoking of opium. In 1878 Lin Tianlin was literary chancellor of Jiangsu, and he issued of his own responsibility certain regulations for the conduct of the students coming forward to be examined for degrees. Graduates or students over sixty [sic] years of age were given twelve months within which to give up opium smoking, and those under sixty were given six months. If within this time they proved incapable of curing or unwilling to cure themselves of habit, they were to be forbidden to present themselves for examination.

Lin died soon after issuing these rules and was succeeded by the present literary chancellor, Xia Tongshan, who has been even stricter than his predecessor in forbidding candidates for degrees to smoke opium.

The consul at Shanghai, in forwarding Mr. Spence's report (30th June 1880), says: "As the sale of the drug by retail dealers all over the province continues to increase more and more as the divans are closed, we may infer that almost as much opium is smoked as heretofore, although the smoking must now be done in private."

NOTES

Correspondence with the Government of India Respecting the Negotiations with China on the Subject of Opium (London: Her Majesty's Stationary Office, 1882), 39–41.

1. wooden collar

2. local constable

3. He is describing the Bao Jia system. This is the mutual responsibility system that the Qing relied on to help enforce order at the lowest level.

4. The two municipalities are the French and International settlements.

Opium and the Exotic East

*China and opium were inexorably linked in the eyes of nineteenth-century West-
erners. China was the classic example of the decadent, stagnant East against which
the modern, active West was contrasted, and the image of the Chinaman was not
complete without his opium pipe. Opium was part of the danger associated with
Asia. It was a threat to the Westerner who traveled there, and the possibility of its
spread to other countries was a threat to Europe and America.*

*This account of opium smoking in North China comes from an account of a
trip that George Fleming, an Englishman, took in 1862. At this point it was not easy
for foreigners to travel in China, and Fleming's book was intended as an account
of the mysterious and inaccessible regions of the country. He, of course, has to say
something about opium and takes a position on its supposed dangers. The selection
opens as he is bedding down in a lower-class inn.*

Scarcely ever was a hard bed so attractive, never came sleep so willingly, but
many of the unthoughtful yellow-skins without had awakened from their first
nap, gorged their paunches, and set to work to amuse themselves according to
their wonted custom. Some smoked tobacco; others played dominoes and
cards, by the help of the faint light emitted from the saucer lamps; a few rattled
dice out of a bowl within a few feet of us. Their earnest grunting voices sang out
as each gambler dashed the cubes on the matting or a little stool, "Hi yo le-o"—
there is another lot of sixes. This medley disturbed our rest, and we sat a long
time gazing out on the strange scene and watching a sensual-looking young man
indulging himself in the opium pipe close to our door, regaling our sense of
smell with the not disagreeable fumes of the burnt narcotic. He could not fail to
see that his nocturnal orgy was the principal attraction in the room for the eyes

of the strangers, though he proceeded to satisfy his craving for the drug with the greatest unconcern. Since we had entered the house, not an inmate of it appeared moved by sufficient curiosity to raise himself from his lair to visit us.

The opium smoker lay with his face in our direction, his head raised a little by a wooden pillow and his whole mind given up to the inhalation of the vapor and replenishment of the bowl by small doses of the drug picked up and stuck on the pipe from time to time. As the quantity he had smoked began to act upon his system, his features kindled up from the solid composed state they had been in previously. After each installment there was a longer interval, as if he wished to prolong the process; and he muttered away in a low tone to himself, while his black eyes sparkled vividly, and the heavings of his indeed chest denoted increased breathing. Still he lay tranquilly in the same posture without any symptoms of uneasiness.

The prescribed quantity, to our gratification, was nearly expended. Once more he stretched out his strong muscular arm toward a little tray on which were the implements employed to charge the "smoking pistol"—the long needle or wire with which the opium is lifted was again in requisition—the almost empty *ka lan,* or shell, was hurriedly scraped by it, and its contents, now changed from a treacly color and consistency to that of a crumb of gingerbread, steadily carried to the *yen-tau,* or cup, of the pipe, which bore a decided resemblance to a magnified gas burner in shape and in the small perforation in the center of its top. The opium is placed on this little aperture, into which the needle is pushed to establish an opening between the interior of the vessel and the external air, then the skewer is thrown away, the open end of the *yeu-ti*—pipe stem—is taken between the lips, the cup is carried down to the flume of the lamp, and the opium becomes faintly red as the deep inspirations of the now drowsy-looking man drew air and smoke into the lungs with a weak sputtering noise.

Suddenly it ceases; the pipe and the hand that held it drop together; the solitary carouse is over; the man of pleasure is overcome, and the object is attained, if not already passed by, for he lies so still that it would be difficult to believe that he was in anything but a profound trance or sleep, one so deep that the shouts and quarrels of those within a few inches of him fail to disturb the vision or rouse his stupefied senses

He looked a sad strange figure in the foreground of that half-wild and novel tableau, stretched out on his back as if dead, the scarcely moving ribs testifying that he was not really so. The hand and the "pistol" were still together where they had fallen, and the head resting on the stool showed the deep yellow features but imperfectly by the partial gleam of the half-extinguished lamp that stood near, illuminating but obscurely the corner where the victim reposed. It revealed the saddle and its load of effects laid up against the wall; the journeying wardrobe, wet and soiled, close to our partition; and the heavy odd-shaped sword within easy grasp of the nerveless hand; while the strong flaring blaze of the large lamp in the background threw marvelously weird-like lights and shadows through the long vista and brought out in grotesque relief the nude beings coiled up and laid out in sleep; the boisterous gamblers dressed and undressed, engrossed with their play, squatting or reclining in every conceivable way, as well as the miscellaneous agglomeration of all sorts of uncouth articles on beams, posts, and beds; all this gave one a vivid impression of a robbers' den, though the lingering aroma of the poppy's juice was rather out of place.

This was the first time I had seen the beginning and ending of an opium smoker's orgy and watched the gradual change through the whole of the stages, from excitement to stupefaction and somnolency. I was satisfied that it was a very quiet and unobtrusive way of getting dead drunk, however injurious it might be in the long run, and was productive of but little annoyance to the lookers-on.

At Singapore, at Hong Kong, but, more particularly at Tianjin, I had often peeped into the interiors of the opium shops, fully prepared to meet with some of those fearful wrecks of humanity that rouse the sympathies and curdle the blood of our people at home, when described in pro-China speeches and books; but I beheld nothing more than what I have just described—in fact not so much, for the dens were seldom so agreeable as to be supportable for a period long enough to enable a visitor to see a votary take his allowance out—and everything as orderly and peaceably as the most sober race of people could desire.

At Tianjin I made many inquires and haunted for some time a number of the shops in our vicinity and gathered as much information as any stranger could well do under the circumstances. The number of the *yai-pian yan-pu,* or opium smoke shops, then was about 300. These are places where opium can be purchased, seethed, and prepared for immediate use, in small quantities, by people who use it in their own homes and where it can be consumed on benches built up in the room usually set apart for that purpose in all these places. There are, besides, many wholesale establishments for the sale of this article to the retail shops but where it is not permitted to be used on the premises by customers.

The smoking shops are generally in low, dirty, out-of-the-way streets and back alleys and are kept concealed from view as much as may be compatible with the trade carried out in them. Ruinous hovels, regular dens, a degree or two more forbidding than our dram shops in the "slums" and lanes of our large towns, and without signboards—for the vice, one would think, is tried to be kept a hidden one—"cribs" that would be passed without any suspicions as to their character by those who had not been told, are met with in every part of Tianjin city and suburbs. You are threading your way through some sickening passage formed by gables and fronts, backs and corners of runagate and advancing houses, handkerchief to nose and mouth in one hand and a strong stick for the benefit of the swarming curs in the other. You are exploring, looking out for novelty and adventure in any shape, but chiefly to study the manners and customs of the people. Every open door has had its share of your attention, every courtyard its scrutiny. Workshops have been entered, the mechanical operations criticized, and the salient characteristics noted. You leave, perhaps wiser, perhaps gratified, and continue your route with the usual disagreeables, until you come to a corner where a great round piece of brown paper clings to the wall, so like the color of the wall itself that you may have passed a dozen such without your eye catching their outline. You are on the trail; the scent is strong. You may be as certain of what is about the vicinity of that brown paper as the North American Indian used to be when he saw a twig snapped from a bough or a scrap of dress fixed on a thorny bush.

A "howff" is near, and you search. There is no corresponding paper on any of the doors, and you penetrate further into the maze, when you remember that a courtyard full of rubbish was passed, at the top of which stood a riddled sort of bothy with the windows thickly patched with paper and the door well fitting, closed. You turn back, peep behind the courtyard gate, and discover another disc of whiteybrown.

Without any warning to those who may be inside, you advance to the door and shove it boldly open. You will find a darkened room as soon as you close it behind you again, with a couple or so of tiny lamps burning in various places, making the darkness darker still and reminding you of those lamps that superstition says are ever faintly gleaming in the old Roman sepulchers and are only extinguished when these are opened to the light of day. You stand at the floor post for a minute or two, during which vision is slowly returning, and the proprietor or manager—though he would rather not see strangers enter his secluded abode—makes you welcome. Three or four dark masses are laid on the everlasting benches. They are labourers or some such members of a poor class taking their daily or afternoon dose, after the benefit of the morning one has passed off. Three have just begun, and the fourth is resigning himself to the dreamy sleep. That is all you can see; and you stay in the mixed flavored dungeon for a few minutes, just to assure the landlord that you intended him a friendly visit.

The sight is a pitiable one—a sad one, but not so repulsive nor so heartrending as that I once witnessed in what might be called a public house on a summer's afternoon in Stam-boul, where the opium chewers were at work and going on like men possessed with demons, until they subsided into lumps of paralytic imbecility, fagging a year of nature in an hour; neither does it affect one-half so much as the glare and the misery, the garish display and the ragged brutalized mob, the stir and commotion, the ribald and profane language, or the indecent quarrel and the savage bulldog-like fight that may, alas, too often be observed by the stranger who traverses our own land, and who, at a distance—for we would advise him not to enter—surveys the "life" at the gin palaces, the taverns, public houses, drain shops, and taproom, decorated by their gay luminous show and superb fittings, to be found in all our great thoroughfares in manufacturing towns and cities and providing plenty of occupation for the policeman, the jailer, and the hangman.

If opium smoking is a great evil among the Chinese people—as it is, no doubt, yet they endeavor to hide it—they are ashamed of it—and it offends neither the eyes nor the hearing by obtrusive publicity. It is not made a parade of by night and by day; neither does it give rise to mad revels and murderous riots. Its effects on the health may be more prejudicial than our habit of alcohol drinking, but yet it is hard to see any of these broken-down creatures that one reads about.

A strong opponent of opium smoking, and a man who spoke the Chinese language thoroughly, took me to an opium shop to see some of these examples, but the exhibition was what we should call a failure so far as the exposure of the unhealthy effects of the drug might be considered.

The room was filled with men of nearly all ages and as robust looking as the majority of their townsmen. They freely answered all questions, and the result was not particularly unfavorable to the reputation of the habit, compared with the number of lives sacrificed every year by the use of alcoholic liquors and the number of strong constitutions sapped by them in other countries.

We can recall to mind one old fellow, fifty-two years of age, who confessed that he indulged himself as often as he could afford it, which was always twice, often thrice, a day. His earnings daily were about two hundred and fifty cash as a coolie, and out of this he spent one hundred in opium. This man had taken it for twenty-two years and left it off twice during that period—once voluntarily—when he was induced to begin it again at the instigation of his friends (?), and the second time to allay the pangs of hunger after he had abstained from smoking for some months. Two boys—his sons—usually accompanied him and remained in the shop while he was engaged with his pipe. How like the gin shop family meetings!

On being asked why he smoked opium, he could not give any satisfactory answer; and his sensations, while under the effects of it, were vaguely described as strength imparted to him, and the production of happiness to a degree he could not find words to express. When he required opium he did not feel well and experienced a sensation as if his breast was being torn open. If it were possible, he said, he would gladly abstain from it, though he feared he could not voluntarily do so; but if confined in a room for several days, and plenty of food allowed him, he supposed he could then do without the smoke.

Another of my friends, also an anti-smoker, used to select cases of infirm-looking Chinese in the streets as objects who were succumbing to the narcotic; but unfortunately for his judgment, the greater portion of these disavowed having anything to do with the drug and gave positive reasons for their sickness. If an impartial observer were to go the rounds of the three kingdoms and direct his attention to the effects of strong drink and the spectacles it affords, and then do the same in China—of course I speak of the north more particularly, as I have had more ample opportunities of investigating this matter there than in the south, with regard to the opium question—I can almost safely predict at what conclusion he would arrive.

One occasionally meets with pictures for sale in the streets, in which are caricatures of emaciated creatures with terrible eagerness clutching the pipe as they lie in a dilapidated house, their clothes in rags and their toes protruding through their worn-out shoes. And in one of the temples at Tianjin, where the Buddhist pandemonium was represented in all its horrors, and the punishments to be awarded the transgressors of Fo's precepts portrayed by plastic models with an almost supernatural talent in devising infernal torture, the opium inhaler is there represented awaiting his doom; yet in spite of these illustrations the custom is on the increase. It is a hidden vice, but Chinamen will tell you that every shop ought to or does pay a secret tax—a "squeeze"—to the mandarins and that the latter are kept well informed as to the number of new openings which take place, consequent on the flourishing state of business in the drug that briefly cheers but deeply enervates.

A slave to the narcotic is perfectly well aware of his danger and the enormity of the offense he is committing against his family and relations—in starving the one and disgracing the other—but he looks with fear and contempt on a drunken European who reels and tumbles about in the street, kicks up brawls, and sheds blood, and wonders why, if the foreigner is determined to get rid of his senses for a time, he does not do so pleasantly and peaceably, instead of acting like a wild beast.

There is little use in a missionary preaching to the Chinaman about his evil propensity, when the man can point to the preacher's countrymen and ask if the *samshu* is not worse than the opium; and if you showed him a print of Cruikshank's bottle, he would tell you—and perhaps you wouldn't quite disagree with him—that opium could never produce such a tableau. It is a vexed subject, as is teetotalism to many people elsewhere and as Chinese gambling might be, if viewed in the same light.

Let us quit the midnight amusements of a strange inn and, bolting with some care the passage door, seek our room. Before consigning ourselves, however, to repose, with the clatter outside still strong in our ears, the expediency of inserting five bullets in each of our revolvers was not overlooked, and the Japanese chopper was placed in the most advantageous position under M's pillow, ready for a half-asleep hack and thrust; for we reasoned that since the Chinese showed such a fancy for lethal weapons, and manifested so much prudence in their disposal at night, there could be surely no valid objections to our doing the same.

NOTE

George Fleming, *Travels on Horseback in Mantchu Tartary: Being a Summer's Ride beyond the Great Wall of China.* (London: Hurst & Blackett, 1863).

Missionaries and Opium

Missionaries were the single most important group of people for the transmission of ideas between China and the West in the nineteenth century. Missionary accounts of Chinese opium use were important in creating new discourses about opium in the West, and missionaries brought these new ideas back to China, where they were leaders in the most important anti-opium efforts of the late nineteenth century.

This account, written by a missionary with fourteen years of experience in China, is a good example of the new discourse on opium. In contrast to George Flemming in reading 3, Justus Doolittle sees the drug as inevitably destructive for any who use it and for society as a whole. This would become a standard position both in China and in the West. Doolittle also connects the opium trade to the failure to evangelize China, an issue of much less importance to Chinese.

If one smokes opium at stated intervals, as every morning or every evening, or once regularly in two days, he acquires in a short time the habit, so that he must smoke it *at just such a time* or suffer the disagreeable consequences of not smoking. This condition causes an incessant thinking about it, and a longing or hankering after it, which in a great degree incapacitates the victim for effort, intellectual or physical, unless he has recourse to the drug again. The habit becomes fixed in a period of time varying from ten or fifteen days to one or two months, according to the constitution of the person and the circumstances of the case. It is not determined so much by the quantity he consumes as by the regularity of his resorts to the pipe. If he smokes at irregular periods, as once in a week, and then once in a day, and then goes for a longer or shorter period before he smokes again, he will not feel this ardent and intolerable longing. He does *not become addicted to the vice;* he is still his own master.

Some originally resort to the drug in order to cure the toothache, or headache, or dyspepsia, under the advice of friends. The pain is usually relieved for the time being, but at the expense of acquiring the habit of smoking opium. When this habit has fastened itself on the victim, the usual quantity will not long assuage the pain as at the beginning, and, in order to relieve it, larger and still larger quantities must be used from time to time.

Friends often invite each other to smoke opium as preliminary to the discussion of business matters or at intervals while engaged in ordinary conversation. It has become the popular way of *"treating"* among some. This fashion of inviting guests or friends among the higher classes to smoke the opium pipe has, perhaps, attained at this place the same popularity, though not the same universality, that the custom of inviting friends who called to drink wine, or rum, or brandy as a token of hospitality, attained in the United States some thirty or forty years ago. It corresponds also very much to the practice now common among many foreign residents in the East, as well as among many Englishmen and Americans in their native countries, to offer wine, or something stronger than wine, to guests.

Opium shops are always provided with platforms, which the buyers of the prepared drug may occupy while consuming the quantity purchased. Here two friends often meet and, reclining on these platforms, facing each other, with the burning lamp and apparatus between them, and their heads resting on pillows, *treat each other,* usually each preparing for the other to smoke the pipe that is furnished for their common use. Most of the poor, and many of the middle classes, prefer, for convenience's sake, to consume the opium at the shop where it is purchased. In the case of some of the middle class, and of most of the wealthy and the higher classes of Chinese, the opium is bought at the retail shops already prepared in a liquid form for smoking and taken home to be consumed. Sometimes, however, they procure the drug in the solid form and prepare it by boiling in their own houses. Perhaps one-half or more of the quantity imported and used here is thus consumed at the homes of its buyers. Many officers, merchants, literary men, the wealthy, and generally all those who have their time at their leisurely disposal, buy the drug by the ball or in smaller quantity and prepare it at their residences, where they smoke it whenever they please.

Extensive native mercantile firms sometimes keep it on hand for their large customers or their personal friends who may call. The best Chinese physicians oftentimes depend on being invited to a smoke at the houses of their patients and take it unkindly if not *"treated."* The official employees connected with mandarin establishments, such as policemen and constables, of which class there is a large number, delay or decline to proceed to the transaction of their business unless first treated with opium when called to one's house, even on the most urgent and important affairs. Many wealthy private families keep the opium pipe and fixtures in readiness for the demands of fashion. They not unusually have a room that is devoted to the smoking of the drug, being provided with a bedstead or platform for the convenience of smokers.

The baneful effects of opium smoking are many and various—social, moral, mental, physical, and pecuniary. It is not designed to dwell at length on the evil influences of this vice.

In the first place, opium smoking sensibly and unfavorably affects *one's property and business relations.* It is comparatively a very costly vice, the expense being graduated by the circumstances of each case, ranging from a dollar or two to ten or fifteen dollars per month, even in regard to persons not of the highest and the most wealthy classes. The lowest mentioned rate, taking into consideration the low price of labor among this people compared with the price of labor in Western countries, is relatively large and burdensome. With all smokers, however, the effect of this vice on their pecuniary standing is *by no means to be estimated by the actual outlay in money for the drug.* Its seductive influence leads its victims to neglect their business, and consequently, sooner or later, loss or ruin ensues. As the habit grows, so does inattention to business increase. Instances are not rare where the rich have been reduced to poverty and beggary as one of the consequences of their attachment to the opium pipe. The poor addicted to this vice are oftentimes led to dispose of everything salable in the hovel where they live. Sometimes, even, men sell their own children and their wives in order to procure the drug and finally end their career by becoming beggars or thieves. In order to understand the EXPENSE of this vice, the Western reader needs perhaps to be reminded that the vast majority of the Chinese are generally poor and that wages are invariably low. It oftentimes, and even usually, requires as much time and toil here to earn a dime as in America it requires to earn a dollar.

In the second place, the smoking of opium *injures one's health and bodily constitution.* Unless taken promptly at the regular time and in the necessary quantity, the victim becomes unable to control himself and to attend to his business. He sneezes. He gapes. Mucus runs from his nose and his eyes. Gripping pains seize him in his bowels. His whole appearance indicates restlessness and misery. If not indulged in smoking and left undisturbed, he usually falls asleep, but his sleep does not refresh and invigorate him. On being aroused, he is himself again, provided he can have his opium; if not, his troubles and pains multiply. He has no appetite for ordinary food, strength, or disposition to labor. Diarrhea sets in of a dreadful and most painful description, peculiar to opium smokers; and if still unable to procure opium, the unhappy victim not infrequently dies in most excruciating agonies. Few, comparatively, recover after the diarrhea has become virulent, unless they have access to opium, and not always then.

The Chinese, in describing the effects of opium smoking on the individual, dwell with peculiar emphasis on the *weakness and indolence* which it induces. The victim is described as *unwilling,* and usually physically *unable,* to perform anything requiring muscular strength or mental application, except under the excitement of opium. His habits of sleep are changed, it being impossible oftentimes, owing to the overwrought mental excitement induced by the drug, for him to fall asleep in the early part of the night, as others do. Frequently it is nearly or quite morning before he is able to compose himself to rest, waking only late in the forenoon or early in the afternoon. The Chinese have a common saying that the smoker of opium "makes the day night, and the night day," alluding to his unnatural hours of waking and of sleeping. His features almost always become strikingly changed, being of unhealthy, pallid, deathlike cast. His shoulders not infrequently become permanently elevated above their natural level, much as when one shrugs them up, at the same time drawing down his head. Such an opium smoker is expressly described as *"having three heads,"* from the high and unnatural appearance of his shoulders. His eyes become glaring and without expression. Most inveterate smokers become spare and thin, owing in part to the direct effects of opium on the human system and in part to the fact that nutritious food is taken in less quantities and at more irregular intervals, through loss of appetite, than is usual in the case of persons not addicted to this habit. They are styled *"opium devils."*

Men of naturally strong constitutions, and possessed of sufficient property to support them without vexatious care and personal labor, may indulge in this vice with comparative impunity for a considerable period. Such sometimes live to good old age; but the longer they smoke, the larger is the quantity required to keep them up. Freedom from care and hard labor, as well as plenty of opium, are requisite in order that the smoker may continue in health and attain a respectable longevity. There is not so much shortening of the lives of rich men who have become victims of this habit as is often asserted, and as seems very natural to suppose, though, doubtless, the lives of such men are in fact considerably shortened by the use of opium. They often live to old age, *notwithstanding* the effects of opium on their physical systems. The greatest destruction of life from this vice in China is unquestionably seen in the poorer and the working classes. These are not able to increase the amount of opium in proportion to the need of an augmented supply, and therefore they soon feel the effects of a limited amount on their health. Besides, when ill, they are not only under the necessity of going without the drug but are often unable to procure physicians and medicines as aids to recovery. In such cases, their previous use of opium renders their illness the more dreadful and intolerable. It has been estimated that the lives of the poor who become slaves to this seductive habit are cut short by it from five to fifty years.

The vice of opium smoking has long since become a gigantic obstacle to the welfare and the prosperity of this people. The consumption of opium is rapidly on the increase in this city as well as in other parts of the empire, and its ravages are becoming more manifest and more awful. Shops where the drug is offered for sale are becoming more and more common. Its unhappy victims are becoming more and more numerous. The nation is becoming poorer and poorer.

The Chinese here have a current saying that *"Opium shops are more numerous than rice shops."* In a certain neighborhood, three or four years ago, there were twelve shops where opium was retailed and seven shops where rice, which is the "staff of life" in this part of China, was sold. The number of opium shops in the city and suburbs is estimated to amount to several thousands. While estimates given by the natives differ greatly in regard to details, they substantially agree in showing the vast number of people who have become slaves to opium.

One of the most common inquiries made by confirmed smokers, *as* well as by young beginners, of those foreigners who express a hatred of the vice and who urge them to break away from it is, *"Have you medicine which will cure it?"* The Chinese entertain the opinion that since the drug comes from a foreign land, foreigners must know some infallible remedy which will counteract its bad effects or destroy an acquired taste for it. Accordingly, the Chinese have opium medicines in abundance, professedly of foreign origin.

Some six years ago I observed some six different kinds of advertisements, or placards, each in large numbers, posted up in conspicuous places in the streets, pretending to teach men how to cure the habit of opium smoking or telling them where they could find the necessary and infallible medicines. The pompous title of one would lead the public to infer that the medicine advertised was prepared in accordance with American receipt; another according to a receipt obtained from Manila; another from India, etc. On one of these placards were large English capital letters, arranged without meaning, in the ordinary style of Chinese writing—that is, in rows from the top to the bottom of the sheet. Such letters were used, doubtless, in order more successfully to impose on the common people, who might be supposed to be more easily duped by the display of foreign characters. Another had what was intended to be an imitation of a sentence written with English letters in the running hand, taken from a Christian almanac published by a missionary here. The original design of this sentence was to illustrate the way Chinese words could be represented by the use of English letters. Here it was evidently used as a kind of certificate of the value or genuineness of the medicine advertised. Few Chinese can read English here, and the sentence probably produced its desired impression on many of the people. These facts show two things—the great demand for opium medicine on the part of the victims of opium and the readiness of some Chinese to engage in the manufacture and the vending of quack nostrums, hoping to make money out of the vicious habits of their fellow countrymen.

There seems to be a bewitching influence connected with opium smoking which renders it almost impracticable to break away from the habit when once formed. The peculiar pains and sensations which accompany attempts to desist from smoking it also have, doubtless, a great influence in discouraging such attempts. Some missionaries and physicians in other parts of China seem to think that many victims have been reclaimed from this vice by the aid of certain medicines, but benevolent efforts to overcome the power of the habit in individual cases have not here been attended with very encouraging success. Few have the fortitude to bear up against the fascination of the pipe and the agonies induced by efforts at reformation, even with the aid of foreign medicines, long enough to become thoroughly cured. They usually, after a short trial of abstaining from the drug, have recourse to it again, although they know that every indulgence with the opium pipe but rivets the chains of their bondage the tighter.

A strange infatuation impels annually many of the Chinese who have never smoked this drug to begin its use, and, after they have been bound fast in the fetters of the habit they have induced, they seemingly arouse themselves to the fact of their thralldom. They know perfectly well that, if they smoke regularly the bewitching pipe, they will certainly soon come within its power, and yet many yearly voluntarily become its fresh victims. With their eyes open to the inevitable consequences of indulgence, they blindly do what will enslave them for life.

Some have attempted to compare the evils of opium smoking in China with the evils of drinking intoxicating liquors in the West. But these vices are so different in some of their principal effects as to render a just comparison exceedingly difficult. The one is soothing and tranquilizing, the other excites and often maddens. Ardent spirits are often taken to stimulate to the commission of violent and bloody deeds; but opium is never smoked for such a purpose, nor with such an effect. Were the subject of the comparative evils of opium smoking and liquor drinking, as seen in China (where the use of Chinese whiskey, or *samshu,* is universal among all classes), to be submitted for decision to intelligent Chinamen, the verdict would be given with promptness and startling energy against opium. It would be unanimous in the condemnation of opium as being the producer of an immensely greater amount of misery, sickness, poverty, and death than Chinese liquors.

The Chinese seldom discuss the evils of opium smoking without excitement, nor do they often refer to the subject in conversation with those foreigners who can understand them without manifesting apparently a very cordial and sincere hatred of the drug, frequently denouncing it in the most emphatic terms. They are well aware of the destructive and baneful influence of opium consumption. I desire to protest against the justice and the truthfulness of the sentiments which some foreigners assert in regard to the feelings and the views of the Chinese on the effects of the use of this drug. They do not regard it as a harmless, innocent luxury. They are not ignorant of its monstrous and its numerous evil effects; indeed, they acknowledge them and depict them in a manner not to be excelled by foreigners. But, after all, they continue the use of that which they appear heartily and sincerely to reprobate. To the question, *Why the Chinese continue the use of opium when they are fully aware of its evil effects on the habits, health, and wealth of its victims, and consequently on the social condition and welfare of the empire,* an intelligent literary man—reverently pointing upward with his thumb in a manner peculiarly Chinese—once uttered substantially the following sentiments: "THE MASTER AND GOVERNOR MUST HAVE A MEANING IN CAUSING IT. HE MUST INTEND TO DESTROY THE NATION. THERE IS NO OTHER WAY OF ACCOUNTING FOR THE LOVE OF THE CHINESE FOR OPIUM. THEY KNOW ITS BANEFUL EFFECTS PERFECTLY WELL, BUT STILL ARE EXCEEDINGLY FOND OF SMOKING. HE MUST PURPOSE OUR NATIONAL DESTRUCTION." Providence does indeed seem to be making use of this drug in humbling this proud nation, not by *causing* the natives to smoke it any more than He *causes* foreigners to introduce it, or their countrymen to purchase and retail it, but by *allowing* them freely and joyfully to smoke it in the gratification of a vitiated taste, in the same sense that He *allows* foreigners to produce and import it in their desire to become rich, notwithstanding the miseries they are instrumental in producing.

Good men in China deplore the use of opium as an extraordinary and most gigantic obstacle to the reception of the Gospel and the spread of it among the Chinese. The beneficent religion preached by men from Western lands and this demoralizing drug are placed by the vast majority of this people in the same catalogue—viz., articles introduced by foreigners. Missionaries, while denouncing the evils of opium smoking, and entreating the people not to indulge in the vice of using it, are very frequently met by the reply, "*You foreigners bring it to sell and now you exhort* us *not to use it. If you do not wish us to smoke it, why did you import it? If you did not bring it to sell, we could not buy it and therefore should not use it.*" Missionaries were often regarded by the Chinese at first as a party to the importation of the drug. The British consul stationed here before the large increase of foreign trade in 1853 was very generally believed by the common people to be appointed by his government principally for the purpose of indirectly fostering the opium trade and of protecting the opium receiving ships which were stationed in the River Min. Generally speaking, only those Chinese who are more or less personally acquainted with the missionaries know that they do not deal in the article. Probably those who have acquired considerable knowledge of Christian doctrines from the reading of the books published by missionaries are led to infer that the authors of those books, or the believers and the doers of the doctrines they contain, would be unwilling to engage in the opium trade. It is doubtless true that, by some good proportion of the Chinese who live at the consular ports, the missionaries are regarded as opposed to the importation and the consumption of the drug, because the use of it is the source of numerous and aggregated evils. It is, however, as undoubtedly true that the mass of the people in China at a distance from the consular ports have no such knowledge and make no such distinction between preachers of the Gospel and importers of opium.

NOTE

Justus Doolittle, *Social Life of the Chinese* (New York: Harper, 1865).

The Philippine Commission

After victory in the Spanish-American War the United States decided to keep the Philippines as a colony, thus becoming an Asian colonial power. The Spanish had allowed and had profited from opium sales during their rule, and the Americans were forced to decide whether to keep or eliminate this system. The Philippine Commission appointed a committee to look at opium in 1903 and charged it with determining an appropriate opium policy for the new colony, as there was at that point no consensus on the effects of opium or the appropriate way to deal with it. Opium use was recognized to be a pan-Asian phenomenon, so the commission visited Japan, Formosa, Shanghai, Hong Kong, Saigon, Singapore, Burma, Java, and the Philippines, taking testimony and examining the legal and economic basis of the trade. Their final conclusion was that the United States should set up an opium monopoly that would sell opium to registered addicts for a brief period until the trade could be entirely eliminated. After 1908 opium importation and use were illegal in the Philippines. This model and the data the Philippine Commission collected would be influential in debates about opium policy all over Asia and led to the 1909 Shanghai, the 1913 Hague, and the 1925 Geneva conferences for the international control of the opium trade.

The selections below deal with the question of the dangers of opium to the health of the individual, which had not yet been entirely resolved.

Interview XI

Interrogatories Addressed in Writing to Reverend Thos. Barclay, English Presbyterian Mission, Tainan, Formosa

Q. During the Chinese regime, was there any attempt to regulate the opium trade in Formosa on the part of the government?

A. During the Chinese regime there was absolutely no attempt to regulate the opium traffic; the traffic in it was as free as in any other article of merchandise—that is, internally, there were customshouse regulations.

Q. Was anything done officially to aid the victims to break away from morphomania?

A. No official cognizance of morphomania was taken. This vice had not attained any great prominence in the island.

Q. At the inception of the existing law, what, in your opinion, was the popular feeling among the natives?

A. Among the opium smokers, of course, the law was unpopular. Among others it was recognized as the right thing to do—by some heartily welcomed. Considering the state of feeling among the people at the time, one could not look for enthusiastic approbation: the mere fact that it was proposed by the Japanese was enough to set people against it. I believe, however, that they were passively favorable and not opposed to it.

Q. Has there been any change in the popular opinion regarding the merits of the law during the past five years, and if so, upon what grounds?

A. Any change of feeling arises from the fact that the provisions of the law have not been carried out. The original plan was that no one should get a permit to smoke opium, except those whose health would suffer or whose lives would be endangered by giving it up; but no such restrictions seem to have been made, anyone being able to get a permit who applied for it and was willing to pay. So much was this the case that the Chinese came to believe that the government had no real desire to stop the practice but looked upon it as a regular source of revenue. This belief was also general among the members of the foreign community: even Japanese have expressed themselves to me in the same effect. The authorities have, however, always denied it. Undoubtedly this caused much offense to the Chinese, who have freely criticized the government for its failure to act as it had originally proposed doing. They blame it for making high moral professions, while all the time its object is to get the trade into its own hands, so that it might raise the price and make a good profit out of this harmful practice. I have heard far more said against failure to carry out the law than I have heard said against the law itself.

Q. Are the provisions of the law rigidly carried out in your section of the country?

A. I am informed that for about three years, I believe, no new permits have been issued and that this is telling rapidly upon the number of smokers. My own inquiries among the people corroborate this. But doubtless you will have fuller statistics than I can give you. The police supervision is, I believe, very strict. The Chinese are quite afraid to be found in the company of one smoking opium. Any one they say found within five feet of a person smoking opium is liable to arrest, if not himself the possessor of a permit, the idea being that he is waiting his turn. So much is this the case that I am told that numbers of persons who do not smoke themselves but have occasion to associate with those who do take out permits—simply as a matter of precaution. I was horrified lately to learn that an elder of our church was the holder of a permit to smoke opium; but I was assured that there was no ground for suspicion. There is, I believe, practically no smuggling.

Q. What effect has the educational movement, which I understand is in operation, had to discourage the opium habit among the younger generation?

A. The educational movement has not yet affected the life of the island to any practical extent, except among a few high school or medical students, etc. It would not have occurred to me to think of it as a factor in the opium question. The rising generation is taking more to cigarettes and drink.

Q. Do you think that the law tends to stimulate the victims of the vice to make an effort toward release?

A. The law tends to stimulate giving up the practice in that it is now felt to be more troublesome; the regulations must be observed. There is uncertainty as to what may be the next regulation. There is a rumor among the people that all opium smokers are to be obliged to wear a red uniform. The practice is less fashionable now: it is not safe to offer the pipe to a visitor until it is known that he has a permit. The drug also is said to be more expensive and less pleasant to smoke. The government is said to be doctoring the drug with a view to weaning the smokers from its use.

Q. Have more cases of this kind come under your observation since the promulgation of the law than prior to it?

A. On this matter I have no personal experience. Cases of this description do not come directly under my observation, except in the case of those who become worshipers; but I am informed that of late such cases are more frequent.

Q. To what extent, in your experience, is there illegal use of opium?

A. On this matter I have no personal experience; but I am informed that illegal smoking takes place to a much greater extent than I would have supposed from the strictness of police inspection. By illegal use I understand the purchasing of opium by one who has not himself a permit in another person's name, the use of another person's pipe, etc. One estimate given me was as high as 10 percent of the whole amount used; but I imagine this is much too high. Of late I have heard of fewer cases of suicide caused by the use of opium. From the completeness of the Japanese registration system and the hold this gives them over the people, I imagine this illegal purchase might be stopped if the government really wished to reduce the amount consumed.

Q. What emendations in the law or what substitute law, if any, would you suggest as being more effective than the ordinances and regulations now in force?

A. As a missionary I am, of course, opposed altogether to the use of the drug except as a medicine. From a government point of view, even, it might have been a simpler, and it might be argued a more merciful, plan to have abolished this practice entirely from the first. It would have caused some suffering, perhaps some deaths (though this may be questioned, and provision might have been made for such cases), but less suffering than has followed its continued use. It might have driven away some of the wealthier Chinese, whom the government was anxious to retain in Formosa. More drastic measures lacking, however, the plan proposed, if it had been faithfully carried out, would have been a great boon to the people. If it is the case that no new licenses are being issued, in a few years a marked improvement should be visible. It ought to be made quite clear to the people that the government is earnest in wishing to put a stop to the matter. This is not generally believed. Persons professing to be cured and wishing to return their permits should be taken at their word and the permit confiscated. They might be kept under supervision to make sure that they have really given up the practice. Our Mission Hospital has no difficulty in getting tenants for the rooms set apart for this purpose. At present there seems to be great difficulty in getting rid of permits. Why there should be this reluctance on the part of the officials I do not know—probably from want of faith in the reality of the cure. The saying among the people used to be that it was much easier to get a new permit than to get rid of an old one. The retention of the permit, of course, makes return to the practice much easier, when the temptation comes—and it always does. Criminals in prison are cured by drastic measures, with I understand uniformly good results. Such persons should have their permits taken from them, so that they might not resume the practice.

Some years ago, as you are aware, a movement for the cure of the habit spread like wildfire through the island. There were objectionable features about the movement that justified the authorities in interfering; but they might have accepted the cures. Had the permits of all who professed to be cured been taken from them, there would be far fewer smokers in the island today. I have been told that today native medical practitioners are not allowed to treat patients for the cure of the opium habit. The patient must apply for the cure of some other disease; then the doctor tells him that during the time he is in his hands he must abstain from the use of opium. By the time he leaves his hands he is cured. There may be no truth in the statement, but it shows how little confidence the people have in the desire of the government to reduce the number of smokers. Had the government been enthusiastically in earnest in seeking the extinction of the vice, and rigidly carried out its proposals, not only refusing licenses to learners but also discriminating among the smokers, determining what part of them really required the drug, in a very few years from now the question would have been practically settled.

Q. Have you observed any instances of Japanese acquiring the opium vice in your district, and if so, how many authenticated cases?

A. I have never heard of any Japanese acquiring the habit and think probably there are no such cases.

As regards the subject in general, I should say that one very interesting point is that the government, whether in Formosa or in the Philippines, should be clear in its own mind that this is a hurtful and obnoxious practice, which it is anxious to bring to a stop and from which it will seek to draw no revenue. In this matter it will have the sympathy of the people and the approbation of right-thinking ones among them. It can in no sense be regarded as a hardship that such regulations should be made. In England and Japan, and I suppose America also, opium is treated by law as a poison, which is to be bought and sold under the same regulations as other poisons. In the ordinary course of events in the case of new possessions this law would go into force along with the whole body of laws, and it could not be felt by anyone as a grievance that this should be so. Whether the fact that the practice is found already existing should or should not affect the question may be fairly considered. In any case, it should be made plain that any legislation abolishing the traffic is in accord with the natural course of events and is not to be considered special legislation directed against the smokers. On the contrary, the exceptional legislation is the permissive legislation, if any such is passed, authorizing the temporary continuance of the practice. Any such regulations are acts of grace on the part of the government, which the people have no right to demand and which the government has the right strictly to limit. It should be made plain that it is not to be expected that any such special legislation is to be permitted to any great extent or for any length of time, but that at an early date the law of the land will come into full operation.

Letter attached to the preceding interrogatories

Tainan, Formosa, November 14, 1903

Dear Dr. Brent:

I do not know how far what I have written may be of service to you. In order that I might not simply send you my own impressions, I submitted your questions to the students of our Theological College, drawn from all parts of the island and able to speak frankly and freely without regard to what they might think I wished to hear. What I have written represents my own judgment after hearing their statements. You may rely on the information so far as it goes. I have put down a good deal of what the people are saying, not as being necessarily right, but at least as showing what they think. I understand, of course, that your Committee is in possession of all the official statistics, etc., which the government has compiled, and that what you wish from me is rather what the people say, think, and do. From my own experience, I do not think the Chinese will resent pretty firm dealing in this matter, so long as it is honestly meant for their good. They recognize the evil that flows from the use of opium, though they have not strength enough to give it up. But they do resent anything like double dealing, professing to seek their good while really wanting their money. I am glad that the government here has taken a firm stand. We shall watch for the results with much interest. I am, very truly,

Thomas Barclay

China. Interview XII

Interview with the Right Reverend Bishop Graves, Who Has Been a Resident of China for the Past Twenty Years

Shanghai, November 4, 1903

The opinion of Bishop Graves, after several years of observation among the poor class of people, is to the effect that the moderate use of opium is pernicious, for generally speaking a man who begins by using the drug moderately increases the dose from time to time, until he becomes a slave to the habit. He states that he has personally known many natives who, from being moderate users of opium, have become immoderate ones and have suffered all the evils consequent upon such a course. He also stated that sometimes men of strong will who find that they are becoming enslaved by the habit attempt to break it off, but that they rarely if ever succeed in so doing. He was of the opinion that the use of opium in the provinces of the interior of China is a great and unmistakable curse to the inhabitants.

The bishop was under the impression that mercantile and other firms are averse to employing moderate users of opium in positions of trust or when money is handled. He stated also that the moderate user of opium becomes dependent upon it, even if he remains moderate in its use, and that while he may perform his work in a satisfactory manner as long as he is able to obtain the drug, if by any accident he should be deprived of it, he would become practically useless.

He mentioned several instances in which excessive users of opium sold their children or wives in order to procure the drug. It was also stated that the men and officers of the Chinese army and navy as a rule use opium, and the supposition was advanced that the demoralization said to exist in these services is due to its use.

Interview XIII

Interview with Mr. G. E. Tucker, Secretary of the Asiatic Department of The New York Life Insurance Company

Shanghai, November 5, 1903

Mr. Tucker placed such information as was in his possession at the disposal of the Committee. He stated that but few users of opium apply for insurance, and an examination of his records demonstrated the accuracy of his statement. A considerable number of Chinese, however, have been insured by the company and among them some who stated that they used opium, but in no case more than 2 mace (1–5 ounces) per diem. Mr. Tucker said that if emaciation or say other sign of injury to the applicant resulting from the use of opium, such as pallor, anemia, etc., is apparent, the application cannot be unconditionally accepted.

Interview XIV

Interview with Dr. N. Macleod, Examining Physician of the Shanghai Agency of the New York Life Insurance Company

Shanghai, November 5, 1903

Dr. Macleod stated that he advises companies with which he is connected to scrutinize with care the applications of all persons (Chinese) who use opium. He believes that Chinese can use opium moderately for years, indeed for a lifetime, with no ill results but that many are injured by it. He has prepared a number of questions to be asked by the agents of the insurance company in the case of Chinese applicants. (A copy of these questions is hereto attached.) He laid stress on the difficulty of determining what is a moderate use of opium and what an immoderate one. Individuals differ in their constitutions and in their susceptibility to the effects of the drug. Dr. Macleod did not believe that the fact of a man's using opium militates against his opportunity of getting work, unless he gives evidence of using it to excess, in which case his chances are diminished.

NEW YORK LIFE INSURANCE COMPANY,
SHANGHAI BRANCH OFFICE

Every Chinese applicant should be asked if he now smokes or ever has smoked opium. The following questions will be considered part of the application:

1. What is the daily amount now consumed?
2. If ever exceeded, when, and how much?
3. If not consumed daily, how often, and how much?
4. When was the habit commenced, and with what amount?
5. If opium is not now taken, when was the habit stopped?

Applicant.

To the Examining Physician:
Note any evidence of the habit, like delicacy, pallor, or anemia.

M. D.

Note: Two mace per diem is the limit placed on the quantity of opium which may be used by an applicant without disqualifying him for obtaining insurance.
1 mace equals cir. 1—10 oz. equals 1—10 tael.

Letter

Shanghai, November 6, 1903

Dear Major Carter:
    The following is the gist of what I had to say to the New York Life Insurance Home Office re opium smoking:
    "In the absence of anything like reliable statistics and as the effects of the moderate use of opium are at least no more evident than those of the moderate use of alcohol, while the effects of opium abuse are certainly not so obvious as those of alcoholic excess, no more definite statement as to the prevalence of opium smoking in China is possible than that it is apparently less than the use of alcohol among the white races. The statements vouchsafed by the users of the drug as to the quantity vary from a few pipes occasionally to 1 to 4 mace, which latter figure, confessed to, raises suspicion of approaching excess. A 'pipe' may vary from three to eleven grains, the latter representing a mass preferred for smoking and known as a 'pipe,' a large one. I should say,

smokers who can afford it have their 'mixtures,' but the quality is of less importance than the quantity. Social pleasure is the usual plea for commencing the habit—seldom pain relief. By excess, health is disturbed and disease resistance and longevity lessened; short of excess, the question of effect is, I believe, on all fours with that of alcohol in moderate use, it may or may not shorten life. The effects of excess are written large on its subject in the form of pallor, loss of weight, expression, the condition of the gums, and the breath odor."

I am sorry I cannot give you anything more definite on the subject. I am,

Yours sincerely,

N. Macleod, Examining physician of Shanghai Office of N. Y. Life Insurance Co.

Interview XV

Interview with Dr. Boone, a Resident of Shanghai for Forty Years, during which Time He Has Been, and Still Is, in the Practice of Medicine

Shanghai, November 5, 1903

Dr. Boone stated that he believes his opportunities for studying the effects of opium upon the Chinese have been rather good, as most of his practice has been confined to these people. Among his clients have been many men of rank and position.

In his opinion the use of opium is increasing and is certainly more common than it was forty years ago. He regards it as very difficult to draw a line between the moderate and the immoderate use of opium, within the physiologic limits even, as some persons are more easily affected than others. He believes that a large percentage (probably 66 percent) of those who use opium moderately for a while increase the dose gradually until they become excessive users. This is the natural tendency, and only a strong will is able to resist the increased use or to diminish the quantity of the dose when that quantity has been recognized by the user as being injurious.

Many, if not most, of the Chinese officials use opium, and while its use is generally on the increase, this is particularly true so far as the women are concerned. Children also—boys from ten to twelve years of age—smoke opium, generally with deleterious results.

Dr. Boone could see no difference in the effect of the drug upon

Europeans and Chinese. Its moral effect on the Chinese is often to make him a criminal. Opium smokers are prone to lying and to acts of malicious mischief, such as incendiarism, etc. The police courts of Shanghai show that the use of opium and crime in Shanghai are intimately associated. Dr. Boone stated that on the death of the father of a family, when he is a user of opium, the friends of the family are wont to urge the widow or the surviving head of the family to destroy the pipes and other apparatus used in opium smoking, in order to prevent the sons from following in the footsteps of the father.

Dr. Boone mentioned a number of cases which had come under his observation of the breakdown of users of opium under mental strain. He stated that while foreigners take chances in employing natives, the Chinese are unwilling to employ in positions of trust anyone using opium, particularly do they decline to employ such persons in positions involving the handling of money.

The Doctor regards opium as having its physical effect chiefly on the nerves, contrasting it with alcohol, the effects of which are confined mainly to the kidneys, the liver, the stomach, and the arteries. There is, of course, alcoholic neuritis. There appears to be no postmortem evidence of the use of opium that is pathognomonic.

He does not think that the use of opium has any marked influence upon the power of resistance in cases of illness or injury or in surgical operations. If a person is in the habit of using opium, it is unwise to compel him to discontinue its use on entering the hospital as a patient, since a condition resembling delirium tremens might be superinduced, exactly parallel with such circumstances in alcoholic cases.

The Doctor was sure that the area devoted to the cultivation of opium in China is steadily increasing, a condition which he believes to be due to the actions of the landowners and high officials, as larger and quicker money returns can be derived from the cultivation of the poppy than from that of any other crop. The statement has been made that the Chinese government desires to produce opium sufficient to drive the importer out of the market and after that has been accomplished to prohibit the cultivation of the poppy and the use of opium. Dr. Boone regards the statement misleading and meant only to serve as an excuse for the increasing of the area planted with the poppy—"to save the face" of the government.

The opinions of Dr. Boone and of an eminent British medical man at Shanghai were requested for submittal to the Royal Opium Commission. Both opinions are said to have been of about the same character as that above set forth. (The Committee, however, has not been able to find these opinions in the proceedings of the Royal Opium Commission.)

Dr. Boone said that there is a demand for "opium cures" in many parts of China, but that as most of the so-called cures contain opium or morphia in some form, they do more harm than good, since the remedy is usually in tablet or pill form and can be carried about with no difficulty and used by the habitué as many times a day as he may desire.

Interview XVI

Interview with Messrs. Yu, Yeng, Chao, Li, and Su, All Leading Chinese Merchants of Shanghai and Holding Daotai Rank

Shanghai, November 7, 1903

Chairman: (Explains the purpose for which the Committee has come to Shanghai.)

Mr. Chao: The wealthy class in China, as a rule, does not smoke opium; the habit is largely confined to the poor, upon whom most of the consequent hardship and injury fall. We would welcome any measure looking to the prohibition of the use of opium.

Mr. Yu: But it would be very difficult to stop the use of opium, as a great many people have already become so accustomed to it that to deprive them of their supply would entail an immense amount of suffering.

I would suggest that opium smokers should be licensed and that only those should be granted licenses who are already addicted to the habit. Opium should be sold only by the government. In that way the government could largely control the matter.

Mr. Li: I would also suggest that the amount of opium an individual be allowed to smoke should be regulated by his needs.

Q. I should infer that all these gentlemen are dissatisfied with the present status of the opium problem in China?

Unanimous assent.

Mr. Yu: A great many begin the use of opium on account of illness or weakness and soon become slaves to the habit.

Q. Are the people satisfied with the present regulations regarding opium, or would they like some change?

Mr. Chao: The people would change the conditions if they could, but it is not an easy matter.

Q. Suppose that a province, we'll say, for instance, this province of Jiangsu, should through its government try to enforce prohibition, would there be any possibility of carrying it out? Would a prohibitive law be possible in any province?

Mr. Chao: It is only through the central government that any such law could be enacted.

Mr. Yeng: Opium is not the very worst thing in China. There is also gambling, which is the worst of all evils; but the addition of opium to this vice makes conditions very deplorable.

Mr. Li: Has the government of the Philippine Islands statistics of the number of Chinese who smoke opium and of the amount they smoke, so that regulations could be made to allow each smoker only the amount that he is actually smoking now? Regulations should be made forbidding a smoker to increase the amount of the dose?

Chairman: We could determine the number of persons that use opium, but we should have to take their statements for the amounts they use.

Mr. Chao: Do you have opium dens in the Philippine Islands, as we do in China?

Chairman: At present, yes.

Mr. Chao: Could opium not be made a government monopoly?

Chairman: The object of this committee is to determine whether such a course is advisable.

Mr. Chao: I am entirely in favor of a government monopoly; it is the only way in which the habit can be controlled. Get the smokers to state the amount they are using at the time they obtain their licenses, and then permit them to buy only that amount, gradually reducing the dose until they become free from the habit. Only with a government monopoly could such a measure be enforced.

Q. Are the other gentlemen of the same opinion?

Unanimous assent.

Mr. Li: A heavy penalty should be placed upon those who are licensed to sell opium, for violating the regulations.

Q. Is there any organization in China looking to the improvement of the present opium regulations?

Mr. Su: There is nothing of the kind at present, excepting church organizations, known as anti-opium clubs or societies. We intend to effect an organization that shall be outside the church, to see if we can do anything to limit or stop the use of opium in China.

Q. Are any of the gentlemen present members of an anti-opium society?

A. None. (None of those present, it should be stated, uses opium.)

Mr. Li: The entire matter lies in the hands of the central government. When you speak to a high official about opium smoking, he says you must not smoke; but a great many prominent persons smoke opium and think lightly of it, a condition of affairs which makes the problem all the more difficult. In the central government rests the power, and the provinces can do only what it says in the matter.

Q. We understand that there is an old imperial edict forbidding the importation of opium. The clause in our treaty referring to opium is based on the assumption that there is such an edict.

Mr. Chao: Under Emperor Daoguang a heavy penalty was placed on the use of opium. That was about sixty-six years ago. It was then held to be a great crime.

Q. Has that law been revoked?

Mr. Chao: No, but the law is not carried out.

Q. Our government does not allow American merchants to import opium into China on account of this law, which, we suppose, is still on the statute books.

Mr. Li: I believe that three months' or so notice should be given to all merchants in the Philippine Islands who are at present dealing in opium, after which they should be made to sell whatever they have on hand to the government at a stated price.

Q. In your opinion, should a young person under twenty years of age be granted a license, that is, if he already smokes?

Mr. Chao: In case such a person has smoked only for a number of months, so that the habit could easily be stopped, no license should be granted to him, but if he has used opium for two or more years, the suffering in his case would be as great as in that of an older person, should he attempt to break off the habit, so that it would be unjust to refuse him the license.

Mr. Li: A great deal could be accomplished by making a moral distinction between a smoker and a non-smoker, by publicly considering the one as belonging to a high class of society and the other to a low class. This would be a great inducement to many to stop the use of opium.

Q. Do you think that instruction in the public schools regarding the evils of opium would influence the people in breaking off the habit?

Unanimous assent.

Q. In employing their clerks and laborers, do Chinese firms and businessmen investigate to find out whether the applicants use opium or not?

Mr. Chao: Yes.

Mr. Li: As a rule we prefer those who do not smoke opium, but there are many instances in which the only person we can secure who knows the ins and outs of the business is an opium smoker, and we have to employ him.

Q. Is it possible for a man to continue smoking all through life with moderation in such a way that it does not affect him in body or mind?

Mr. Chao: No, it makes a great deal of difference; the use of opium is always dangerous. No man can smoke opium for a long time without harm to himself.

Mr. Su: One of the signs that distinguishes an opium smoker is the dilly-dallying and slowness with which he performs his work. He is lax and careless in all his habits.

Q. Would you compare the moderate use of opium with the moderate use of cigars or the moderate use of alcoholic drinks?

A. All concurred in the opinion that the use of opium is much worse.

Mr. Yu: An opium smoker must have his daily dose; if he cannot buy it, he steals it.

Q. Is that true also in the case of a man who is a moderate user of opium?

Mr. Yu: There is no difference.

Mr. Li: There is, however, a difference between the well-to-do and the poor people in the extent to which the use of opium injures them. The well-to-do are better fed and clothed and as a result have more resistance, enabling them to smoke opium with less injury and suffering.

Q. How do you regard the increasing growth of the poppy in China? Do you think this is unfortunate or otherwise?

Mr. Li: We do not regard it as good; but it cannot be helped. The farmers find the cultivation of opium much more profitable than that of cereals, and even if the government should forbid it, they would still continue to cultivate the poppy.

Mr. Yeng: In the province of Shanxi especially.

Mr. Li: You have a very good religion, and it would be a very good thing if no opium smoker were allowed to become a member of a church.

Mr Chao: Bishop Graves (of Shanghai) told us that the admission of moderate opium smokers to membership in the church was tried by one of his missionaries but was so disastrous that it had to be given up.

Mr. Su: Any plan for the suppression of opium which is to accomplish anything must come from above, must come from the central government, and not from below.

Mr Yu: The importation of morphia, which comes into the country in the little cigarettes called "Pinhead Cigarettes," should be carefully looked into. A laborer who makes ten cents a day at first spends two cash daily for Pinhead cigarettes, but as he continues their use, he gradually increases the number he daily smokes, until all of his earnings are required to satisfy his craving for them, finally leading to his ruin.

Mr. Yeng: It is only the low class of people that buy these cigarettes: the better class do not smoke them. Those who begin to use them seem to become so addicted to the habit that it is almost as difficult for them to break it off as in the case of opium. Their sale has increased until it amounts to more than 3,000,000 annually.

Q. Where are they made?

Mr. Li: They are made in America.

Chairman: They are sold also in the Philippines. We shall have them analyzed.

Mr. Chao: All the so-called anti-opium medicines that are being sold throughout China contain morphia in some form. They are sold very extensively.

Q. Where are these remedies made?

Mr. Chao: They are prepared here. The morphia is imported in large quantities and the remedies put up here. If the present treaty is enforced, importation of morphia will be prohibited.

Q. In your judgment, would it be wiser for the government to control the preparation of opium and to have direct administration of all that pertains to it, or would you recommend farming out the work to such reliable men as might be chosen?

Mr. Chao: It is better to keep it entirely in the hands of the government.

Mr. Li: I would suggest that the government of the Philippine Islands get hold of the leading Chinese and in consultation with them make rules that will be best for the regulation of the matter.

Chairman: The government has already consulted with the leading Chinese of the islands. Two ideas were advanced by them, one, total prohibition, the other, government monopoly.

Mr. Li: The Chinese should be consulted for several reasons, among others because they understand the inner workings of the Chinese mind and can make suggestions that might be helpful to the government in the control of the traffic.

Chairman: We thank you very much, gentlemen, for your kindness.

Interview XVII

Interview with Reverend Timothy Richards, Who Has Been a Resident of China for Thirty-Three Years

Shanghai, November 7, 1903

Q. Is the moderate use of opium common in China?

A. A very large number of Chinese use opium moderately, as moderately as we use tea or coffee. I am aware that there are many who would express a different opinion.

Q. Does the moderate use of opium seem to have no effect on the individual?

A. Well, I should not say "no effect," at least no serious effect.

Q. When mercantile or other firms employ Chinese, do they investigate to find out whether the applicant for employment uses opium or not?

A. I do not believe any inquiries are made in that regard as a rule.

Q. Is that true of both Chinese and foreign firms?

A. There are many Chinese who are very strict about it; but these are the exception rather than the rule. Opium is taken as a matter of course, more or less just as we in England take beer or wine; but that does not justify those who take it in an extreme manner. The great mass of business-men in Shanghai use opium moderately.

Q. What is the effect on the moderate user of opium when he is deprived it?

A. Well. I should say that he contracts a sort of malaria and in general is out of sorts and can do nothing very well.

Q. I suppose that this condition finally passes away entirely?

A. Yes, but it takes considerable time, and it is only men of strong will who are able entirely to break off the habit. There is a fact that might be mentioned in this connection. There is quite a large number of persons addicted to the use of opium who were obliged to take it to relieve sickness or suffering. After once commencing its use they became dependent upon it and if deprived of it would die. There are innumerable instances of this kind. They resort to opium because they are on the point of death, and it is only the opium that sustains them. I have seen a number of cases where opium was abandoned at the cost of life.

Q. Is the proportion of those who begin by using opium moderately and gradually increase the dose until they become excessive users considerable?

A. Yes. There is a tendency in that way. In this one respect opium differs from alcohol. There is a tendency gradually to increase the use of it, and once the habit is contracted, it is a thing that the user must get every day. This is not true of beer and wine; I know lots of people who take a glass of beer only when they have company and never think of using it at other times. In the case of opium, however, there is in most cases a daily craving for it, when once the habit is permanently established it is an exceedingly difficult thing to get rid of.

On the other hand, I learned this very interesting thing from a friend of mine who came from the interior that in a certain province they smoke opium only on certain days when they attend market, never touching it while at home. That resembles a custom in England. Many people take a glass of beer with their friends on market days and do not think of touching it until they come to market again.

However, my observation during most of my life in China has been that there is a daily craving for the drug, very much the same as in the case of a man who is in the habit of smoking and must have his cigars daily, only much more so in the case of opium. From what I have heard, it is generally used moderately.

Q. They use it as some people who are addicted to the use of coffee or tea?

A. There is more truth in that comparison, in my judgment, than is generally allowed by those who are in the habit of running down the use of opium. I think that there have been extreme statements on both sides. Some say that the use of opium has no bad effect whatever; that I believe to be an extreme statement. Others say that a person who uses opium is bound to go in rack and ruin; that also, in my opinion, is an extreme statement.

Q. Is opium used in all ranks of society?

A. Yes. In many provinces from 80 to 90 percent of the people use it.

Major Carter: That bears out Dr. Osier's statement. He says that the majority of the inhabitants of the East use it, referring chiefly to China and India.

A. Yes. In the western provinces of China fully 80 to 90 percent use the drug.

Q. Are they any less vigorous than the people in those provinces where it is not used to such an extent?

A. That I cannot answer. I have not observed the conditions sufficiently to make a satisfactory answer. It would be a random answer, which is of no value.

Q. We have heard the statement made that the Chinese government is encouraging the cultivation of the poppy, with a view to supplying all of the opium that is wanted in the country, after which it is the purpose of the government to stop the raising of the poppy and prohibit the use of opium. Is that statement correct?

A. I have heard that statement made. I should not be at all surprised that a few of the most rabid officials would do so with all their hearts; but I have not the facts.

Q. Do you know anything concerning the action of the government?

A. I could not place my hands upon any documents. The regime of a tariff on opium is a definite proposal by the officials themselves. I believe the statements made by such a man as Dr. McKay to be perfectly correct. The only objection the officials have to the use of opium is that the silver goes out of the country. They do not say so in their proclamations, but there is no question about it. The Chinese government for the last fifty or sixty years has been anything but a high moral tone. Everything is done from an inferior motive; the welfare of the people is one of the last things considered by the government. The government has deteriorated immensely from what it was at one time. Its main motive now is money.

Q. Do you think there is any regulation that might be put into force in China that would decrease the use of opium, or are matters now conducted as well as they could be?

A. If it were the purpose of the government to stop the use of opium it could very easily be done. Let them place so high a duty upon all opium produced in the country that the cultivation of the poppy would have to be suspended, and then let them raise the price of the drug to such an extent as to make it prohibitive. The thing is done instantly.

Q. But the different provinces have practically independent governments; in other words, the only government there is in China is the provincial one, is not that true?

A. Certain things the central government reserves to itself.

Q. Do you know of any instance in which a province has taken a definite stand against the use of opium?

A. There are several provinces that have taken fits and starts in the matter, but they have never done it to such an extent that it would convince anybody that they were thoroughly in earnest. A proclamation is issued to the effect that the cultivation of the poppy is absolutely prohibited. Then the governor goes along the road, for he is obliged to visit the whole province at least once during his time of office. When the proclamation is issued, there are many who think that he will make it hard for those who raise the poppy, and when the people learn that he is likely to come along a certain road they are careful to see that not a poppy is in sight. This I personally know to have happened in the province of Shanxi. Outside the main route, however, the thing is going along as usual.

Zhang Lu has the reputation of being the most vigorous opposer of opium. He insisted that every prefect and every district magistrate should see that the poppy was not grown, and he raised the duty upon opium during his term of office, but it lasted only for twenty months, when another man came into office. This amply demonstrates that the Chinese government, as a government, has no intention of stopping the use of opium.

Q. Is there any Chinese government?

A. If a viceroy does not obey the central government, he will find himself high and dry. It is a government to that extent. The appointment of all high officials is in the hands of the central government.

Q. Is there any difference in the proportion of Chinese that use opium in the cities and in the outlying districts?

A. Yes. There are many places where opium is but little used and quite a number of districts where practically no opium is used. In the province of

Shandong there is village after village, with as high as 10,000 inhabitants, where scarcely anyone takes opium.

Q. Is there any important port there?

A. Yes. Chefoo [Yantai].

Q. Can you give us any reason for this?

A. No, I cannot give any definite reason for it. But I suppose that there is a sort of hereditary opinion among them in regard to the matter. They pride themselves that they have not used opium. In a village of 500 there may be only four or five families who take opium. There are many such places. It is observed that wherever there is much trade with foreign countries, and especially with the people that come from the West of Asia, the opium habit is prevalent.

Opium is also used as a medium of exchange. Paper money issued in one district can seldom be used in another, and traders can carry opium more easily than silver. Opium can be sold everywhere. Everybody is handling it. It is this kind of a thing that prompts the people to the use of it.

Q. Do you know of any village or community which was free from opium and in which its use has recently been begun?

A. No, I cannot recall any such place.

Q. The reason I ask the question is that the statement is made that the members of a community who have just begun the use of the drug and are not accustomed to it are in a much worse condition than those of a community where the drug has been used for several years. I have not been able to find on what this statement is based.

A. I could not give you any light upon that question. Chinese farmers have found that they get much more money from their land by cultivating opium than by cultivating corn or other cereals; but in spite of that they are much worse off than they were before. When everybody was cultivating cereals, the people were able to secure enough of the necessaries of life at very moderate prices. Cereals were heavy and could not be easily transported, so that they were consumed on the spot where they were produced. But since the people have gone in largely for the cultivation of opium, cereals have become scarce and now they have to buy the necessaries of life with the money that is obtained from the growth of the poppy. The money gained is lost through the increased price they have to pay for cereals. It is a very complex problem.

Q. Do you think that the Chinese people, as a rule, would be inclined to favor any measure looking to the prohibition of the use of opium?

A. A very large number of people, as a matter of sentiment, would hail it gladly, especially the poor, who attribute their poverty to the curse of opium. The hardheaded men, however, who have studied the subject in its bearings apart from sentiment would be differently inclined. What the ultimate results of such a measure would be I do not think can be said; the question has so many *pros* and *cons* and becomes immensely complex the moment you touch it in this way. The sentiment against opium may be classed with that against gambling and vices in general. If such a measure should be proposed, everybody would say, "Yes, this is a good thing," and would speak of it highly at once. Anyone who introduced such a measure would become popular all over the land.

Q. Could such a measure be carried out?

A. That I question very much; it would be almost next to impossible. You have tried to stop the use of liquors but have not succeeded. Such, in my judgment, would be the result in the case of opium.

Q. In the event that the use of opium should be discontinued, would there be any danger of the Chinese resorting to the use of alcohol or some other stimulant in its place?

A. I do not think so, for this reason: Where they do not smoke opium, for instance, they do not use alcoholic liquors. It is an exceedingly rare thing to see a drunken man in China. I have not seen in China, during my thirty-three-year residence here, over a dozen drunken men who could not take care of themselves.

Q. Your experience has been quite broad?

A. I have spent about twenty years in the interior and thirteen on the coast. I have seen all classes of men, both high and low.

Q. Do you think there are more excessive users of opium in the cities than in the inland districts?

A. In the cities a larger number of people take opium than in the country, as I have already said. In the western provinces its use is almost universal. As to Canton, I do not know, as I have not been down there.

NOTE

Report of the Committee Appointed by the Philippine Commission to Investigate the Use of Opium and the Traffic Therein (Washington, DC: Government Printing Office, 1905), 71–83.

READING 6
Opium and the New China

Although the Qing had been attempting to reform by "self-strengthening" since the end of the Taiping Rebellion, the New Policies period, after the Boxer Uprising, was a radical departure. The Chinese government was fundamentally remade in the years before 1911, and so were the popular conceptions of the problems that faced China and the correct solutions to them. This reading, from a leading Shanghai newspaper, discusses opium in relation to establishing a "constitutional" form of government.

Those who seek a cure must first clarify the origin of the problem. Those who wish to rectify harm must first cut off its root. To raise plants first get rid of grubs and weeds, then you water them. When using medicine first come in out of the cold and damp and eat some nourishing food and then take medicine. People's affairs and government matters are the same. To promote beneficial undertakings you must first abolish harmful influences. . . . Since our country began commercial intercourse with the Europeans our greatest failing has been opium. It has drained our wealth, weakened our race, and enslaved our people. For over a hundred years men of ideals and integrity have cried out against this disease and encouraged people to cure themselves, but the people have not been cured, and there have been no results. Those in power are more interested in collecting taxes and fear to raise the issue. Those who wish to cure themselves have no method to do so, and while few are cured the number of smokers grows daily. According to the current decree establishing a constitution, the court is making vigorous efforts to establish prosperity and renew all under heaven, but it will rely on the efforts of all, rich and poor, strong and weak. Although this has been declared to the people, will they comprehend the court's determination to eliminate opium? If opium is not eliminated, a constitution cannot be established, and China cannot be saved. Curing the opium problem and establishing a constitution are closely related. For those who do not understand, let me make it clear.

First, the relationship between opium and physique. In constitutional countries the people are all practically soldiers. Not one does not pay attention to hygiene, and all are fit to be soldiers. Take a trip to England or Germany. The people's spirit is lively and their physiques powerful. Regardless if they are old or young, rich or poor, none lacks vigor. In event of war they will not disperse but will blunt the thrust of an invading force. Opium smokers are like so many dull axes from constantly taking this medicine that weakens their bones. If you look at the situation after the opium has poisoned us, China is big, but its suffering gentry, merchants, workers, and officials are weak. Sixty to 70 percent of them cannot free themselves. They have weak spirits, and because their bones are weak they cannot bear labor. Because they cannot concentrate mentally their will is lacking. Because their will is lacking they cannot arouse themselves. Their lives dribble bit by bit into the opium box, and their souls flicker away to the light of the opium lamp. Officials who smoke cannot attend to public affairs, scholars who smoke cannot study, soldiers who smoke cannot kill the enemy, merchants who smoke cannot turn a profit, the men are deficient and weak. The majority of our countrymen smoke opium, and every day they weaken themselves. Can our 400 million people establish a constitution or self-government in this state? As I say these words I sigh. Of all the race of the world, ours is the lowest.

Second is the relationship between opium and state finances. In the constitutional countries things are constantly being changed, but nothing can be done without money. In China today there are countless things that cannot be done for lack of money, and this is because of the millions that opium has drained from us. At present we lack the capital to set up a new government because for decades chests of opium have been flowing in and silver has been flowing out. Opium must be eliminated to generate the money we need. Ignorant rascals work all day, and can earn the price of three days of rice, but then dissipate it in a single puff of smoke. When a body smokes opium that body takes the strain of it, and when a family smokes opium that family takes the strain of it. When one person in a family smokes opium the whole family suffers because of that person. The opium smoker suffers even more if they are not wealthy enough to afford opium, selling land or women, resorting to theft or other disgraceful acts. If this is not stopped famine will result. As Mencius said, "only after the people are fed and clothed can they know righteousness." When the people are starving to talk to them of patriotism or civic-mindedness, or the importance of education or physical fitness is like putting on furs to slake your thirst, it is obvious to anyone of understanding that it will not work.

Our people want a constitution? First they must make the weak strong and the poor rich, and opium makes both of these impossible. The physique grows weaker by the day, causing the weakening of the race. Our stupefaction grows deeper daily and so does the fear of starvation. When we reach the point where the army is useless and the nation can no longer feed itself, and there is no time left to save the situation, how can we possibly establish a constitution? A wasp merely stings and a snake only bites. A flood only goes to its high-water mark. Wild animals can be tamed by a Duke of Zhou. Opium's harm, however, goes so deep that it cannot be cured. If we drift along without finding a way to deal with it we will not be able to establish a constitution in 5 or even 10 years. It is like training soldiers and not giving them guns. The court understands this, and that is why after announcing a constitution they made opium suppression a top priority. I say that opium cannot be suppressed without a method. What is that method? It must start with the officials, but people of all sorts must work together. The rich should provide money; officials of all sorts must supervise and nurture; the soldiers, scholars, merchants and craftsmen, and ordinary people must contribute in their own ways. Those who, after a given time, do not quit smoking should be executed without mercy. Those who fail to inform on others should be executed without mercy. Those who plant opium or run an opium den after the time limit should be executed without mercy. The time limit should be lenient, but the execution of the law should be meticulous and universal. There must be vernacular propaganda so that everyone will know that if opium is not eliminated a constitution cannot be established. Orders must be appropriate in order to be effective. To emphasize taxes . . . is wrong. As the number of smokers declines, the profit of the growers will shrink, and they will switch to other occupations. An embassy must be sent to England to revise the treaties. Once all these holes are plugged up, the nation's potency will increase. Scholars will study and become more capable, soldiers will drill, and the army will become strong. Due to diligent work, production will be improved. Local rectification will lead to progress in self-government. After the river's flood subsides it flows to the sea, and after the darkness comes the dawn. After opium is eliminated there will be a New China. I perform the three bowings and nine prostrations, offer a libation, and say long live our anti-opium comrades, long live the Chinese constitution.

NOTE

Shenbao, October 6–7, 1906.

The Guangxu Emperor's 1906 Edict on Opium

This is the imperial edict that launched the great anti-opium campaign of the Late Qing, a campaign that would continue into the early Republic. This edict was only one of the many New Policies reforms that were intended to create a modern state in China. It was, at least in the short run, one of the most successful of the reforms and one of the few that called on ordinary Chinese to do anything other than pay higher taxes. It was also the only reform linked directly to foreign control. Article X mentions that the Qing court was attempting to negotiate a treaty to end the import of Indian opium. The treaty was signed in 1907 and provided for the elimination of imports over a period of ten years.

This edict gives the outline of a system of opium control not too different from that proposed in the nineteenth century as a way of raising revenue. Additional edicts set up a unified system of opium taxation, which the Qing had been working on as a source of revenue, but now it would be aimed at providing temporary revenue while the trade was abolished entirely.

Regulations Prohibiting Opium Smoking (Issued November First, 1906)

Article I. To limit the cultivation of the poppy is the way to eradicate the evil. The poppy obstructs agriculture, and its effect is very bad. In China, in the provinces of Sichuan, Shanxi, Gansu, Yunnan, Guizhou, Shaanxi, and Kianghuai, the poppy is widely cultivated, and even in other provinces there are places where poppy cultivation is largely pursued. Now it is decided to prohibit and root out the habit of smoking opium within ten years. It is therefore necessary to limit the cultivation of the poppy so as to effect the prohibition. Viceroys and Governors of provinces have to instruct the Magistrates of departments and districts to report upon, after registering, the actual area of land used for cultivation of poppy. Unless land has been hitherto used in the cultivation of the poppy it is not to be used for that purpose in future. For the land already being cultivated with the poppy special title deeds must be obtained. Of the land at present in use for the cultivation of the poppy one-ninth must be annually withdrawn from cultivation, and if such land is suitable, other crops are to be cultivated thereon. Magistrates of departments and districts are to pay surprise visits in order to ascertain whether there is any violation of this regulation.

By this means the cultivation of the poppy will be exterminated in nine years.

Any person violating the rule will forfeit his land, and any person ceasing to grow the poppy and adopting some other crop before the time required in the decree shall be considered as meriting special reward.

Article II. The issuing of certificates will prevent the possibility of new smokers. The bad habit of opium smoking has now been indulged in for such a long time. About three- or four-tenths of the natives smoke opium. Therefore we must be lenient to those who have already acquired the habit but must be strict for the future. First of all, all the officials and gentry and licentiates shall be prohibited to smoke opium, so as to show examples to the common people. Those who smoke opium, without distinction, whether he be an official, one of the gentry, or a servant, shall report the fact at the local yamen. If the place of their living is remote from the local yamen, they may report themselves to the police bureau or to the gentry of that place, who will collect such applications and send the same to the local yamen. The local officials then will issue a proclamation ordering them to fill up a form with their names, age, residence, profession, and the amount of opium each smokes per day; such forms will be ordered to be sent in at a fixed date according to the distance of the residence from the yamen. After the forms have been collected at the yamen a list will be compiled, and one copy of the same will be handed over to the higher yamen, and certificates will be issued under the official seal. Such certificates will be of two kinds: one for those who are over sixty years of age and another for those who are under sixty years of age. Those who receive the second kind of certificate are not allowed to receive the certificate of the first kind when they reach sixty. In the certificate the name, age, native address, amount of daily consumption of opium, as well as the date of the issue of the certificate, are mentioned to certify that they are allowed to buy opium. If there are any who, having no certificate, buy opium secretly, such persons will be duly punished. Once a registration has been made and certificate been issued no future application will be allowed.

Article III. By ordering gradual reduction of the amount of smoking opium, a cure of such habit may be effected. Those who are over sixty years old are treated leniently because of their age, but those who are below sixty and have received a certificate of second kind are ordered to reduce the amount of smoking annually either by two-tenths or three-tenths and to determine the date of ceasing to smoke opium. Those who cease to smoke and obtain the guarantee of their neighbors will be presented to the local officials, who will also inquire into the case, and then the name will be erased from the book of registration, and the certificate will be returned to the officials. A list of such withdrawals will be sent to the higher yamen for record. The date of prohibition of opium is quite lenient, and therefore if there is anyone who does not give up the practice within term, such person shall be severely punished. If there is anyone who has a certificate of the second class and does not stop smoking, if he be an official, he will be cashiered; if he be a licentiate, his title will be taken away; and if he be an unofficial person, his name will be registered. These names will be sent up to the higher yamen to be placed on record, their names and age will be put up in the street, and their residence will be made public, and no honorary positions will be given to them. They are not allowed to be reckoned as equals of the general public.

Article IV. By closing the opium shops the source of the evil can be cleared away. Until the terms for the date of prohibition come it is impossible to close the shops where opium is sold. However, there are opium shops where there are many lamps for smoking opium, and many youngsters are induced to come there and gather together with many bad characters. Therefore such shops shall be closed by local authorities within six months, and the owners shall be ordered to change their occupations. If they do not close their shops in time, these shops shall be officially closed by sealing the door. The restaurants and bars shall not keep opium for the use of their customers, and the guests shall not be allowed to bring in any opium pipe in order to smoke opium in these places. If there are any who violate the rule, they shall be severely punished. Those who sell opium pipes, opium lamps, or other utensils for opium smokers shall be prohibited from selling these goods after six months, or they shall be severely punished. The taxes on opium lamps shall not be collected three months after date.

Article V. By registering each shop where opium is sold, the exact number of them can be known. Though the shops where opium is sold cannot be closed at once, yet they can be gradually closed and no new shops be allowed to be opened henceforth. In every city, town, or village, the shops where opium or opium dross is sold are to be investigated by the local officials, and their numbers shall be duly registered and kept on record. Certificates shall be issued, which certificates will be reckoned as permits to follow that business, and no more new shops shall be allowed to be opened. These shops shall show the certificates whenever they buy their merchandise, or they are not allowed to sell the same. These shops shall report upon the quantity of opium and opium dross they sell at the end of each year and report the same to the local officials, who will keep the same on record. After calculating the total amount of opium and opium dross consumed in a district, annually, the proportion of annual reduction necessary for the abolition of opium smoking in ten years shall be calculated. Any surplus at the end of that time shall be destroyed and double its value forfeited as a fine.

Article VI. The government shall manufacture medicine to cure the bad habit. There are many prescriptions for curing the habit of smoking opium, and each province shall select the best medical students to undertake research for the best cure suited to the circumstances of each province. Such cures shall be made in pills, and shall in no case contain opium or morphia. After being manufactured such pills will be distributed to each prefecture, subprefecture, department, and district, at reasonable prices, and then these will be handed over to the charitable societies or medicine shops, where the cure will be sold at cost price. Whenever there are any poor people who cannot afford to buy the medicine, the cure may be given to them gratis. It is also granted to local gentry to manufacture the cure in accordance with the official prescription, so as to have the cure distributed as widely as possible. If there is anyone who will distribute the cure for charity's sake, and if such cure has the proper effect, the local officials shall give them reward.

Article VII. The establishment of anti-opium societies is a worthy proceeding. Lately, many persons cured have voluntarily organized an anti-opium society and have endeavored to eradicate bad habits. This is really praiseworthy. Therefore the Viceroys and the Governors of provinces shall instruct the local officials, with the local gentry, to organize anti-opium societies and to endeavor to stop the opium-smoking habit in the locality. Then prohibitions will surely have better effect. Such society shall be purely for the anti-opium smoking, and the society shall not discuss any other matters, such as political questions bearing on topical affairs or local administration or any similar matter.

Article VIII. The local officials are relied upon to use their utmost endeavor to carry into effect these regulations, and with the effective support of the local gentry there should be no difficulty in carrying out the prohibition. The Tartar Generals, the Viceroys, and the Governors of provinces shall make up a list of people who smoke opium, and those who cease to smoke annually, and the number of pills which are used as cure, together with the number of anti-opium societies. These lists, when compared, will easily give the comparative results of each province, by which the responsible officials will be either rewarded or reproved accordingly. The annual statistics shall be sent to the Government Council, where their merits will be duly dealt with. In the city of Peking the police authorities, officers of gendarmerie, and the officials of the city are held responsible. If in any district opium smoking is stamped out before the expiry of the ten years' limit, the officials of that district should be duly rewarded. The petty officials are to be warned to have no irregularities in reducing the area in which the poppy is cultivated, in issuing certificates for opium shops and shops where opium and opium dross are sold, or in dealing with those who smoke opium. Any such irregularity will be followed by severe punishment, and any who receive bribes will be punished on a charge of the crime of fraud.

Article IX. The officials are strictly prohibited from smoking opium so as to set examples to others. The prohibition within ten years is for the general public. The officials shall be examples to common people, and therefore they shall stop such bad habits before the general public, and such prohibitions shall be strictly enforced upon the officials, and the punishments upon them shall be more severe. From now all the officials without distinction of rank, metropolitan or provincial, military or civil, who are over sixty and suffering from opium-smoking habits, are exempted from the prohibition just as are the common people, for they are too far gone for cure. However, those who have not reached sixty years of age, princes, dukes, men of title, high Metropolitan officials, Tartar Generals, Viceroys, Governors, Deputy Lieutenant Military Governors, the Provincial Commanders-in-Chief, as well as Brigadier Generals, being all officials who are well treated by the Throne and high in rank and position, are not allowed to conceal their affairs, and if they smoke opium, they shall report themselves and the dates when they should stop the same. During the cure of the habit these officials shall not retire from their official duties but shall appoint acting officials; and when they have proved themselves cured of opium smoking, they may return to official duties. Moreover, they shall not be allowed to take opium under the pretense of illness longer than the terms promised. The rest of the officials in metropolitan or provincial service, either military or civil, substantive or expectant, shall report themselves to their principal officials in regard to these matters, and they shall cease to smoke within six months, at the end of which time they will be examined. If there are any who cannot be cured in time, they shall give reasons, and if they are hereditary, they shall retire, and, if they be ordinary officials, they will retire with original titles retained. If any conceal their actual conditions, such officials shall be impeached and be summarily cashiered as a warning to others. If there are any who are misreported by higher officials, they may memorialize and the case will be tried accordingly. Those who are the professors and students of ordinary schools and colleges or of military or naval schools and colleges are also hereby ordered to cease smoking within six months from date.

Article X. The prohibition of the import of foreign opium is one of the ways to root out the source of opium smoking. The prohibitions of cultivation of the poppy and of the opium-smoking habits are within the jurisdiction of the internal administrations. Foreign opium, however, concerns foreign powers. The Waiwubu [Foreign Ministry] is hereby instructed to negotiate with the British minister to Peking to enter into a convention to prohibit the importation of opium gradually within a certain term of years, so as to stop such importations before the term for the prohibition of opium smoking. Opium is imported from Persia, Annam, Dutch colonies, and other places besides India, and the Waiwubu shall also open negotiation with the ministers of these treaty powers. In case of a power where there is no treaty China can prohibit the importation by her own laws. The Tartar generals, lieutenant generals, viceroys, and governors shall order the commissioners of customs to find a way to stop such importation from the frontiers either by water or by land. It is also known that morphia is injected, and the habit is worse than opium smoking. It is mentioned in Article *n* in the Anglo-Chinese Commercial Treaty, and in Article 16 of the American-Chinese Commercial Treaty, that except for medical purposes no morphia shall be imported to China, and it is also strictly prohibited to sell or manufacture morphia or syringes for injecting the same by Chinese or foreign shops, so as to stop the bad habit.

These regulations shall be promulgated by the local civil and military officials in cities, towns, and villages, for the information of the general public.

NOTE

H. B. Morse, *International Relations of the Chinese Empire* (New York: Longmans, 1910), 486–91.

The New Policies in Action

Under the terms of the Anglo-Chinese opium treaty of 1907 British imports of opium were to be reduced gradually as the Chinese reduced domestic production. This linkage between Chinese and Indian opium was demanded by the government of India, which was willing to give up its lucrative opium trade if it had to but was not willing to surrender its profits to Chinese competitors. British officials would eventually end up touring the Chinese countryside looking for signs of opium production and certifying Chinese provinces as free of opium. This is one of the first reports on the success of the campaigns against opium sent in by the British embassy. The British ambassador, Sir John Jordan, was personally opposed to the opium trade and always stressed the good faith of the Chinese attempts to carry out their obligations under the treaty.

As a year has now elapsed since the issue by the Chinese government of the eleven regulations framed for the enforcement of the Opium Edict of the 20th September, 1906, it will be of interest to review the results which have been so far obtained and the measure of success which has attended the stupendous task of attempting by legislation to eradicate a national and popular vice in a country whose population is generally estimated at 400,000,000.

China has not hesitated to deal with a question that a European nation, with all the modern machinery of government and the power of enforcing its decision, would probably have been unwilling to face.

Though it is too early to expect any very definite result, the amount of success (and it is appreciable) that has hitherto been obtained produces the impression that the task that the Government has undertaken can be fulfilled and shows conclusively that the Chinese people in general consider opium smoking a vice, from which they would willingly free themselves, inspired by what a missionary has aptly described as an ill-defined moral and patriotic motive.

The Court attaches great importance to the conscientious fulfillment of the Decree and Regulations, and the fact that the Central Government has found it necessary to adopt the unusual course of repeating the instructions at frequent intervals would seem to show that they are not altogether satisfied with the response which has been made. Moreover, the Decree of the 10th October, 1907, removing from their offices a number of high dignitaries and Princes who have failed to break off the opium habit within the limit of the prescribed time, indicates the determination of the Palace to insist on obedience.

If this example of the Court is upheld and followed by the authorities in the provinces, there seems no reason why the object of the Decree should not be attained in the specified term of ten years. The Vice Presidents of the Censorate and of the Law Reform Committee, who were confirmed opium smokers, have recently died in consequence of having to give up the habit. These sad results of virtue have caused the stringency of the Regulations to be relaxed, and those past 50 instead of 60 years of age are now to be allowed to continue smoking, while those who have been addicted to the habit for ten years may continue to smoke in diminishing quantity during the ten years allowed for total abolition of opium.

The steps to be taken towards a general suppression of opium smoking practically only commenced in August last, and as the poppy is in most places a winter crop, and is usually sown in the late autumn, no reduction in the area under cultivation could be made last year in obedience to the Decree, while, as the seed is only now being sown, it is too early to judge how far the Regulations are being carried out in this respect.

Before explaining the action which has been taken in each province to carry out the Imperial Decree, it will be well to mention the difficulties with which the Government has to contend.

Foremost among these is the increasing difficulty experienced by the Central Government in enforcing their wishes in the provinces. The opium habit is one indulged in by all classes of society throughout the vast Empire and is practically the principal, if not only, national stimulant. If opium goes, its place will not long be empty, and if its substitute is one which produces aggressive action rather than sedative inaction, the change will scarcely be a good one.

The loss of revenue will, under present conditions, be less severely felt by the Central Government than by the provinces. In a country where official statistics do not exist, and where there is often great irregularity of procedure, it is difficult to obtain figures which are absolutely reliable, but competent authorities assert that out of the total annual revenue of about 6,500,000*l* collected on native opium only 1,750,000*l* reaches the Central Government, the remainder being employed in the provinces. Formerly taxation on native opium varied in different provinces, but in July 1906 it was abandoned in favor of a uniform tax of 115 Kuping taels per picul, known as *tungshui*, leviable on all native opium, whether for export or local consumption. Once paid, the drug can circulate free throughout the Empire. Owing to the difficulties of enforcing this tax in the province of Sichuan, the Central Government have permitted a return to the tax formerly levied, viz., 27.28 taels per picul and an additional 5.28 taels levied for railway purposes, which reduces the price of the drug in the province but increases it in others, where it still has to pay the 115 taels *tungshui* on entering. Foreign raw opium pays 30 taels (Haikwan) import duty and 80 taels *likin* and receives a Customs stamp which accords free circulation in China.

The prospective loss of revenue, however, is a matter which would not seem to have caused much anxiety to the Central Government, and, as far as can be ascertained, no concrete proposals have yet been made to replace the eventual loss to the Exchequer. In the provinces, however, the progress of the movement has been greatly hampered by the revenue difficulty and the prospect of dislocated finances.

Whether China can completely obtain the goal she seeks without Government control of opium, both native grown and imported, is somewhat doubtful. At present she is debarred from doing so by Article V of the British Treaty of Nanjing of 1842 and Article XIV of the French Treaty of Tianjin of 1858, which run as follows:

> *Article V of the British Treaty of Nanjing, 1842:*
> The Government of China having compelled the British merchants trading at Canton to deal exclusively with certain Chinese merchants, called hong merchants (or co-hong), who had been licensed, by the Chinese Government for this purpose, the Emperor of China agrees to abolish, that practice in future at all ports where British merchants may reside, and to permit them to carry on their mercantile transactions with whatever persons they please; and His Imperial Majesty further agrees to pay to the British Government the sum of 3,000,000 dollars on account of debts due to British subjects by some of the said hong merchants, or co-hong, who have become insolvent, and who owe very large sums of money to subjects of Her Britannic Majesty.

> *Article XIV of the French Treaty of Tianjin of 1858:*
> No privileged trading company can henceforth be established in China, nor any other coalition organized for the purpose of exercising a monopoly over trade. In case of infringement of the present article, the Chinese

authorities, subsequent to the protest of the consul or his agent, will take such steps as required to dissolve associations of this type, of which they will make every effort to prevent the existence of through prior prohibition, so as to eliminate every possible interference with free competition.

Both in former years and since the issue of the Edict attempts have been made both in the direction of interfering with the importation of foreign opium and the establishment of official monopolies and successfully opposed by Great Britain as contrary to Treaty stipulations.

The financial side of the question in connection with the establishment of a State control or monopoly is a very serious obstacle to be overcome should the matter ever come within the bounds of practical politics. In the cases where State control was recently commenced it was found necessary to seek the assistance of the native opium merchants in order to overcome the difficulty. Although China can deal with native-grown opium as she wishes, wherever the interests of British opium merchants have been effected by these monopolies complaint has been made, and they have in consequence been abandoned, except in the non-Treaty cities or ports where they have been established.

Official control of any undertaking is in these days regarded in China with suspicion and dislike by the non-official classes, who would find no difficulty in convincing the people that the officials so far from endeavoring to suppress the use of opium were converting the traffic to their own advantage. However, it is evident that China cannot establish State control of foreign opium without the consent of the Treaty Powers, and, to judge from the past, it is questionable whether she would obtain the consent of all without having to pay very dearly by way of *quid pro quo* to some and also doubtful if all would be prepared to approach the question from a purely moral standpoint.

The position of the Chinese Government in regard to the opium question is not dissimilar to that in which His Majesty's Government would find themselves if they desired to suppress the distillation and consumption of whiskey in the British Isles without being able, owing to Treaty stipulations, to introduce efficient Government control or prevent the importation of the spirit from abroad.

The amount of opium produced in China in 1906 has been estimated at 330,000 piculs (a picul equals 133 lbs.), and the accompanying map shows the various provinces and the amount of opium attributed to each, though the Province of Fujian is probably under-estimated. It will thus be seen that Sichuan alone produces close on two-thirds. Of this total production only 4,730 piculs were exported to foreign countries in 1906, of which the chief items were 4,013 piculs to French Indo-China and 147 to Hong Kong, *en route* probably to Formosa.

Foreign raw opium imported in the same year was as follows:

TABLE 8.1.

	Piculs
Indian	
Malwa	14,465
Patna	25,486
Benares	13,479
	53,430
Other kinds	795
Total	54,225

Thus China may be said to have required for her own consumption, 1906:

TABLE 8.2.

	Piculs
Native opium	325,270
Foreign opium	54,225
Total	379,495

or 50,599,333 lbs. weight, or 22,588 tons, of which about one-seventh comes from India.

It is said that, during the pourparlers which preceded the Anglo-Chinese Commercial Treaty of 1902, a suggestion was made by the Chinese negotiators that the Chinese Government should annually purchase the Indian export of opium with a view to controlling the sale of the drug in China but that the question went no further. Indian opium is stronger than that grown in China, and, moreover, the latter is frequently adulterated, which adds to its inferiority. It may be said that a smoker who requires to take 3 mace of Indian opium to produce a certain effect would on the average require 4 to 4½ mace of the native drug to obtain the same result. The Imperial Anti-opium Edict of the 20th September, 1906, is as follows:

Since the restrictions against the use of opium were removed, the poison of this drug has practically permeated the whole of China. The opium smoker wastes time and neglects his work, ruins his health, and impoverishes his family, and the poverty and weakness which for the past few decades have been daily increasing among us are undoubtedly attributable to this cause. To speak of this arouses our indignation; and at a moment when we are striving to strengthen the Empire it behooves us to admonish the people, that all may realize the necessity of freeing themselves from these coils, and thus pass from sickness into health.

It is hereby commanded that within a period of ten years the evils arising from foreign and native opium be equally and completely eradicated. Let the Government Council (Zhengwu Chu) frame such measures as may be suitable and necessary for strictly forbidding the consumption of the drug and the cultivation of the poppy; and let them submit their proposals for our approval.

And was supplemented by the eleven Regulations issued two months later for the enforcement thereof and the Imperial Edict of the 26th June last in the form of a reminder.

Considerable latitude is not infrequently taken in China by the provincial authorities both in the interpretation of the spirit of an Imperial Decree and in the steps they decide to take to enforce its provisions; but the Imperial wishes have undoubtedly been brought to the notice of most of the inhabitants of the Empire, and in every province special Rules and Regulations of some kind have been drawn up with a view to carrying out the desire of the Throne.

The average price per picul of raw native opium in the district in which it is produced, and before taxation of any kind, is 250 taels. In certain districts the price is as high as 500 taels, while in Sichuan Province, where, roughly speaking, as much as two-thirds of the native drug is both grown, prepared, and smoked, the average price is from 150 to 200 taels per picul.

Native raw opium when prepared (that is, boiled) is reduced to about 65 percent of what it was before that process. Indian opium after a similar process works out at about 75 percent. These figures, however, are only approximate, and it is quite impossible under present conditions to reach anything more trustworthy.

The important point in this report being to show what really effective steps have been taken by the provincial authorities to carry out the Decree, it will, in regard to good intentions, be sufficient to say that the special Rules and Regulations they have issued in their districts have generally been in the right direction, though of great variety. In some instances they have been quite inadequate and in others either not enforced or disobeyed.

In taking each province by itself, therefore, mention will rarely be made of the different local enactments, and the account will be restricted to a statement of what has actually been done to obey the Decree.

These accounts are chiefly based on reports supplied by His Majesty's Consular officers, who have been kindly and ably aided by the British Protestant missionaries in their Consular districts, many of whom, from their long residence in China and intimate knowledge of the country and people, have afforded both reliable and valuable information, often from remote spots where they are perhaps the only European inhabitants.

Many of the replies which have been received from the missionaries to the questions put to them on the subject have been negative and allow that in numerous districts little or nothing has been done or even attempted to carry out the Regulations; but wherever the local authorities are sincere, energetic, and enlightened a beginning has been made and the fire of enthusiasm lit; still, as one Consul has remarked, it is necessary that someone should continue to apply the bellows.

In any case the information from which this Report is composed is undoubtedly the most far-searching, reliable, and accurate which exists on the subject at the present time.

Jiangsu Province.—Production, 5,000 piculs. This province is the foremost in China in anti-opium measures.

In Nanjing 100 dens were shut and their appliances destroyed because the proprietors refused to pay the new prepared opium tax. Effective measures of suppression are said to be in force among the student and military classes.

The official monopoly of prepared opium was to have commenced on the 8th September but was suspended on the protest of His Majesty's Government that it came in conflict with Treaty provisions. The whole scheme is now in abeyance, and meanwhile all dealers in opium, raw or prepared, carry on their business as before, though no lamps are allowed on the premises. Rules relating to raw opium and the registration of smokers await the reply of the Viceroy's Memorial to the Throne.

Zhenjiang.—All dens in the native city are closed, though some are still allowed to sell prepared opium for consumption off the premises, but only to known confirmed smokers. This was effected under the personal supervision of the *Daotai,* who, finding two proprietors smoking in their divans, administered 200 blows to the one and locked up the other.

The British Concession at Zhenjiang is the only British one in China where opium establishments existed; these have now been closed, an order having been issued by the Municipal Council prohibiting the sale of prepared opium within the Concession, thus anticipating any similar action on the part of the Chinese authorities. No real hardship was entailed by this order, for the licensed opium dealers, six in all, had each denied that he dealt in prepared opium.

Suzhou.—All shops registered at the Prepared Opium Bureau received a license and paid the tax. A Proclamation has been issued that the price of prepared opium is raised by one-tenth, and of this increased taxation two-fifths goes to the *Likin* Bureau and three-fifths towards the expenses of the Anti-Opium Bureau. This Bureau has opened a department for the care and treatment of those addicted to smoking.

First-class patients pay 6 dollars until cured; second-class, 3 dollars, half of which will be returned when the patient is cured, third-class are treated gratis. Accommodation is provided for 100 persons at a time. The proctor of the Anti-Opium Bureau has been cashiered for lack of zeal.

Shanghai.—Here the authorities had to contend with the powerful influence and opposition of the rich commoners who derive their wealth from opium. These authorities, as well as the gentry and respectable merchants, were in favor of the Decree, and the closing of the dens became a fashionable and popular movement. Though trouble was anticipated, the closing of the 700 dens in the native city was peacefully and successfully carried out, the Opium Guilds having given way and supported the *Daotai*. Their suppression, however, did not appear to diminish the consumption of opium, shop sales rather increasing than otherwise. Finally the shops were closed.

Zhejiang Province.—Production, 5,000 piculs.

Hangzhou.—The gentry and better classes are favorable to the movement. The officials have registered themselves as smokers or non-smokers, mostly signing documents of a non-committal kind to the effect that if they smoked they should be given six months' leave in which to cure the habit and that, if then still addicted, they would consent to be handed over to the police.

The dens are all closed, and the Anti-Opium Society has opened a school for opium smokers, where they can learn trades, and advances loans to approved ex–den keepers in order to enable them to start some other business. The Society also purchased the old smoking utensils, 5,000 of which were publicly burned. Anti-opium pills are distributed gratis. A thriving trade is done by selling opium in the form of anti-opium pills, so that the people can change smoking for eating opium, which is cheaper and more convenient. It is stated on very reliable authority that it is far more difficult to cure opium or morphia eating than smoking or injection. The Anti-Opium Society is adopting similar measures in the country districts.

The Provincial Treasurer has been suspended on account of his opium tendencies.

At Quzhou, in the south of the province, the local officials have either given up the habit or are endeavouring to do so, and one is said to have died in the attempt. The dens are all closed, and the trade of the opium shops is reduced to one-sixth of what it was last year.

At Yanzhou, in the east of the province, all the dens are closed, and anti-opium medicines are distributed gratis under the auspices of the leading officials and gentry.

Ningbo.—Activity in the movement has been delayed owing to the circumstances that the revenue is chiefly derived from opium and cannot be dispensed with until a new source is found.

Both the Prefect and the Magistrate are said to have given up the habit, while two-thirds of the population are in favor of the Decree.

Apparently there is no decrease in the poppy-growing area.

All the dens in the city and in the Settlement are closed.

Jiangxi Province.—Production, 500 piculs. Generally throughout the province the dens have been closed and without any trouble, though shops selling raw opium are still open. The people are in sympathy with the Decree. But little opium is grown in the province. In the northeastern portion only two-thirds of the old poppy ground has been taken up for the same purpose; but this is said to be due, not to the decree, but to the high price obtainable for rice and flour. In any case it is not possible to form a reliable opinion till the winter crop appears.

At Yaochow(?) the head of police, said to be the only opium-smoking official in the city, has been suspended for six months pending his cure.

Fujian Province.—Production, 2,000 piculs—probably underestimated.

In Fuzhou a native Anti-Opium League has been started, and, owing to the energy exercised, some 500 dens have been closed.

The high officials are said to have given up smoking. Three large and successful refuges have been opened in the city, and the treatment is gratis.

In the surrounding district all the dens are closed, and a very heavy fee is imposed for licenses to opium shops. Four refuges have been opened and financed by the gentry also many private ones. Admission is 2½ d. a day for food and treatment, and free for the poor. Each building holds about twenty.

At Xinghua all the dens are closed, six proprietors having been cangued for refusing. A meeting has been held by the officials and gentry, when it was decided to open refuges.

Amoy (Xiamen).—For some time no active measures were taken, but as soon as the Fuzhou *Daotai* sent officials to inquire why nothing had been done the local *Daotai* hastily issued a Proclamation on the 10th of July and closed all the dens by the 19th, which shows what can be done in China when the officials are in earnest. Opium can still be purchased in retail shops but may not be consumed in public places.

The poppy area is small, and some 50 miles north of Amoy has been reduced, owing, it is said, to the attitude of the Government.

The more important officials are endeavoring to give up the habit, also some of the literati.

Szechwan Province.—Production, 200,000 piculs, of which 182,000 is consumed in the province, practically no foreign opium entering this part of China. When these figures are compared with 330,000, the estimated total annual production of opium in China, it will be readily perceived how important a place this province holds in connection with the opium question.

The area of the province is said to be 167,000 square miles; that of the British Islands is 136,000. Sir Alexander Hosie, the Acting Commercial Attaché in Peking, who has spent five years in the province, has given the following account of the cultivation of opium in Sichuan:

> The province was at one time the great wheat producer and exporter, but since the rapid extension of poppy cultivation that export has ceased and has been replaced by opium. It is too readily taken for granted that the cultivation of the poppy trenches on the food crops of the people, but it must be remembered that it is a winter crop, and shares the ground with wheat, rape, beans, peas, and barley. Sichuan still (in 1904) produces sufficient flour for home consumption, and the export of wheat of former years has given way to opium, which the farmer finds a far more profitable crop. An English acre of wheat will, on the average, yield grain of the value of 4l. 5s. 6d., whereas a similar area will produce raw dry opium of the value of 5l1. 16s. 8d.

The population of the province is estimated at 45,000,000, and Sir Alexander is of the opinion that 17 percent of the adults and 7 percent of the entire population are addicted to smoking.

In regard to the province generally, it may be said that, to start with, the authorities did not carry out the provisions of the Edict with any degree of completeness or sincerity and that but little was done to abolish or restrict the habit. Matters have now improved, and official activity is more noticeable in many directions.

It must not be forgotten that the question is much more difficult to deal with in Sichuan than in other provinces on account of everyone being personally interested in opium to a far greater extent than the inhabitants of any other province.

In Chengdu, the capital, the following steps have been taken to carry out the Decree.

Refuges for the cure of the habit have been opened, and though they are not much patronized there appears to be a real attempt on the part of the non-official and shopkeeping class to overcome the habit, while the officials do little or nothing to stop their own smoking.

The 500 dens in the city have been replaced by 300 well-appointed official divans for consumption on the premises, and though this arrangement carries out neither the letter nor the spirit of the Decree, it is a step in the right direction, and the complete prohibition of smoking in a city of 400,000 inhabitants where 50 percent of the male population smoke would undoubtedly have caused disturbances.

All persons using these official divans have to register themselves, but except in the case of the coolie class the authorities are unable to enforce this order with any degree of thoroughness. The richer classes have either laid in a store of the drug or purchase it secretly. Smoking is effectively prevented in colleges, schools, industrial institutions, the police, and the army.

At Kaixian, the largest opium-producing district in the province, where every available spot is under poppy, slight steps have been taken to obey the Decree. The Mandarin himself has given up the habit, and the yamen people have reported themselves. Some of the dens have been closed, and people have been beaten for smoking, but they are hostile and destroyed four out of the twenty offices erected for collecting the opium tax.

In view of the unpopularity of the *tungshui* tax, which in some places the authorities were unable to collect, and in order to ameliorate the position of the opium merchants, the Acting Viceroy asked permission of the Board of Finance in Peking to revert to the former tax on opium, the objection of the people being that the tax deprived the poor of their pipe by making the price of opium prohibitive except as a luxury for the rich.

The result of the appeal to Peking was that the *tungshui* tax was abolished in July in favor of a tax of 27.28 taels per picul, with an additional tax of 5.28 taels for railway purposes on all opium, whether for local consumption or for export, this amount of 27.28 taels in the case of opium for export being divided into 20 taels as customs duty and 7.28 taels likin.

At Chongqing half the dens were closed two years ago at the time the opium tax was increased, which shows the effect which taxation can have on the question.

An official Prepared Opium Office has been opened in the city for registering smokers, licensing smoking premises, and supplying the Government with prepared opium. The closing of the dens has been modified: 46 were allowed to remain open, 2 in each ward of the city, and this number was subsequently increased to 100; the proprietors themselves and the rich have mostly laid in a store which makes them independent of the Government supply. The authorities show energy, fines, blows, and the cangue being administered and a crusade carried on against unlicensed houses, illicit sale, and unregistered smokers.

The licensing system has not yet been adopted in the country districts, but it is to be on the basis of one guaranteed store in each village. In these districts most of the dens have been closed.

From Fushun a missionary reports that the dens have been reduced from thirty-six to seven. The officials are energetic, and great sympathy is expressed for the thousands of poor who work in the salt-well district and are unable to continue work without the drug. Heavy taxation has reduced consumption, and less ground is under the poppy than last year.

In the Luzhou district many dens have been closed definitely, others reopened under the name of "The Silver Exchange."

In the northeastern portion of the province many of the gentry have given up the habit; some have entered hospitals, others are said to have cured themselves. Many dens have closed of their own accord, and the gentry have combined together to purchase and manufacture anti-opium medicine.

At Suifu the dens have been closed three times without disturbance, but many have reopened clandestinely, and though the police occasionally make ostentatious raids, they usually connive what they dare not suppress.

Guizhou Province.—Production, 15,000 piculs. All dens have been closed at Guiyang, the capital, and a number of persons punished for taking in smokers.

An official Prepared Opium Bureau has been opened, also two refuges where 100 and 80 patients respectively are to be treated gratis.

In September, one had 10 indoor and 1,400 outdoor patients; the other, 7 indoor and 400 outdoor patients. Ninety days are allowed for the cure, which is said to be unnecessarily long, ten to fifteen being sufficient.

Yunnan Province.—Production, 30,000 piculs, of an estimated value of 1,000,000l.

The serious efforts of the Viceroy are looked upon by his subordinates, not only without sympathy, but with positive dismay. He has dismissed all opium smokers from his yamen.

In the neighborhood of the city of Yunnan-fu there has been a considerable decrease in the area under poppy, but this is reported to be due less to the Decree than to the fact that the 1905–6 crop could not be sold at a profit and that a large stock remained on hand. Both shops and dens have been inspected in the city, and the latter were subsequently all closed without disturbance.

An Anti-Opium Bureau has been opened to license, regulate, and restrict the sale of opium, and in regard to the latter the authorities announced that the first year would be for exhortation, the second for zealous prohibition, the third for force.

TABLE 8.3.   Native Production of Opium (piculs)

Province	31st Year (1905)	32nd Year (1906)	33rd Year (1907)
Fengtian	3,080	3,662	1,284
Jilin	378	812	604
Heilongjiang	1,744	1,805	818
Zhili	3,004	3,870	1,477
Jiangsu	9,794	9,919	8,022
Anhui	5,020	4,048	3,423
Shandong	5,217	6,863	3,155
Shanxi	13,573	9,666	4,946
Henan	2,640	5,283	4,074
Shaanxi	10,743	10,815	8,088
Gansu	4,818	7,988	4,142
Xinjiang	144	187	178
Fujian	1,500	1,514	1,324
Zhejiang	3,716	4,724	4,206
Jiangxi			78
Hubei	3,800	1,293	1,242
Hunan	120	158	137
Sichuan	51,134	57,463	44,519
Guangdong	89	77	66
Guangxi	(under) 1	(under) 1	(under) 1
Yunnan	7,574	7,928	15,950
Guizhou	14,532	9,959	12,250
Total	142,698	148,103	119,983

Source: Dispatch from His Majesty's Minister in China Forwarding a General Report by Sir Alexander Hosie Respecting the Opium Question in China (London: HMSO, 1909), 20.

The Bureau is actively at work, and eighty shops have taken out licenses. To commence with great difficulties were encountered in making a return of smokers owing to their reluctance to admit their vice. The manufacture and sale of opium utensils has ceased. Emissaries of the Bureau have visited each house and taken down particulars of every smoker and the number of lamps used. Preparations have been made to obtain returns of the area under poppy cultivation, which is to cease in the spring of 1910.

The sale of opium is to cease in July 1908, and an official Company is to purchase what is grown and sell it to those confirmed opium sots over 60 years of age who have been registered and also, no doubt, to the Tonquin Regie (though this is not mentioned).[1]

The Director of Agriculture has proposed that opium sots over 60 shall wear the red garb of a criminal and be labeled, "So-and-so, Opium convict,"

TABLE 8.4. Sale of Foreign Opium

Province	31st Year (1905)	32nd Year (1906)	33rd Year (1907)
Fengtian	25	98	11
Jilin			
Heilongjiang			
Zhili	225	282	150
Jiangsu	18,077	19,384	19,994
Anhui	1,626	1,633	2,428
Shandong	440	627	375
Shanxi			
Henan			
Shaanxi			
Gansu			
Xinjiang			
Fujian	6,600	7,007	7,064
Zhejiang	4,041	3,164	3,240
Jiangxi	1,715	1,459	1,874
Hubei	264	308	238
Hunan	298	303	356
Sichuan		1	1
Guangdong	18,587	19,818	18,845
Guangxi			
Yunnan			
Guizhou			
Total	51,920	54,117	54,584

Source: Dispatch from His Majesty's Minister in China Forwarding a General Report by Sir Alexander Hosie Respecting the Opium Question in China (London: HMSO, 1909), 21.

and the Governor has favorably received this proposal. There are some thirty-seven anti-opium drugs in use.

Thus it will be seen that a serious effort is being made to carry out the wishes of the Government.

Dengyue.—Here the Regulations are not taken seriously by the people. Exhortation is not expected to have much effect on them, and the authorities dare not use force.

At Dali the people are reported to have restricted the poppy area of their own accord and to be growing other crops.

Gansu Province.—Production, 5,000 piculs. Practically no official action has been taken in this far-off and conservative province. Few dens existed, as the people prefer smoking at home, but where they were found they have been generally closed. More poppy is grown than ever, and in one district an official encouraged the people to plant for all they were worth and to make hay (or opium) while the sun shone; in consequences, five times as much was sown. One missionary sends a discouraging report that the high price of opium has induced people to take to drink, while another states that those in his neighborhood are trying various medicinal herbs as a cure.

NOTES

Correspondence Respecting the Opium Question in China (London: His Majesty's Stationary Office, 1908), 31–39.

    1. The Tonquin Regie was the official opium monopoly in French Indo-China.

Opium and Imperialism

The course of the 1907 Anglo-British agreement was interrupted by the Revolution of 1911. Despite some backsliding during 1911 the anti-opium campaigns continued and grew. The new government was even more enthusiastic than the old, which caused problems for the British. The treaty had allowed the Chinese to regulate the retail trade in opium in any way they wished, while allowing certified foreign opium free passage through those provinces where it was permitted. The treaty did not clearly define the meaning of "retail trade," however, and many local officials read this clause very expansively. As a result, it became impossible for even legal opium to circulate in some provinces. This was potentially disastrous for the British opium merchants. It had been assumed by many that the certified opium would remain legal forever and that wealthy Chinese addicts would want to purchase a lifetime supply. Speculation drove the price of opium up, but by 1911 the merchants were beginning to panic at the thought that they might not be able to unload this opium at any price. The first document in this section deals with the refusal of the government of Zhejiang to allow foreign opium to circulate. Sir John Jordan, the British ambassador to China, was not sympathetic to the plight of the opium merchants, but he later dispatched the gunboat Flora *to Anqing, Anhui, to deal with the refusal of the Anhui govt. to allow opium to circulate there. This is a classic example of gunboat diplomacy and its weaknesses.*

Foreign Banks to Senior Consul

Shanghai, June 15, 1912

Sir,

   The undersigned banks have the honor to draw the attention of the consular body to the critical state of the opium trade. For many years past it has been the custom of the different banks to finance shipments of opium from India to this port and in the ordinary course of business to make advances on the same when it has been stored here waiting sale.

In making such advances they have provided for the ordinary market risks but have depended on the Chinese Government fulfilling its obligations in the matter of international treaties and agreements.

Since February last the Zhejiang authorities have prohibited the importation and trade in Indian opium, in absolute contravention of existing treaties, causing accumulation of stocks in Shanghai and heavy deprecation in the value of the same.

Owing to this high-handed and illegal action the opium market has been paralyzed, the merchants having been unable to move off their stocks and repay the money the banks have advanced to them, and should the present state of affairs be allowed to continue, disastrous failures may result involving the banks in heavy losses.

The amount of money at present locked up in this trade amounts to several millions of pounds, a considerable part of which has been advanced by us.

While prohibiting the trade in Indian opium, it is a matter of common knowledge that the Zhejiang authorities have allowed the cultivation of the native drug in that province to continue unabated and that it is sold freely in Shanghai.

We recognize the difficulties of the Peking Government in providing protection for foreign trade in distant parts of the Republic but fail to see how it can be seriously contended that it is unable to exact obedience to its wishes in a province so easily accessible as Zhejiang, and we therefore respectfully beg to ask the consular body to transmit this protest to their respective Ministers at Peking and request them to protect our interests, either by insisting on the Government enforcing the adherence of Zhejiang province to existing treaties and agreements or by obtaining a promise from them to make good any losses we may sustain by this illegal interference with legitimate trade.

As the matter is one of considerable urgency, we beg to suggest that the foregoing be transmitted to Peking by telegraph.

We are, &c.

For the Chartered Bank of India, Australia, and China:

W. S. LIVINGSTONE,

Manager, Shanghai

For the Hong Kong and Shanghai Banking Corporation:
    Manager
For Deutsch-Asiatische Bank:
    H. FIGGE, Manager
Banque russo-asiatique:
    JEZIERSKY, Manager
For the Yokohama Specie Bank (Limited):
    K. KODAMA, Manager
Banque de l'Indo-Chine:
    ARDAIN, Manager
For the International Banking Corporation:
    H. C. GULLAND, Manager
Banque Sino-belge:
    W. A. HOHN, Manager
For the Mercantile Bank of India (Limited):
    R. MILLER, Sub-Manager
For the Bank of Taiwan (Limited):
    M. ESAKI, Manager
Netherlands Trading Society:
    LAGRO, Manager

Consul-General Sir E. Fraser to Sir J. Jordan

Shanghai, October 12, 1912

Sir,

I HAVE the honor to report my proceedings on the mission to investigate the circumstances of the seizure and destruction of seven chests of Indian opium at Anqing, which I was directed to undertake by your telegram No. 106 of the 30th September.

On the 1st October Captain Corbett informed me that he was directed by the commander-in-chief to put His Majesty's ship *Flora* at my disposal for my visit to Anqing, and we agreed to set out at 1:30 P.M. on the 2nd instant. . . .

After telegraphing to Mr. Bai, Tutu of Anhui, that I should call on him on the afternoon of the 5th October, on a case which you had instructed me to investigate in conjunction with him, we started at the appointed time.

In the hope of preventing any popular misconception of the nature of my visit, I authorized Mr. Phillips to inform the *North China*

Daily News of its purpose; but I regret that that paper, as well as others, native and foreign, persisted in ascribing to me the exercise of pressure and the presentation of demands for compensation and redress.

On our reaching Wuhu, Mr. Pearson handed me a telegram from Anqing to the Shanghai consulate, declaring that Mr. Bai was on a visit to Nanjing and the date of his return uncertain.

He also gave me copies of telegrams exchanged with that tutu which, as the enclosed copies and translations show, proved that he ignored entirely the terms of China's agreements with Great Britain.

Surmising that Mr. Bai should have been ordered to return at once, I proceeded to Anqing to find that he had, in fact, arrived on board a Chinese cruiser on the evening of the 4th October.

One of his secretaries met our boat at the landing and came off in her. He stated that the seizure and burning of the opium were done by the direct orders of the tutu, who was prepared to explain and justify this action if I would call.

Accordingly, at 5 P.M., I went with Captain Corbett, his first lieutenant, and Mr. Jones to the tutu's yamen, where we were received by the head of his Foreign Affairs Officer Mr. Bi Wei, who was formerly employed at Nanjing.

Mr. Bai, escorted by a dozen military officers, appeared after a few minutes and proved eager to descant on the evils of opium smoking and his own zeal in eradicating the vice in Anhui.

He admitted, in answer to a question, that there was an agreement regarding the gradual cessation of import from India, but he held that that applied only to the trade at open ports. Once opium Indian or other passed into native hands and away from a port we had no further concern with it.

I produced the agreement of last May with the relative papers sent me in your circular of the 19th June, 1911, and, showing him article 3, asked whether he had reported to Peking the total suppression of poppy cultivation in Anhui so that you might be moved to agree to the province being closed to the Indian drug. After some beating about the bush, he admitted that he had not done so; but, at the instigation of Mr. Bi, he asserted in a blustering fashion that the closing of a province was entirely an internal question and that no previous acquiescence on our part was required by the agreement. His vigorous measures, which would include sending troops to shoot down every person found growing the poppy, brought his province within the terms of the article.

I proceeded to call his attention to article 4 and the other provisions of the agreement as well as to the papers appended and asked if he recognized that his Government had accepted as valid all the engagements of its predecessor.

He displayed considerable uneasiness and greedily scanned the papers shown him with every appearance of being quite unfamiliar with any of them.

Encouraged by Mr. Bi, he now took up the line that this was not a diplomatic question worthy of my being sent in a cruiser but a mere matter of finance to be adjusted, if his Government, to which he had sent reports, should not uphold his action, by payment of some compensation. And he proceeded once more to inveigh against the vice and assert for China an absolutely free hand in dealing with it, our only claim being for compensation to our dealers should China decide to stop importation at once instead of spreading the prohibition over a term of years.

His attention was again called to the papers in my hand, and especially to the penultimate paragraph of the Waiwubu's circular telegram of the 15th June, 1911. I added that the important point in the case was precisely the international question of the due performance of solemn engagements between friendly nations. That this instance referred to opium was a mere accident: if China could go back on this agreement and her own official interpretation of its meaning, all her treaty engagements became untrustworthy and her position in the world one of serious danger.

Mr. Bai, who had been reading the documents while listening to my words, seemed at last to perceive in what an awkward position his rash act had placed him; but Mr. Bi again intervened with voluble assurance that they had carefully studied all the treaties, even last year's agreement, and were prepared to prove they were within their rights. He sent an attendant for a book of treaties, but, though sent back more than once, the man returned empty-handed. He explained, meanwhile, that the Tianjin Treaty specially provided against foreign interference with opium once it left the foreign importers' hands (presumably referring to the second sentence of the first rule of trade).

I explained that the proper interpretation of treaty terms was a matter for the parties making the treaties, that is, for the Governments concerned, and no good purpose could be served by our arguing on a matter already explained authoritatively by his own country's Government. Besides, my instructions were simply to investigate a specific case and its circumstances; I desired, therefore, to obtain direct answers to certain questions concerning it:

1. Were the seven chests seized and destroyed by the tutu's direct order? The answer was, "Yes, they were."

2. For what reasons?—Because Anqing was not a treaty port and because the owners were not foreigners. The treatment of all opium under such conditions was purely a matter of internal administration in the absolute discretion of the provincial authorities.

Prompted by Mr. Bi, the tutu, in a confused manner, added that the seven chests had not all the necessary papers—transit certificates and bills of lading—and the opium had been changed.

They all seemed astonished when I said this was scarcely possible, as the Imperial Maritime Customs kept the most careful track of every ounce of Indian opium sent inland and would have supplied any information required in case of suspicion of irregularity. Mr. Bai then said the opium had been left on the hulk unclaimed for some days; and I replied that this was quite usual and did no harm, as the hulk keeper was bound to keep cargo securely.

We took leave after arranging that Mr. Bai would return our call on Monday, the 7th October.

During the 6th my servants and the Wuhu writer traversed the city in search of proclamations and news. They found one proclamation freely posted; copies of this and of one other are enclosed; both are signed as well as sealed by Mr. Bi, and I myself saw them posted freely in the city. It will be observed that at first Mr. Bai went beyond the Waiwubu's standing order only by confining the sale of prepared opium to certain official shops—a monopoly of which, I believe, Mr. Pearson complained. This process, however, seemed to him too dilatory, and he has, in fact, recently closed all the shops in the city, though, I believe, secret sales continue.

About 6 p.m. on the fifth, Mr. Bai sent me a note of which copy is enclosed, alleging a cold due to the sudden change of temperature as sufficient reason for sending Mr. Bi to return my call on board "the steamer." A reply was returned declining to receive any substitute for the officer whom I was directed to deal with in person.

I had trustworthy information that Mr. Bai was up and about and had spent most of the day consulting with his subordinates. His note may have been due not only to a wish to belittle us but also to my having told his secretary that I desired to return to my regular work as soon as was consistent with the fulfillment of my mission.

Late on the night of the 6th instant, Mr. Bai again wrote that his doctor warned him against the risk of aggravating his ailment by exposure to cold; and the next morning I rejoined that my own health would benefit by rest and I should await his recovery, only asking him to let me know as soon as possible the time of his visit in order that I might telegraph to you, whom I had already told of his sudden indisposition.

On the evening of the 7th, Mr. McCarthy, the British master of the American Church Mission School, who is in friendly relations with Mr. Bai and the other native authorities and who had heard the tutu at a recent feast dilate on his determination to suppress the use of opium by any means he thought fit, called with a letter giving the result of inquiries by one of his Chinese assistants who has a friend a secretary in the yamen. Mr. McCarthy erroneously described this as posted on a wall near the mission, which led me to describe it in my first telegram of the 8th instant as a manifesto. He also stated that he had been hurriedly called to consult with Mr. Bi and another secretary as to what was the best course to pursue. They admitted that all that ailed Mr. Bai was anxiety over this case and reluctance to call lest he be treated rudely or even with personal indignity. Mr. McCarthy, who specially asks that his name be kept private, pointed out the impropriety of leaving unreturned the official call of a British officer sent by his Government on one of His Majesty's ships.

As to the act complained of, which they tried to excuse solely on the ground of supposed defect in the papers covering the opium, he suggested that Mr. Bai might ask leave to explain to the president in person why he has taken so unprecedented a step. But they said the tutu was too busy to go to Beijing—a curious answer in view of his visits to Nanjing on his own affairs.

On the same day, Mr. Jones had obtained from the hulk keeper copies of the letters sent him by the chief of police which preceded the removal of the opium. The material part of these has already been sent you by telegram in Chinese; full copies with translations are now enclosed.

On the 9th instant Mr. McCarthy, whom a perusal of the agreement of last year and the relative papers had convinced of the impossibility of defending the tutu, for whose zeal against opium smoking he has every sympathy, had another interview with the secretaries and again urged the evil impression produced by his delay in calling and the advisability of his putting himself in the hands of the president.

On the evening of the 8th instant, as our inaction might lend to lessen the salutary impression produced by our visit, I had sent the Wuhu writer to the tutu's yamen with polite inquiries after his health, and he had been told that he might probably be well enough to call on board on the 10th.

Meanwhile the pilot had insisted that the unusual lowness of the water, which was falling steadily, rendered it imperative that the "Flora" should get below Wade Island without delay, and our departure was fixed for the morning of the 10th instant, my enquiry having been completed by my obtaining the transit certificates covering all the opium seized, some twenty-five in all, and the tutu showing no intention of calling.

About 9:30 A.M. on the 10th instant Mr. Pai came on board with several officers. He told me that the matter was beyond his province, and he had therefore sent a full report to his Government whose instructions, whatever might be their tenor, he would carry out scrupulously.

This decision appeared to me not without cleverness, since if Beijing should direct him to reverse his previous policy, he could tell his provincial assembly and the native public that his well-meaning efforts to eradicate the vice had been thwarted by his superiors at the bidding of Great Britain, whereas if he yielded to my representations he would have to confess that he had acted ill-advisedly. . . .

Further consideration confirms my belief that Mr. Bai is a genuine fanatic on the subject of opium, inexperienced in government administration and ignorant of the treaty stipulations and, owing probably to his sojourn at a military college in Japan, imbued with the belief that China has been the victim of foreign aggression, from which it is a patriot's duty to free her. The native newspapers, especially the organs of the Tongmenghui, have doubtless persuaded him that the mutual jealousy of the Powers assures the success of the popular policy of recovering the sovereign rights invaded under an effete dynasty, and such sciolists as his foreign secretary, Bi Wei, have encouraged him to interpret the wording of treaties in the sense that suits this policy. For the attitude of Mr. Bai and the other tutus there is, unfortunately, the excuse that certain foreign anti-opium enthusiasts and some foreign papers do not hesitate to preach the morality defying the solemn agreements of China which interfere with their zeal for the immediate stoppage of all traffic in Indian opium. These advocates of dishonesty seem blinded to the danger of the precedent they seek to set up being later turned against treaty rights which very nearly affect their own interests; and meanwhile they proclaim that our support of the opium trade is devoid of the sympathy of our people and our Parliament. Mr. Bai's telegram to Mr. Pearson shows that he relied on the truth of these representations in his policy.

Mr. McCarthy has trusty informants throughout the province who assure him that the last crop of native opium was abnormally large, that public works are neglected, schools vacant, and the revenue very scanty. The 7,000 or 8,000 troops in the province are at least three months in arrears with their pay and exists by forced credit with the rice and other shops. The people pray for the return of the former Governor, Zhu Jiabao, whose elaborate dykes are already falling into decay under the new governor, Mr. Bai, whose supporters are few, if noisy, and drawn solely from the half-educated classes.

It speaks well for the inhabitants of the province that they pursue their usual avocations peacefully on the whole, under officers with neither training nor knowledge; but this quiet is probably due for the most part to the absence of any attempt to exact the regular taxes, the absolute needs of the exchequer being met by "borrowing" from the merchant and shopkeeping classes. The execution of the tutu's threat to send troops to shoot the poppy growers would, there is little doubt, be met by violent resistance.

Under these circumstances I venture to maintain my belief that it would conduce, not only to the due course of the opium trade, but also to the peace of the province, if Mr. Bai were summoned to Beijing to explain his conduct. His visit, I am sure, would dispel any doubt as to his unfitness for a post that involves the observance of international obligations, while such a summons must serve as a beneficial warning to other tutus as ignorant and as self-confident. Even were he under from Beijing to pay compensation for the results of his illegal destruction and detention of Indian opium at various places and to refund the fine of 1,200 dollars exacted by his magistrate at Datong, and also to issue a satisfactory proclamation reversing his previous declarations, I fear that he would make no effort to enforce the terms of our agreement, even if his anti-opium zeal did not lead him to work against the enforcement.

The appearance of His Majesty's ship *Flora* undoubtedly had a good effect on the tutu and all classes, and one of our messengers who visited the opium dealer's hongs was told that an emissary from Mr. Bai had come and asked if they would withdraw all complaints in return for compensation at the rate of 3,000 taels a chest. As there was no security that the money, if ever forthcoming, would not be withdrawn on some pretext later on, the hongs professed that the matter had passed out of their hands. I understand their heads had come to Shanghai for safety before we arrived.

After the tutu's reluctance to call had been overcome there seemed no reason to prolong our visit. He would certainly render no assistance, and any statements made by him were not likely to be trustworthy. He had appealed to Beijing and meanwhile could not, without loss of prestige, alter his policy. We had obtained unexpectedly complete documentary evidence of his conduct in the case to be investigated, and to remain idly at anchor while the tutu professed to be indisposed could only lessen the impression produced by our visit, and familiarity with our presence might encourage Mr. Bai and his secretary to even more drastic measures against smokers, which we could have done nothing to prevent. Even if we had instructions to use force we had not the means to hold the city. For these reasons I preferred to withdraw, with an intimation that my present commission was fulfilled but that I might be ordered to revisit Anqing under a fresh set of instructions.

Enclosure 5

Proclamation Issued by Bai, Tutu of Anhui

(Translation)

FOR more than 100 years the opium poison has been circulating in China, destroying the bodies of the people, paralyzing their energy, and wasting the wealth of the nation in such a way as gradually to bring ruin on the State and Extermination of the race.

In the time of the Manchus many things were mismanaged, and the work of opium prohibition alone was rather satisfactory. The Republic being now established, all stains must be cleansed away and thorough reforms instituted.

How can we tolerate such evil shapes appearing once more in broad daylight before us?

I am filled with great loathing against opium, which is a vice requiring to be completely stamped out, and I am now about to adopt most forcible measures to pull up this deadly poison by the roots.

The provincial council has passed eleven concise rules for the prohibition of opium which should be very effective, and it is my duty therefore to promulgate them. In these circumstances I hereby notify all the officials and people throughout the province for their information. All must comply at once with the appended rules for prohibition of smoking, planting, and transporting. If any presume to defy these orders he will be forthwith severely dealt with. If after the lapse of one year there should be found anyone disobeying these rules he will be executed in accordance with military law. The punishment will accompany the issue of these orders, and no mercy be shown. Let all obey! A special proclamation.

Enclosure 6

Proclamation Supplementary Rules for the Prohibition of Opium

(Translation)

1. PLANTING of opium is entirely prohibited throughout the province of Anhui. If any shall in breach of the regulations secretly plant opium a fine of 50 cents for each stalk shall be inflicted. If there are more than 100 stalks then, in addition to the fine per stalk, the land shall be confiscated.

2. From the date the dispatch naming a fixed period arrives the license system shall cease, and all prepared and raw opium shops shall shut down. Any kind of opium discovered, whether prepared or raw, shall be destroyed with salt.

3. Those under fifty addicted to opium smoking are given a limit of three months within which to break off the habit; those over fifty are given six months; while those over fifty who are really ill are allowed a limit of ten months. Any breach of this rule will involve a sentence of penal servitude of the fifth grade or a fine not exceeding 1,000 dollars.

4. Those who for the sake of gain start opium dens for supplying opium to smokers shall be punished with penal servitude of the fourth or lower grade. A fine not exceeding 300 dollars shall be inflicted and the premises confiscated.

5. Manufacturers of opium, sellers of opium, and those found in possession of opium with the intention of selling the same, and those who have imported for sale opium from outside shall be punished with penal servitude of the third grade, and the opium shall be destroyed.

6. Manufacturers of implements used for supplying opium to smokers, sellers of such implements, and those found in possession thereof with the intention of selling the same, and those who have imported for sale such implements from outside shall be punished with penal servitude of the fourth or lower grade, while the opium implements shall be destroyed.

7. Any customs officers and people assisting them who may import opium from outside or supply opium implements, or allow others to import, shall be punished with penal servitude of the second or third grade, while the opium and the opium implements shall be destroyed.

8. Any police, officials, and person assisting them who become aware of offenses committed against rule 5, and in consequence do not award a suitable penalty, will also, in their turn, be punished in accordance with rule 5.

9. Anyone offending against rule 6 shall be deprived of civil rights either completely or in part. If an official, he shall be removed from office.

10. In addition to the investigation and report made from time to time by the inspecting officer, anyone should publish information in regard to offenses against the above rules as well as against the sections in the Criminal Code dealing with opium. If a false charge is made the accuser shall be punished instead of the accused.

11. The above rules shall come into force from the date of their promulgation.

NOTE

The Opium Trade (Wilmington, DE: Scholarly Resources, 1974), 6:13–14, 100–105.

The Chen Family Opium Den

This is an account of a family-run opium den in the city of Yichang. An opium den was a place for people to come to buy and smoke opium. Although the dens could be well-appointed places for a respectable clientele to socialize, most were not, and the bad reputation of opium smoking was connected in part to the bad reputation of the opium dens where it was consumed. Yichang is on the Yangzi River in Hubei and was a key transshipment point for Sichuan opium. Chen Deyuan's story is probably not that different from those of opium den operators in other parts of China, although it does have some unique features. Chen's background was somewhat unusual because, although his family was fairly well connected, he himself could probably be called a liumang *(hoodlum).*

Unlike most opium den operators Chen was able to avoid government regulation for a long time by taking advantage of extraterritoriality. During the 1930s the Nationalist state made steady attempts to close or regulate opium dens, in addition to providing the ordinary police harassment that such establishments could expect. Chen Deyuan was relatively independent also because he boiled his opium himself, which kept him from being dependent on a larger, often government-controlled, opium wholesaler.

This reading comes from a local history magazine, wenshi ziliao, *from Hubei. The Communist government encouraged people of all sorts to record their experiences under the old society. These recollections have become very valuable resources for historians, but they must be approached with care.*

During the Republic Yichang had many opium dens, one of them run by my father, Chen Deyuan.

To discuss the origins of our family's opium den we must begin with my father. After the defeat of the 1898 reforms and the execution of Tan Sitong and others, Tan's compatriot Tang Caichang returned from Japan and created the Establishing Righteousness Society and the Independent Army to unify members of the Elder Brother's Society all along the Yangzi for an uprising. My grandfather Chen Futing joined the Independent army. The army was defeated in the fall of 1900, and Zhang Zhidong, the Hunan-Hubei governor-general, executed the leaders. Chen Futing fled to Shanghai, leaving behind his wife, Chen Sanliang, and their son, Chen Deyuan.

In 1908 Chen Deyuan returned to Yichang from Wuhan. He had worked in a restaurant run by an Anhui man and not only learned how to cook but also the martial arts. At this point he was 15 *sui*. After returning to Yichang he joined the Red Gang.[1] At that time he had no set profession and ate the bread of idleness, cheated at dice, and gambled.

In 1909 he took advantage of an introduction and got a job on a steamship. He was young, hardworking, and good looking. One day in 1910 he saw his father, Chen Futing, on the ship. Chen Futing had already put aside his family affairs and taken the tonsure and was on his way to Mount Omei in Sichuan.[2] He told his son that the Manchu Qing dynasty had controlled the country for hundreds of years. It was corrupt and incapable and had weakened the nation. It was time for it to be overthrown. "You have studied the martial arts, why not consider using your skills to serve the nation?" Chen Deyuan, hearing his father's charge, immediately went ashore. It was in the same year that he married Li Guoxiu, and not long after he was married he went to work on the Sichuan-Hankou railway.

When the revolution broke out in 1911 the revolutionary party in Yichang organized 100 men into a revolutionary army. Chen Deyuan joined, and because he had joined at the beginning of the uprising he was made a squad leader. At the capture of Jingzhou he was promoted to platoon leader. Chen Deyuan was Chen Sanliang's only child, and she was afraid that he would be killed at the front, where bullets fell like rain, and so she brought her son back home. As she was afraid that he would return to the army she gave him opium. Chen Deyuan slowly sank deeper and deeper into this quagmire and became an opium addict.

Chen Deyuan's wife urged him to open a teahouse. He saved up a little money and bought a small place, hanging up banners in the street announcing the "Drunken Moon Bar." Chen Sanliang saw that there was good profit to be made in opium and urged Deyuan to open an opium den, but he refused. There was a group of northern soldiers who came to the Drunken Moon almost every day, and after they had eaten and drunk their fill they would smash plates and wreck the place. Soon Chen Deyuan was out of business. This was in 1919.

After Chen Deyuan closed his bar he was still unwilling to open an opium den. After his mother moved in with him he was forced to accede to her wishes and open one. Chen Deyuan was an opium den owner for 20 years, from its opening in 1920 to its closing in 1940, due to the fall of Yichang to the Japanese.

The Flat Altar

The Chen family opium den was in a good location near the south gate, and it always did a better business than any other opium den. Chen Deyuan was a real expert in the opium business. He always went personally to buy his opium, and a few times when he was sick he took me along. He bought his opium from a nearby opium wholesaler. The wholesaler was also named Chen and his son, Jinggou, was a classmate of mine at the Huaying middle school. Chen Deyuan always wanted to use Yunnan opium for his paste. Yunnan opium came in two grades, with the better grade being a bit more expensive. Actually, all Yunnan opium was expensive. I remember it took a whole handkerchief full of banknotes to buy five or six ounces of opium. To save money some wholesalers would mix cheaper Sichuan opium with the Yunnan, but Chen Deyuan never did this. After buying the opium it had to be boiled, which took skill. If it boiled too long it had a scorched taste, if it was not boiled long enough it would be too runny. Chen Deyuan did the boiling himself and was known as being a good opium boiler. He put the opium, old ashes from the bowls of the opium pipes, and water in a wood-handled copper pot. He would then put it on the stove and let it simmer down into a paste. . . .

The Chen family opium den had five or six opium pipes, one of which, called the "Flat Altar," had a special bowl. Of the tens of opium dens in Yichang the Flat Altar was one of the two most famous pipes. (The other was the Ma family's "Little Dream Maker.") The Flat Altar was famous because when someone smoked from it they got high a lot quicker. With other pipes you had to smoke two balls of opium to get high, with it one was plenty. This was enough to make an opium addict's day, and customers loved to come to the Chen family opium den. What was the secret of the Flat Altar? Ordinarily each day after we closed the ashes would be cleaned out of each bowl. After emptying the ashes out of the Flat Altar, however, Chen Deyuan would put a little bit of raw opium inside the shaft of the pipe. As the smoker heated the opium in the bowl the opium in the pipe would melt and give a much stronger smoke than any other pipe. Chen Deyuan invested a bit in the raw opium, but it brought customers back and was thus profitable.

With the Flat Altar bringing in customers the Chen family opium den prospered, and Chen Deyuan left behind his unsuccessful past. Two years after the den opened, in the fall of 1921, Yichang became a battlefield. Sichuanese troops and northern troops were fighting on both banks of the Yangzi. Chen Deyuan fled, along with many others, and he took the Flat Altar with him. As the fighting continued, Chen Deyuan took his wife and son to Wuhan. On the ship the Flat Altar was hidden on my body (I was seven or eight *sui*). The Anti-Opium Inspectors confiscated quite a few pipes and opium paraphernalia, but did not find the Flat Altar. When Yichang fell in 1940 I went to work in Jianshi County and later brought my family along. My father brought the Flat Altar with him, but it was stolen soon afterward. By that time he was no longer running an opium den and his opium addition was cured as well.

With the fame of the Flat Altar the Chen family opium den was always full of customers and did a great business. Inside the opium den were six opium couches, each with its own teapot filled with scalding hot tea. After smoking the customers always wanted tea. The first couch had a special teapot decorated with flowers and palms and was reserved for wealthy regulars.

Labor and Management in an Opium Den

The proprietress of the Chen family opium den was Li Guoxiu. First thing every morning she would pack the boxes. Opium boxes were square and came in various sizes, and each morning she would fill several tens of them with the appropriate amount of paste. Preparing food for the customers, collecting money, and keeping the accounts were all her responsibilities. She also kept track of regulars' tabs on either a biweekly or monthly basis.

Li Guoxiu was a very strict person. Although she ran an opium den for twenty years she never smoked a single ball of it. Sometimes when she was sick Chen Deyuan would try to get her to smoke a little to make her better, but she always refused. Other than Chen Deyuan she did not allow anyone else in the family to smoke. I once broke my left foot and due to the pain had trouble sleeping. My maternal grandmother felt for me and wanted to have me smoke a little opium for the pain, but my mother would not agree. I lived in an opium den for over ten years, but because of my mother's stubbornness I never became a prisoner of opium.

Our family only ever had two employees. The first was Zeng Zicheng from Wuhan. Our family gave him room and board, and his wages were paid by giving him a box of opium every day. He would pay his sundry expenses from tips. The Dragon Boat Festival, Moon Festival, and New Years were the best times to get tips. When he wished customers a happy new year he got a large tip. Zeng would open the doors around six or seven in the morning. He would serve the customers by getting opium, collecting money, lighting the lamps, and changing the pipes. He would also boil water, fetch food, and do similar tasks. He also had less pleasant duties like fanning the fire while the opium boiled, and he was usually busy until about 12 at night when he closed up. Zeng Zicheng was an honest and sincere person, and both our family and the customers liked him. He worked for us for a long time, but when the Resistance War broke out he returned to Wuhan. He wrote to tell us that he had quit smoking opium and was working as a rickshaw puller.

The other employee was Zhang Xiaoer, from Sichuan. He came to work for us when he was about 22. He was crafty. He got tips out of customers by doing cigarette tricks. After Ichang fell my family fled to Sankeping. We heard that Zhang Xiaoer had become a bandit. Not long after he was executed in Sankeping.

About 1925 the opium dens of Yichang changed their method of preparing opium. Instead of providing it in boxes it was prerolled into balls that could be put directly in the opium pipe. The Chen family den hired an expert opium roller. The first was a young Sichuanese called Lefty. He was said to be from a wealthy and educated family and to have been driven out because of his opium addiction and ended up in Ichang. We rewarded him for his skill in rolling opium balls by letting him keep some. He was also good at serving our richer customers and got more opium balls this way, as well as tips. Lefty worked in the Chen opium den for two years, until his mother sent someone to bring him home. The other ball roller was named Zhang. He came from Yanxi, and he also had been driven out of his home for smoking opium. He worked for us for half a year and later opened his own opium den.

Operating an Opium Den and Opium Suppression

The Chen family opium den was originally on Neidihui Street, but Chen Deyuan lost it gambling. About that time an Italian *ronin* fled to Yichang, and in 1924 he bought a building on Neidihui Street and opened the "Heavenly Virtue Company."[3] The building had two floors, and he got ten opium den owners to open opium dens inside. Among them was one Pei Wenqing, who had been an officer in the Beiyang army and opened this opium den after being demobilized. The Italian made him the manager, in charge of collecting rent and insurance charges. Chen Deyuan rented space there and opened an opium den.

The Heavenly Virtue Company had an Italian flag over the door. This flag was very useful, since neither Beiyang warlord police nor Nationalist police would dare to enter and cause trouble for fear of creating an "international incident." The opium dens flagrantly sold opium, but they were uncontrollable. The Italian sat back and got rich. When the Resistance War broke out he lowered his flag and went home.

After the Heavenly Virtue Company closed, Chen Deyuan's opium den moved back into an alley. We rented a place, and the family lived on the lower floor while the opium den was on the upper. The upper floor had a window with a view of the street, and when the police came the customers could hurry downstairs and out the back door. If the customers were caught they could be fined or put in jail, so it was in the interests of the opium den to protect them. Some of the customers were quite wealthy and socially prominent, and they especially needed protection. The safety of the customers was one of the key ingredients in an opium den's success.

To run an opium den a certain amount of money had to be given to the police. Both the local patrolman and the chief would want something, as would the policeman in the sentry post down the street. I remember that in the spring of 1938 they wanted more than we could pay, and the police came to arrest people. The customers fled out the back, but my father jumped out of the window and broke his left foot and became deaf in one ear, becoming a cripple. My mother was arrested and put in jail, but thanks to the intervention of a gentryman named He Yuangan she was later freed. That winter I was coming home, and I saw a policeman sitting on a bench. In his right hand he was holding our family's Flat Altar. My crippled father was kneeling beside him begging for mercy. Once the policeman had gotten his money he left. Even now remembering that scene makes my heart ache. When I went to school my classmates would tease me, calling me "Little opium den boss" under their breath. Opium suppression is a good thing, I agree, but the Nationalists only used the name of opium suppression for extortion. It was just a legal way of destroying people.

The Chen family opium den was a middle-rank place. The different classes of opium dens were distinguished by their size, decor, and number of pipes and the quality of their opium. Middle-rank and above places used southern opium, low-rank places used Sichuan opium.[4] Yichang had very few high-class opium dens. I knew of two, the "Sincerity North" and "Sincerity South." I went to the Sincerity South once. It was set up for the gentry. The opium booths were ornate, and the opium tools were also very beautiful. They also had women to bring out the opium balls. Sincerity South was large, and it was on a street near the south gate, and when you pulled back the door curtain you would see many opium booths. There was no need to fear being arrested there, however. The manager had connections in the government and paid a bribe to the police every month and thus could afford to be so bold.

Opium's Harm to Customers

British imperialism forced opium on China with the guns of its warships. For over a hundred years millions of people suffered from it. Yichang got a foreign concession early (before Chongqing or Changsha), and when the imperialists set up a concession as an opium distribution center the damage was even worse. Of those who smoked opium most were weak willed and became addicts and ended up as low-class degenerates. Among the customers at the Chen family opium den there were several examples.

Chao Daifeng (a Northerner) and his wife both liked to smoke opium and drink. When they did not have money they would sell their own daughter and daughter-in-law as prostitutes. They would use the money to buy opium and liquor. Chao Daifeng's wife went crazy shortly after setting up a brothel in her home. She would come to the opium den, and after smoking many balls she would rave and gibber. Opium turned her into two different people. It happens that there was a similar case. She was a middle-aged woman named Dai Ma, and she had a daughter in middle school. Dai Ma had no job or profession, but she did have an opium addiction. She relied on the money her daughter made selling her body to buy opium. The daughter was an unlicensed prostitute who would go to rich people's houses to provide "outside activities" on a half-year contract. Dai Ma was a regular customer at the Chen family opium den, and she would sometimes bring her daughter with and have her prepare opium. The daughter was intelligent and kind, and all of those in the opium den were sorry for her.

In those days those who suffered from the "three evils" of opium, prostitution, and gambling were not always different people. Many became prostitutes because of their opium smoking. The Yangzhou brothel had one women who was a regular customer at the Chen family opium den. When she would come she would be accompanied by either her old attendant or a young man, as they feared she would escape. She was about 27 or 28 and was blind in her left eye and grew her hair long to hide it. She would often go across the railroad tracks to the "House of Dreams" to serve the foreign sailors. She had been ruined to the point she did not seem human. She was deep in the pit of opium, using it to give her the strength to endure her sufferings. Second Alley was a place for low-class prostitutes, and "Second alley wild chicken" was a common epitaph. These prostitutes were all deeply addicted. They usually had only enough money to go to low-class opium dens; the managers and pimps were at the middle-level dens. The Chen family opium den was near Second Alley, and we saw a lot of them swallowing clouds and spitting up smoke.

An opium den also opened the gate to gambling for many people. One was a young man called Zheng Bainian. He did odd jobs at the boat landing. He was a thief and would steal things from the warehouses at the landing. He would steal relatively valuable things like gold jewelry, watches, and Russian wool blankets. Sometimes when he could not get rid of things he would pawn them at the Chen family opium den. Money came easy to Zheng Bainian, and his opium addiction grew with each smoke. He would bring a friend called Zhou Changkou, who was also a thief, along to smoke with him. After the fall of Yichang Zheng Bainian returned to Qingtan and relied on swindling people to get his opium money. Zhou Changkou became a robber and was later shot. He was 21 when he died.

There was also a man named Chang from Sichuan. He was a leader in the Han River Society. In the Yichang Han River Society he also held a high post. He was very good at martial arts. He became addicted to opium and became a thief to get opium money. He was a "smash and grab" thief, stealing things from people's houses, prying open doors, and breaking locks; there was nothing he would not dare to do. He often smoked opium at the Chen family opium den. There was also a litigator named Chen, who opened a place at the mouth of Alley #4. He had money and influence (as a lawyer he was always going to government offices), and he would often use his influence to bully people in the opium den. Once he got into an argument over the Flat Altar with Chen Wufu, and Chen hit him in the eye. The next time Chen Wufu came to the opium den he could not stand and had to drag himself in on his hands. People said that he had been caught stealing something and had his legs broken. Opium smoking had brought him to a miserable end.

The Qing, the Beiyang government, and the Guomindang all loudly proclaimed opium suppression, but the more they prohibited the more people smoked. The prosperous business the Chen family opium den did during the Resistance War is proof that all their efforts accomplished nothing. It was only after Liberation, with the anti-opium and drug movement, that opium's long harm to the Chinese people was ended. I leave to the people this bitter history.

NOTES

Chen Hongru, "Yi jia yapian yanguan de jiushi" (The story of one family's opium den), *Yichang wenshi ziliao* 8 (1987): 118–26.

1. The Red Gang is a secret society.

2. That is, he had become a Buddhist monk.

3. *Ronin* is the Japanese term for a masterless samurai. The Chinese equivalent was often applied to Japanese adventurers resident in China.

4. Southern, in this case, means Yunnan.

Opium and Warlordism: Huang Shaoxiong

This is an account of the opium trade in Guangxi by Huang Shaoxiong. Huang was a member of the New Guangxi Clique, which ran Guangxi Province from 1921. Huang broke with Li Zongren and Bai Zhongxi, the other main members of the clique, in 1930. He would later serve in central government posts under Chiang Kai-shek and held minor offices under the Communists. This reading mostly deals with the early years of the clique, when it was deeply involved in the opium trade. As Huang points out, the province produced little opium, but it was an important transit point for opium from Yunnan and Guizhou going to Guangdong. Opium profits were crucial to the independence and national influence of Guangxi, and like many other governments the Guangxi Clique made considerable progress in refining their control over the opium trade.

The New Guangxi Clique and Opium

Opium began to poison China a hundred years ago, injuring bodies and draining finances, a worry for everyone. During the Qing Daoguang period the Guangdong-Guangxi governor-general, Lin Zexu, declared opium prohibition and strictly prohibited it in Guangdong. This led to the English imperialists launching the "Opium War." The Qing court was afraid of both the military power of the English and the revolutionary resistance of the people as well as loss of territory and indemnities and so begged for peace. Lin Zexu was banished to Xinjiang, which was truly regrettable. After that there was no real opium suppression. Indian "big opium" flowed into China in great amounts. Not only that, on the suggestion that it would help keep the profits at home, poppies were brought from India to China. Soon poppies were blooming all

GUANGXI PROVINCE

HUNAN

GUANGDONG

GUIZHOU

Xiang Jiang

Li Jiang

Wuzhou

Xun Jiang

Youngan

Yujin

Qian Jiang

Yu Jiang

Liuzhou

GUANGXI

Hongshui

Nanning

Yong Jiang

Longan

Zuo Jiang

Longzhou

You Jiang

Lingyun

Bose

Pingma

Jingxi

Zhenfeng

Boai

Guangnan

Xingyi

Xilong

Jiuzhou

Xilin

YUNNAN

VIETNAM

Scale: 1 inch represents 100 kilometers

over the country. Chinese opium production soared, and Indian imports dropped, as Indian opium could not penetrate the interior. Domestic opium proved to be an immeasurably worse problem than the Indian.

After the first year of the Republic the Beiyang government decreed opium suppression and threatened to punish those who disobeyed. Under the Beiyang regime, however, and especially under the pressure of the provincial warlords and their wars and exactions, "opium suppression" was only on paper. This paper suppression was useful to warlords, corrupt officials, local bullies, and evil gentry, however, as the chief source of finance for their civil wars. So-called opium suppression fines were the economic foundation of warlordism. The Opium War was a war between England and China, but the decades of warlordism can be considered a huge and continuous opium war.

The author was a member of the New Guangxi Clique, and this essay is based on his experiences. It is not only relevant to opium and the New Guangxi Clique, however. Of all the warlord struggles in all the provinces there was not one that could not be said to be connected to opium. This essay thus provides the key to many problems.

Under the leadership of the Chinese Communist Party and Chairman Mao, the opium poison that had afflicted the Chinese people for over 100 years was eliminated in a few years. People today do not see elegantly phrased anti-opium proclamations, nor do they see people being imprisoned or executed, and yet in the cities and villages you cannot smell the scent of opium smoke, and even in the most remote borderlands you cannot see a poppy flower. It is indeed a miracle. How can this miracle be explained? The simple answer is that it is due to the leadership of the party and the excellence of the Socialist system.

The Opium Situation in Guangxi under the Qing and the Old Guangxi Clique

After the Opium War opium prohibition was relaxed everywhere. When I was a young boy the county seat of Suxian had a population of under 10,000, but it had two "opium centers." They sold opium paste, and they were all run by gentry. One of them, called the "Fusheng," was opened by one of my friend's uncles. Fusheng can mean "enriching people's lives." What sarcasm. At that time (the 34th year of Guangxu, 1908) I wanted to go to the city to study, and so I left the countryside and moved to that capital of opium, Guilin. Opium paste was divided into standard opium and plain opium. Standard opium was originally made with Indian big opium and was more expensive. Plain opium was made with domestic opium and was less expensive. Later, when Indian opium became rarer and domestic opium more common standard paste came to be made from Yunnan opium and plain paste from Guizhou opium. Those who came to the opium shop were not from the local declining wealthy households; some were the addicted laborers. The rich addicts would buy and boil their own opium and would not go to the shop to buy it. Opium was sold both in the day and in the evening, and it was said that those who smoked opium wanted to smoke both during the day and in the night. Actually, those who were lightly addicted liked to smoke at night. Those who were heavily addicted wanted to smoke in the morning, afternoon, and evening. When the shop sold less that a 1/10 ounce of opium it was wrapped up in a leaf or in a triangle of red paper. Larger amounts were put in small porcelain containers, although sometimes customers brought their own boxes. The Fusheng would sell four or five ounces of opium paste a day. If each person took .05 ounces the opium shop would have about 100 customers. For the whole county seat there were about 600 or 700 smokers, and the other counties were about the same, showing how deeply the poison had spread. My father was a scholar, and he knew how dangerous opium was, and he hated opium smoking. In my father's generation opium smokers were relatively few among country people. I had an older brother who fell in love with a country girl. When my father found out he scolded him, saying "Don't act crazy. I've already arranged a marriage, and I will soon give you a wife." The same brother later became an opium addict, and when my father found out he was furious. My father tied him up, took off his robe, and beat him with a bamboo stick, cursing as he beat his back black and blue. We younger brothers did not dare to look. In spite of my father's beating and cursing and his own promises to reform, my brother continued to smoke secretly. Later another older brother became an opium addict, and my father died of regret.

We landlords had a saying to warn our sons about opium: "The hole of an opium pipe is as small as a needle, but you can put a water buffalo in it, and you can also smoke hundreds of *mu* of land through it." They did not want their sons smoking opium to protect their lands from being lost. The Shanxi bankers, on the other hand, encouraged their sons to smoke opium so that they would not go out and gamble. Since the bankers had far too much money the cost of opium could not damage them.[1]

Above I said that my father's generation did not smoke opium, but among the generation after my grandfather 6 of the 11 in my family became opium addicts by the time of the Resistance War. This shows how the opium poison became rampant during the Warlord period. Among the officials, the warlords' and the feudal landlords' opium smoking was very common. My clan is a typical case.

During the Republic Guangxi was controlled by the Old Guangxi Clique.

Under Yuan Shikai's dynasty there were some opium suppression orders issued, but under the exactions of the provincial warlords it was say one thing in public and do another in private. The warlords and their armies needed money. As the saying goes, "The more salt smuggling is prohibited, the easier it is to sell it," which can be altered to, "The more opium is prohibited the easier it is to sell it." You could see this everywhere, but Yunnan and Guizhou troops were particularly bad. Among Guangxi troops, however, there were not many smokers. It was an open secret, however, that the garrisons and roving troops secretly used opium to fill their pockets.

The Transshipment of Yunnan and Guizhou Opium through Guangxi

Not much opium was planted in Guangxi. Not because either the Old or New Guangxi Clique did not consider it, but because the climate was not suitable. What opium was harvested in Guangxi was of low quality, so we relied on the neighboring Guizhou and Yunnan counties of Xilin and Xilong, which planted more and got a better yield. Opium was planted in the ninth lunar month and harvested in the third month of the next year. It liked cool and foggy areas, and so Yunnan and Guizhou were the best southern regions for it. The quality of the Yunnan opium was higher, and the prices reflected this. Guangxi was the route through which Yunnan and Guizhou opium moved to Guangdong, Hong Kong, Macao, and Guangzhouwan, with a certain amount also going to southern Hubei and Jiangxi. The opium took one of four routes through Guangxi, but the routes were not fixed. It depended on the attitude of the local garrison, level of banditry, and the amount that would have to be paid to move through an area. Opium was like quicksilver, flowing into any hole, and it might take any one of these routes or create a new one. It was impossible to completely stop it up.

The town of Bose was the most important market for Yunnan and Guizhou opium, and as I was in the Bose garrison and participated in shipping opium and in the New Guangxi Clique's first connections to opium I must discuss this.

In the old society when people heard "Bose" they thought of opium. Bose is in northwest Guangxi, at the headwaters of the Shi River, and it was a river port, with small steamboats going east to Nanning. There was a land route west through Lufeng and Boai to Guangnan in Yunnan (small boats could go as far as Boai). There was a land route north to Nanlong, Xingyi, Zhenfeng, and other important opium-producing areas in Guangxi. This made Bose the most important market for Yunnan and Guizhou opium.

How were Bose's commercial affairs arranged? On the surface there was a great disparity between its imports and its exports. Imports (things being sent from Nanning) were much more numerous than exports (things sent to Nanning). The most important imports were colored yarn, imported goods, and salt, all valuable goods. Most of it went on to Yunnan and Guizhou. Exports were cattle hides and mountain goods (medicinals, fennel, etc.), none of any great value. Boats coming up from Nanning were always full, and those going down were nearly empty, to the point they had to be ballasted with rocks when the water was high. Exports and imports were in balance, however, because the most important export was opium. Opium could be packed small and hidden so it could not be seen. (All the steamboats on the West River had special hiding places for opium.) On the streets of Bose you would see yarn shops and foreign goods shops and mountain goods shops, but there was not one that was not involved with opium. The head of the Bose merchants association was the biggest opium dealer. At that time (1921) Bose city had a population of about 10,000, but at the riverbank were three "floating brothels" with over 100 prostitutes.[2] This was the world of the opium merchants and gangs and the troops who protected the opium.

Whether a port above Wuzhou had good nightlife or not depended on if it had a floating brothel or not, although there were of course also regular brothels. It is said that originally city people were afraid of the bad influence of prostitutes on local customs and so forbade them to open brothels on land, leading to their being established on the water. This is the origin of Canton's floating brothels.

Under the Qing Bose was the base of the You River garrison. This may have been because of its closeness to French Vietnam. After the establishment of the Republic, when Guangxi was under the yoke of the Old Guangxi Clique, there were constant civil wars, and nobody paid attention to border defense. Bose was still seen as important by the Old Guangxi Clique, however, and troops who did not have an exceptionally good relationship with the clique were not stationed there. The garrison could make an excellent income protecting opium shipments or confiscating private opium under the pretext of suppression.

In the winter of 1920 Ma Shaojun and his Model Battalion were ordered to leave Wuzhou on the Guangdong-Guangxi front and move to Bose.[3] This was not because Ma and his unit had an exceptionally good relationship with the Old Guangxi Clique but because the clique distrusted them and did not want them on the front and in easy contact with the Guangdong troops. When we got our orders to move those who were not in the know were covered with smiles, thinking that this was a great honor and a sign that we were especially trusted by Tan Gaoming. When our troops arrived in Bose the head of the merchant's association, Lu Bichen, invited us to enjoy flowers and wine on a boat. Ma Shaojun had an outward image as a Taoist and did not do such things. Seeing that this attack did not work, Lu tried another, inviting the various officers. First they were hosted by the head of the merchant association, then the owners of the shops, and then the opium gangs. For two weeks it was as if the night never ended. During this period they were very warm to us, working on the most susceptible and building personal relations. Later they gradually brought up the importance of protecting opium. They explained opium's key position in Bose's commercial affairs, what previous garrisons had done to protect the trade, and cited examples of how some troops had not cooperated with the merchants, leading to an economic slump. The merchants had become angry and denounced them to their superiors, and everyone suffered. Their meaning was that if the garrison and the merchants worked together the city would flourish and we would not fail the merchants' and officials' expectations. This of course could not be explained to Ma Shaojun, but through the subcommanders and his two younger brothers he gave tacit permission, and we below did the work. Ma Shaojun may have cultivated the air of a Taoist, but when money was concerned he didn't let it show and looked the other way. In the situation it was no use for me individually to say anything. From that point I began working with the opium gangs protecting opium shipments.

Bose's Opium Gangs and Problems with Escorting Them

An opium gang was the opium merchant's armed detachment. Each gang would have several tens of rifles and pistols. Their leaders were all old military officials, wandering "heros," or bandits, like the leaders of the Old Guangxi Clique. Lu Yan, my sworn brother from Yongan, and his neighbor Su Yuanchun served in the army and then moved to Bose and became important members of the gentry. There was also Liu Yuchen, who was the nephew of Liu Refu, the head of the self-government troops, as well as others like Lan Yunan, who had served as officials in the old armies. They got on well with an opium gang leader named Chen Rongting. Chen Rongting was notorious; he had been everywhere. At every stop on every road in Longzhou, Jinsxi, Zhenbian, and Yunnan he had a wife and a household. Wherever he went it was like he had never left home. He was the best known of those in the Guangxi opium gangs. Lu, Liu, and Lan were the leading providers of protection for goods in Bose. For foreign and other goods coming up to Guangxi and Yunnan they served openly as guards. Bandits would not attack them, and even officials and regular troops would not give them trouble. On the way back they would guard secret opium shipments, organizing military units to provide security. Since opium was officially contraband anyone could give them trouble or even confiscate it. These attacks were known as "confiscating opium." Asking for official troops made it possible to get the approval of the local garrison, but they would only send a token force, and more military power would be needed.

The opium gang leaders would make up a group of merchants, goods, and money to go by foot and mule from Bose to Yunnan or Guizhou. This was called "making a caravan." There would also be a number of independent peddlers dealing in opium or other things who would find out what day they were leaving and tag along. The whole caravan could total 1,000 men and mules, a vast array. After they arrived at their destination the goods would be sold to local merchants the shippers were connected with or sold in the street. Then they would buy up opium and head back. The most opium I ever recall them bringing back was 500,000 ounces.

The protection fee for the official troops was arranged by the leader of the gang. He would charge the merchant about 30 cents an ounce for protection and then distribute about 20 cents an ounce to the soldiers, keeping the rest for himself. He would also trade on his own account and could make a lot this way. Thirty cents an ounce was the price for protecting the opium from Yunnan to Bose only. From Bose down to Wuzhou protection would cost another 60 to 70 cents. The merchants hoped to be able to cover all this from the sale price in Guangdong and make a profit besides. If they could not make a profit they would ask the military to reduce their protection fees, like asking for tax relief. If the military was inflexible and refused the merchants' request they would change routes, as there were plenty of roads going east. The military also did not provide complete protection for their money. If faced with a powerful force that they could not resist the troops would not take responsibility.

A couple of months after Ma Shaojun's troops came to Bose I escorted my first opium shipment. It was about 100,000 ounces, and the total protection money came to 30,000 dollars. Needless to say, no matter how secret we tried to be everyone knew about the shipment. Those who had not received a share of the money reported it to Ma Shaojun. When the money was divided the higher-ranking people got a large share and the lower-ranking ones a small share. I got a large share, but Ma Shaojun got a small share. He was furious when he found out and sent for me. "I hear that you have been escorting opium shipments and have been making a lot of money from it. If I hear of you doing things like this again I will have you thrown in jail." It seemed as if he wanted to have me dragged away right then. I thought to myself, "I have been shipping opium and you only found out when people told you? All this is only because I did not distribute enough money. If I do get hauled away I will denounce those who denounced me and who also got a share of the money. In the future I need to be careful to distribute more money." This method turned out to be effective, and I never heard about it again.

As I said above, protecting opium shipments was not absolutely safe. One could unexpectedly meet with a more powerful force on the road who would seize the opium. The troops would run off orders and their guns would be lost. Therefore I always went along to order the troops to open fire and bring back both the opium and the guns. Ma Shaojun did not dare to do this, however. At that point we did not understand that guns and opium were more important than the life of a commander.

At that time (the spring of 1921 to the collapse of the Old Guangxi Clique) Bai Zhongxi could be said not to have been stained by the opium trade. His troops were stationed on the road between Bose and Yunnan at Lufeng and Luyi, and he diligently drilled his troops. After arriving at Lufeng, however, his troops began to desert and even killed an officer named Lao. Lao drilled them too hard, but they also killed him because the local opium gang (they operated between Lufeng and Luyi and moved a thousand or so ounces of opium at a time) thought that Bai was stealing their rice bowl by being stationed on their route. They encouraged the troops to bring their guns and join the opium gang. They were also motivated by seeing me and my troops make a lot of money while doing very little drilling. Ma Shaojun would not send Bai Zongxi to catch the deserters, for fear that it would just lead to more desertions. I was sent instead, and I relied on the help of the opium gang leaders, since they not only knew the territory but the smaller opium gangs as well. We spent a week on Bajiao Mountain and came to an agreement with the small gang that they would return the guns. At the same time outside troops were running around the area, but they did not catch anyone. I got a commendation, as did Ma Shaojun, and Bai Zhongxi did not get a demerit.

Good times never last long. Ma Shaojun had only been in Bose about a year when the Old Guangxi Clique collapsed. Cantonese troops took Nanning, and Ma Junwu became provincial governor. Ma Shaojun was ordered to do police work, and Guizhou troops under Hu Ying lu were ordered to Bose by Sun Yat-sen. Guizhou of course produced a lot of opium, and they brought a lot with them. Their routes to Huangyi, Luoli, and Jiuzhou in Guangxi were all in their own rear area, so they did not need any protection from us, and our income declined.

Soon after this the Guangxi troops were transferred to Liuzhou. The remnants of the Old Guangxi Clique, Liu Refu, Ma Yucheng, and Lu Yungui, knew that Ma Shaojun's troops were poor and that Bose was the most lucrative post-ing in Guangxi. After they had been defeated at Longzhou by Guangdong troops under Huang Duwei and Wang Mingtang, they fled to Bose, and Ma Shaojun found his opium profits getting even smaller. Once troops arrived in Bose they no longer drilled and soon became an undisciplined rabble. Although we were all under the Guangdong flag at this point, it was clear that there would be conflict among the Guangxi troops over control of Bose and its opium profits. In the end Liu Refu and Lu Yungui encircled Ma Shaojun and disarmed his troops. Ma Shaojun lost Bose because of opium and his relation-ship to it.

Those who were out escorting opium shipments at the time escaped the defeat at Bose. Bai Zhongxi, Xia Weiying, and a couple hundred troops were warned in time and fled into Guizhou. There they joined together with the opium gang leader Lu Yan (my sworn brother) and the commander of the Nanlung garrison, Liu Xinyuan. Lu and Liu were fellow students and had worked together on opium shipments.[4] They and the opium merchants gave Bai and Xia 20,000 dollars to support themselves. I had been captured at Bose, and Liu Refu had ordered me to be shot. Thanks to the intervention of Liu Yuchen, an opium gang leader and cousin of Liu Refu, I was freed, however. I sneaked off to Huanglan, about 100 *li* from Bose. I did not want to share the problems of Bai and Xia, so I used some of my acquaintances from my opium escorting days and weapons provided by two Xilin County bad gentry to quickly put together a force of two or three hundred men.[5] At this time local bullies and evil gentry were always looking to organize military forces to increase their power and give them chances to make money.

After the Guangdong troops defeated Liu Refu and took Bose they assigned Ma Shaojun to the Guangxi fifth route army in Pingma. This was not at Ma's request but at the gentry's request, since they could profit by getting rid of him. Our troops were not strong, and we were reluctant to move, even though Pingma was not that far away. We organized ourselves in southeastern Liufu County. I was one leader, with Lu Yan, Huang Bingxuan, and the other opium gang and opium-related people. The other leader was Bai Zhongxi, with Xia Wei and Feng Yunsong. All told there were six or seven hundred men. We moved to Pingma, but to keep the troops' spirits up we deceived them, and rather than telling them that we were planning on returning to Bose and that Pingma was just a temporary stop, we told them that the local troops were too powerful and if they tried to go back they would be cut to pieces. When we got to Pingma we were joined by Feng Chunlin (later one of my most capable fol-lowers) and Huang Yubao. Huang Yubao was a woman of the Zhuang nationality with a reputation as a fierce warrior. She had advanced political ideas, which led to her joining the Communist Party in the 1930s. She was killed by Bai Zhongxi. It could be said that Ma Shaojun's troops were in fact the troops of Bai Zhongxi and Huang Shanghong's New Guangxi Clique, as half of them were opium smugglers or bandits. These were the sorts of troops who garrisoned the banks of the You River, and unlikely as it seems, we were soon sent to reinforce the provincial capital, Nanning.

When I sent off for Nanning (Ma Shaojun, Bai Zhongxi, and their troops had already left) I made a strong force with Xia Wei, Feng Yunsong, and Feng Chunlin in the vanguard, with Lu Yan, Huang Bingxuan, and the opium smugglers in the rear. Self-defense forces controlled Fengan County, but the vanguard troops quickly forced them to retreat from Fengan city, and both they and the opium smugglers moved in. The opium smugglers had never had any military training, and their discipline was lax. When they entered Fengan city they recklessly robbed people at gunpoint and committed countless outrages; order fell apart completely. The looting of Fengan was both painful and educational for me. I resolved to emphasize military discipline; we would no longer take instruction from opium gang members, rather the New Guangxi Clique's army would be founded on military discipline. After this I got rid of all the opium smugglers, and later, after Guangxi was unified, I not only purged the opium smugglers but many of the old-style troops as well. They were critical of me, saying that I was "catching the fish and discarding the net."

After we withdrew from Nanning we roamed around Guangdong with nothing to eat. The few thousand ounces of opium that Lu Yan had brought along were our final support. I led my troops back to Yulin, where we joined with Li Zongren, and eventually we and Li's fellow Guangdong army member Li Jishen occupied Wuzhou. At that point I still had the habits I had picked up hanging out with opium smugglers and always offered guests a pipe of opium. Li Jishen and Yan Da came by once and were very surprised. Yan Da angrily said, "What is this! Among the revolutionary troops this is not done. If you want to join the revolution you must cure yourself of this." I resolved to cure myself, and although I was deeply addicted I managed to do so at the cost of a little time. To this day I am grateful to Yan Da, the friend who put me on the right path.

After curing myself I put the troops in order. The opium gang chief Lu Yen was very hardworking but not appropriate to command troops, so I made him opium prohibition officer of Wuzhou. Using an opium smuggler to suppress opium might be thought of as making a joke of opium suppression. All over China, however, governments were making a joke of opium suppression. Of opium suppression officials, how many did not smoke opium? And there was not one who was not using opium suppression to line his pocket. As I saw it, putting an opium smuggler in charge of opium suppression was just making appropriate use of him.

The Yunnan-Guangxi War and Opium

I have discussed the Yunnan-Guangxi War elsewhere. It arose when Yunnan's Tang Jiyao, frustrated in his ambitions in Sichuan, turned his scheming to Guangxi and Guangdong. On the surface the whole thing was about military control, but the underlying cause was opium. Prior to 1920 both Yunnan and Guizhou were under Tang's control, and their opium was exported either north to the Yangzi or south to overseas. The northern route went through Sichuan and western Hunan and Hubei to the Yangzi to supply the northern provinces. The southern route went through Guangxi to the Pearl River. In the 1913 Second Revolution Yunnan troops moved into Sichuan, making it easier to ship the opium and increase profits. Yunnan could be called a poor province, but before 1920 Tang was able to recruit troops and campaign because of opium. When the Yunnan troops were defeated by Gu Pinzhen and driven out of Sichuan it could be called a conflict between Yunnan opium and Sichuan opium. After Tang had been defeated and driven back he obviously could not support as many troops and had to accept the support of Sun Yat-sen. Tang joined with the Yunnan troops from Guangxi and returned to Yunnan and killed Gu Pinzhen and took back control of the province. Those who had supported Tang returned to Guangxi and joined Sun Yat-sen in fighting Chen Jiongming. The repeated changes in Yunnan showed that without a way to export opium an army could not be supported or expand its territory.

When the Yunnan troops entered Guangxi they brought a great deal of opium with them to support the expedition, and many merchants carrying opium went along with them. They were all hoping to get down to Canton to take advantage of the price difference. The leading officers would do very well for themselves, and the merchants would make a tenfold profit. They were unwilling to sell the opium on the way, but Fan Shisheng and I were able to encircle Long Yun and Hu Ku'en at Nanning. Tang Melu and Zhang Nuyi's troops were encircled by myself and Bai Zhongxi. I don't know how much opium they had, although they certainly had some, but it was almost all destroyed in the fighting. The period from the winter of 1924 to the spring of 1925 was one of continuous warfare for Guangxi. On the Guangxi side we were almost out of supplies, and I had no choice but to give the pursuit to Bai Zhongxi and retreat to Wuzhou to get some money. Not long after, the Yunnan troops in Nanning managed to get their opium through to Canton and sell it. This was because of the poor encirclement. The Nanning opium merchants also sent out a shipment of 200,000 ounces, but that was intercepted by the Guangxi troops. The opium money and the protection fees all went to the Yunnan troops. This was a great embarrassment, but if you want to know who wins you must wait until the final victory. We usually caught the shipments, and this was the basis of the New Guangxi Clique and the reason for our final victory in the Yunnan-Guangxi War.

Opium and Guangxi's Finances

After the New Guangxi Clique unified the province I became governor. I fully understood the benefits of opium and paid particular attention to controlling, unifying, and opening up the trade. We used the label of opium suppression, but our real goal was to bring opium profits to the government. This was in 1926, so you could say that we were the first to openly put opium revenues in government accounts, but later Nanjing and the other provincial governments would follow us.

How much did Guangxi make from opium per year? I don't have exact figures, but according to the *Guangxi Government Record* during the rule of Huang Jiuchu over half of the income was from opium, which shows how important it was. What percentage of the opium that entered Guangxi was sold locally and what percent re-exported? To answer both of these questions, here is a section on "opium fines" from the *Guangxi Government Record.*

Opium fines and opium medicine taxes are both opium taxes.[6] Guangxi does not produce opium. It is imported from Yunnan and Guizhou to Guangdong, and as the amount is great the number of addicts in the province continues to grow. Prior to unification of the province local garrisons would collect opium taxes. In 1926 under the old Finance Department's unified assessment method, a transit tax was intended to suppress through taxation.[7] In July of 1926 the provincial government was established and began a program of gradual suppression. They decided in principle to gradually increase taxes and decrease the amount. The old regulations were abolished and new ones issued. Yunnan and Guizhou opium that was being shipped through the province now had to be declared to the Opium Suppression Office, which would certify the amount. It would be shipped along approved routes, stored in government warehouses, and escorted by soldiers assigned by the Opium Suppression Office. All opium was to be sealed and pay taxes, regardless of whether it was to be sold in Guangxi or Guangdong. The opium suppression fine was 50 dollars for

1,000 ounces, half that for opium ashes.[8] The proceeds were to be divided into three parts, with 2/3 going to the central government and 1/3 to the provincial government. The provincial government was to keep the value of any smuggled opium that was captured and the rewards for capturing it. In 1932 the rules were changed, and opium to be sold in Guangxi was required to pay an additional 200 dollars. In August of the same year an Opium Suppression Inspectorate was set up to coordinate shipping and anti-smuggling activities with the Guangdong Opium Suppression Office. The Guangdong office stationed people in Wuzhou, Yulin, and Nanning to help coordinate shipments.[9] Opium that was being shipped through Guangxi to Guangdong would first be inspected in one of these three places, pay its taxes, and then be escorted to Guangdong. Each month 1,100,000 ounces were to be shipped, with anything above that being excess. Guangdong agreed to pay 45 percent of the taxes it collected on any excess opium to Guangxi to finance anti-smuggling efforts. In 1934 the rules were revised again, with all the revenue now going to the provincial government and none to the central government.[10] In January of 1937 a branch of the Anti-Opium Inspectorate was set up in Guangxi.[11] By its orders opium suppression fines were renamed opium taxes. Yunnan opium was taxed at a rate of 820 dollars per 1,000 ounces, Guizhou at a rate of 800 dollars per 1,000 ounces. Each also paid 100 dollars to support anti-opium clinics. In January of 1938 a progressive tax of between 200 and 400 dollars per thousand was added.

According to this source, the total amount shipped to Guangdong each year was over 13,200,000 ounces, with any amount over that being excess, and 45 percent of the Guangdong taxes being returned to Guangxi to fight smuggling. If you add in the amount Guangxi sent to Hunan, the total was probably over 20,000,000 ounces at the 1931 tax rates of 500 dollars per 1,000 ounces. According to the *Guangxi Government Record* total income for 1932 was 31,000,000 dollars, of which opium income was 15,880,000 dollars. At a rate of 500 dollars per thousand ounces this would mean that over 30,000,000 ounces of opium moved through Guangxi, a surprising amount. Over the next three years the amount declined, but never to less than 10,000,000 dollars and 20,000,000 ounces. In 1936 it fell to 4,000,000 because of the "6.1" incident.[12] With Chiang Kai-shek in control of Yunnan and Guizhou he was able to cut Guangxi off and force the clique to accede to his wishes.

I had suggested this system of unified transport between Guangxi and Guangdong to the Guangdong finance minister, Feng Shiwan, in 1928. At that time Guangdong's opium income was only half of Guangxi's, but he turned me down, saying that "Clear water has no fish." By this he meant that if the transit system kept the merchants, soldiers, and government officials from profiting personally they would oppose it. In 1932, however, Chen Jitang set up just such a system, and it can be considered one of his most brilliant moves.

Opium and the Financial Reconstruction of Guangxi

During the time that the Old Guangxi Clique ruled the province the Bank of Guangxi issued more banknotes than they could redeem, mostly connected to their decade-long (1911–21) attempt to control Hunan. By the time the Old Clique collapsed in 1921 Bank of Guangxi notes were wastepaper. When the New Guangxi Clique unified the province we wanted to manage the bank properly, but had no capital. Liu Rifu had originally been in the self-defense forces and had long been stationed in Bose. He eventually saw an opportunity to go to work for Li Zongren, and after the unification of the province he was made a brigadier. In 1926 Li Zongren took his 7th Army on the Northern Expedition (Liu remained behind), and I became the most powerful person in the military and government of Guangxi. Liu Rifu, in order to win my favor and consolidate his own position, sent me a telegraph saying that he had seized 700,000 ounces of smuggled opium, which he was presenting to the provincial government. At this point I was looking for money to finance the bank with, and the report was a godsend. Where did these 700,000 ounces of opium come from? To this day I'm not entirely clear. If a garrison caught an opium gang with "smuggled opium" they could confiscate it, and this often happened. Liu Rifu often sent me opium he had confiscated as a way of currying favor, and this was the extent of "opium suppression" at the time. Liu Rifu gave the opium to me so I would not dismiss him, but in fact I had no intention of dismissing him, as he got on well with the local people and was well liked by them. I converted the 700,000 ounces of opium into 700,000 dollars cash, which became the capital of the Bank of Guangxi. I had silver coins made in Hong Kong. Prior to this, the old Guangxi banknotes being worthless, most trade was done with coins. Although when I was in Wuzhou (1924) I allowed a merchant named Liang Quanheng to set up a mint, the markets of Guangdong and Guangxi were flooded with inferior coins. Many of them seemed to be silver on the outside, but were actually copper or lead. When the new Bank of Guangxi notes were printed and I issued them people were grateful and were even willing to pay a premium to get the new notes. I gave orders that at first the new notes were to trade at 1:1 even for bad coins. The coins were then remelted into 3,000,000 dollars of new coins, which used up the 700,000 ounces of opium.

These coins were the capital of the Bank of Guangxi. The Nanjing government's Farmer's Bank also got its capital from opium.[13]

At that time (1926 to 1928) the bulk of the Guangxi forces were not on the Northern Expedition but in Guangdong, and the money to support them was all supplied locally. Not many troops were left in Guangxi, and the government apparatus was rudimentary, so these could be supported by current taxes. We used the resources of the Bank of Guangxi to build new highways, building over 3,000 km in these few years. We also set up public loan offices in the important counties, offering loans as low as two or three percent a month. We also set up a number of small factories, such as the Wuzhou sulfuric acid plant, the Liuzhou ethyl alcohol plant, and the Nanning shoe factory. In the field of education we established Guangxi University and many upper-middle and middle schools, as well as agricultural experiment stations. The "reconstruction" of the so-called Huang Shaoxiong period was all based on 700,000 ounces of opium.

Opium's Effects on the Trends of the Guangxi Government

As stated above, some 20 to 30 million ounces of opium moved through Guangxi in these ten years, and half the province's income came from opium. All this opium money of course had a great effect on Guangxi's social and economic life and on the government of the province. Regardless of whether it was the Old Guangxi Clique or the New, no Guangxi government could afford bad relations with Yunnan and Guizhou, as these were the sources of our opium. Although Yunnan troops invaded us twice, it was always Guangxi that sent representatives to Yunnan to try to smooth things out, as they had other options for shipping their opium. After the 1936 "6.1" incident, when Chiang Kai-shek told Yunnan's Long Yun and Guizhou's Wu Zhongxin to stop sending their opium through Guangxi, our revenue dropped from 10,000,000 to 4,000,000 dollars. Chiang was able, within three months, to subdue Li and Bai, demonstrating the great importance of opium for the New Guangxi Clique and China's warlord system.

NOTES

Huang Shaoxiong, "Xin gui xi yu ya pian yan" (The New Guangxi Clique and opium), *Wenshi ziliao xuanji* (national edition) 34 (1986): 175–95.

1. This is a common story about rich people in general and Shanxi bankers in particular.

2. A floating brothel was built on top of two or three barges. The top floor was used by customers for banquets, and the bottom floor was a rabbit warren of little rooms used by prostitutes and guests.

3. At this point Huang Shaoxiong was a company commander in the Model Battalion.

4. "Fellow students" (*tongxue*) meant that they had attended the same school, although not necessarily at the same time. This could be a very important relationship.

5. The Chinese word for "bad gentry" is *tuhao lieshen*.

6. "Opium medicine taxes" refers to the tactic of taxing opium but calling it anti-opium medicine.

7. "Suppression through taxation" was a common term for trying to tax opium so heavily that people quit using it. The phrase was usually used as a cover for an opium monopoly.

8. Ashes were often added to raw opium as it was boiled down to make prepared opium.

9. These towns are all in Guangxi.

10. At this point the Guangxi Clique was in conflict with the central government.

11. The Anti-Opium Inspectorate was Chiang Kai-shek's main opium control organization. It was based in Hankou and by 1937 already controlled the wholesale opium trade in most of the provinces south of the Huai.

12. The "6.1" incident was an open break between the Guangxi Clique and its allies in Guangdong and Chiang Kai-shek. The Guangdong and Guangxi forces found themselves without allies and soon had to submit to the central government.

13. The Farmer's Bank of China was created by Chiang Kai-shek to handle the financial side of the Yangzi opium trade. It was one of four banks allowed to issue legal tender banknotes.

Sun Yat-sen on
Opium, 1924

Sun Yat-sen was regarded as the father of the Chinese Republic and of the Guo-mindang party. He was China's premier revolutionary until his death in 1925, and he enunciated many of the key principles that animated political debate. After his death his thought was made the center of Nationalist ideology, and his statements on opium became canonical. Sun did not talk much about opium during his life, and what he did say was often not in keeping with the positions of anti-opium activists. In his 1894 memorial to Li Hongzhang he suggested encouraging Chinese poppy cultivation in order to keep foreign opium out of the country, pointing out that Chinese opium had a much better fragrance than foreign opium and would easily drive the foreign product from the market.

The document that follows is his only extended condemnation of the opium trade. It has an obscure origin and an interesting history. It was not a formal speech but an answer to a question posed to Sun prior to the 1925 Geneva Anti-Opium Conference. The question was asked by a member of the Anti-Opium Association and was probably intended to elicit a response that could be used by the association as propaganda. Sun's words were elevated by the association to the status of his Anti-Opium Will, which was implicitly equal to his ordinary Will, the chief sacred document of the Nationalist revolution. While the association put Sun's picture and his Anti-Opium Will in all their publications they usually used only the first paragraph, not the later sections that put opium suppression off to a future date. At the time of these comments Sun's government in Canton was running an opium monopoly, a policy that he briefly defends in this document.

Dr. Sun Yat-sen and Opium Suppression

In my opinion, the problem of Opium Suppression in China is synonymous with the problem of Good Government. For traffic in Opium cannot coexist with a National Government deriving its power and authority from the people. Until political workers in China are in a position to assert victoriously the Supremacy of the Civil Authority in the administration of government there is little hope for the effective suppression of the Opium Evil.

So long as lawless militarists encourage, and even make compulsory, the cultivation of the poppy plant in territories under their control, it is futile to devise measures for opium suppression. Crops of the poppy are easily grown and quickly harvested; they yield a far more remunerative return than crops of ordinary food cereals, fruits, and vegetables; and the farmers do not dare, and indeed do not care, to refuse to cultivate the poppy wherever the militarists command them, of course with a view to participation in the profits by doing so.

As a measure of tardy justice to the Chinese people, there should be no reluctance on the part of the delegates of the Powers at the League Conference to make more stringent regulations forbidding the export to China of opium and its more terribly insidious derivatives, morphia, heroin, and other narcotics. The disruption of government in China has not only resulted in the recrudescence of poppy cultivation but has also tended greatly to retard the development of the country's foreign trade, to the enormous loss not only to Chinese but foreign merchants and manufactures of legitimate articles of commerce. The huge sums that are being squandered in the smuggling and illicit trade in opium, if diverted to proper trade channels, would assist not inconsiderably to secure the much desired revival of trade and reestablish the volume of legitimate commerce between China and her foreign suppliers.

The view expressed in some quarters that, because of the admittedly widespread recrudescence of the opium traffic in China, the opium trade should again be legitimized and foreign opium openly admitted through the Maritime Customs—thereby providing increased revenue for the national exchequer—is totally reprehensible. *For it is incontrovertible that Chinese Public Opinion—the opinion of the average peaceful and law-abiding, decent, and respectable citizen— is strongly opposed to the Opium Evil and any, even temporary, surrender in the fight against the illicit opium traffic, much less the proposal to readmit the legitimacy of the opium trade, is revolting to the nation.*

There can be no parleying or armistice, and although conditions in China just now are deplorable and the anti-opium fight is being waged against fearful odds, with apparently little success, it would be a betrayal of the nation were responsible Chinese governmental organs to haul down the flag even temporarily from motives of expediency and shortsighted national self-interest. Surrender in any shape or form is a direct flouting of the national conscience. Not even the lawless militarists and warlords, who are benefitting hugely by the illicit traffic in opium, have dared to acknowledge openly and to glory in the opium traffic. What is being done is done surreptitiously and shamefacedly.

Owing to the lack of roads and other facilities for easy communications in the interior districts and the increased economic burden thrown on the shoulders of the people in consequence of the present ascendancy of the militarists, the natural and normal tendency of the farmers to confine themselves to the growth and cultivation of ordinary agricultural products is being effectually thwarted. Provinces like Guangdong, where the government is strongly opposed to the evil, are confronted not only with the smuggling from adjacent provinces but also with the greater evil of smuggling of both foreign and native-grown opium by the more facile and expeditious sea routes. In these circumstances, while at present a province like Guangdong attempts under great difficulties to regulate and control the illegal traffic in opium—always with a view to curbing the evil and with the aim of devising effective measures for ultimate suppression when greater control is established—we find our efforts of little avail at present, owing to the smuggling that is rampant by land and sea routes.

It must be regretfully admitted that local action cannot become effective unless concerted measures under a National Government are introduced. Until the greater and more destructive evil of militarism is crushed and a National Government is established assuring the supremacy of Civil Authority, the present efforts toward opium suppression can achieve little. When the greater menace to the life and liberty of the people is destroyed, the public conscience of the nation will very soon assert itself over the suppression of illicit opium traffic. But until militarism is first suppressed and Civil Government becomes effective throughout the length and breadth of the Republic the best that can be hoped for, as the foregoing remarks are intended to indicate, is to keep alive the struggle against the illegal traffic by encouraging unceasing vigilance and publicity on the part of the popular anti-opium societies. The firm and uncompromising determination to fight on, however discouraging and unsuccessful the situation may appear to be for the moment, must be incessantly proclaimed. The policy of "No Surrender" must be unflinchingly pursued.

NOTE

"Dr. Sun Yat-sen and Opium Suppression," *Opium: A World Problem* (English Journal of the National Anti-Opium Association of China) 1, no. 1 (1927): 3–5.

The Anti-Opium Association

The National Anti-Opium Association was founded in 1924 for the purpose of representing China at the 1925 Geneva Anti-Opium Conference. It was originally largely composed of educated Shanghai Christians, but it aspired to be a truly national organization. By 1928 it had branches in many major cities and took on the role of chief critic of the Nationalist government's opium policies. The association was the leading voice in the storm of criticism that forced Nanjing to abandon plans for national opium monopolies in 1928 and 1931. It was unable, however, to force Chiang Kai-shek to abandon his lucrative involvement in the Yangzi River opium trade.

The following article is the leading editorial from the first issue of Opium: A World Problem, *the association's English-language monthly.*

The Mission of Opium: A World Problem

Opium and its allied narcotics constitute one of the most complicated and difficult problems that confront young China in its process of national reconstruction and often give unnecessary entanglements to sino-foreign relations. The past history of what opium has done in humiliating China is too evident to need repetition; nor is it necessary to relate here the heroic efforts China has taken in eradicating the horrible scourge in years past. The disorganization of the Central Government, however, was immediately followed by the recrudescence of the cultivation of poppy and extensive trade in native opium. All former heroic efforts to suppress opium were thus spent in vain. This is not all for disintegrated China! As the Chinese proverb says, "Over snow is added frost"; to the scourge of native opium, which is already big and difficult enough for any highly efficient government and any enlightened public opinion to handle with, is added the infliction of foreign opium and its derivatives. These derivatives of opium, that is morphia and heroin and another narcotic, cocaine, are manufactured chiefly in Japan and European countries and have, on account of various reasons, flooded from all directions into China. There is no doubt that the amount of opium produced in China probably reaches hundreds of tons and that the tonnage of imported and smuggled foreign opium can also be counted by the tens. This is not hard to believe when one recalls that a single shipment by the British Steamer *Luchow* from Hongkong, discovered in Shanghai, on Nov. 21st last year, amounts to 100 cases of foreign opium, valued at $1,000,000. As to narcotic drugs, according to the estimate of Dr. Wu Lien Teh, the foremost medical authority of China, not less than thirty tons are imported every year. Thus China is hopelessly poisoned both from within and without!

In view of these horrifying facts and their effect upon the moral, social, economic, and political welfare of the nation, the National Anti-Opium Association of China sprang into existence in the fall of the year 1924, through the cooperative efforts of forty organizations of nationwide significance and representing the educational, religious, social, and commercial interests all over China. The Association has as its sole purpose to free China from the bondage of opium and narcotic drugs. These drugs, in the opinion of the Association, are one of the most demoralizing influences in Chinese society to day, capable, if unchecked, of undermining not only the physical health of large numbers, but also, in an ever more serious way, the will power and moral integrity of the Chinese people. To fulfill its purpose, that is, to save the youth of China from becoming addicted to opium and narcotics, the Association makes use of three weapons: thorough going investigation, extensive popular education, and world wide publicity.

The one way in which we use the last mentioned weapon, that is, publicity, is our publication of the *Chinese Anti-Opium Monthly*, which is being read with increasing enthusiasm by the Chinese public. But as opium is a world problem, the need of an official organ in English to serve as a medium of worldwide publicity among foreign friends and sympathetic organizations has been equally acute. Without an English paper of the kind, it is naturally difficult for foreign friends to get access to true facts about opium and narcotics in China or to know what part they can play in encouraging the Chinese national movement against the world evil. To meet this long-felt need, this issue of *Opium: A World Problem* now makes its first appearance. It will be continually published as a quarterly magazine, and its mission may be briefly outlined as follows:

1. The primary duty of this magazine is to present to the world true and reliable facts about the cultivation of and traffic in Chinese native opium and the importation and distribution of foreign opium and other narcotics. It is not intended to white wash China in order to "save her face" in her international relations, but rather to represent China as one with the world in her suffering from the damage done by opium and other narcotics, as in all other respects. The presentation of true facts, we believe, is the best way towards international understanding and cooperation with respect to the problem of dangerous drugs.

2. This paper, though fully aware of its limitations, will also strive to represent the Chinese public opinion—the opinion of the average peaceful and law-abiding, decent, and respectable citizen—with regard to the problem of opium and other narcotics. That Chinese public opinion is strongly antagonistic to opium and narcotics is clearly shown by the wonderful success China has achieved in suppressing opium in years past. Although on account of various causes, and many that are beyond her control in her present state as a nation without complete sovereignty, the opium scourge has again held its sway, Chinese public opinion is still as strongly antagonistic as ever to opium and other narcotics. This paper attempts to trace and present the developments of this strong public opinion till it wins a complete victory.

3. It is also the aim of this paper to promote international understanding and good will in the world campaign against opium and other narcotics. The Association firmly believes that nothing but international cooperation can give a death blow to the opium evil for good and all, since the problem of opium and narcotics in one country is inseparably interwoven with that of other countries. So while trying to represent the Chinese public opinion in regard to opium, this paper will at the same time stand for a common forum, in which various phases of the opium problem will be discussed from a world wide standpoint and nations are free to exchange their respective opinions.

4. Another thing that needs to be mentioned in this connection is that the National Anti-Opium Association has recently been recognized by the Advisory Committee on Traffic in Opium and Other Dangerous Drugs of the League of Nations as the communicating body of the Chinese people. This naturally throws upon this paper another important duty to perform, that is, to present the facts about opium and other narcotic in China and her people's anti-opium movement as to be a faithful eye of the said Advisory Committee of the League of Nations.

The foregoing statements briefly summarize the noble mission of this humble paper. The mission we will try our utmost to perform in spite of the limited means at our disposal and our insufficient knowledge of the English language. If in some way through the medium the world will be kept informed of the true situation of opium and narcotics in China and thus throw in their lot with China in her war against the world evil, the task assigned to this paper will be more than accomplished. We welcome all timely contributions and friendly criticisms.

NOTE

From *The Mission of Opium: A World Problem* (English Journal of the National Anti-Opium Association of China) 1, no. 1 (1927): 1–3.

A Private Crusade against Opium: Mei Gongren

Mei Gongren was a minor Guomindang functionary with a deep interest in the opium problem. In 1935 he published Opium's Destruction of the Nation and the Race, *a 350-page collection of documents and newspaper clippings about opium in China. The selection here describes the development of Mei's ideas about opium, in particular how he went from being relatively indifferent to opium suppression to seeing it as central to China's revival. It is one of the few accounts of the development of an individual's ideas about opium and also explains how opium could be linked to other problems that China faced.*

When I was a child the prohibition of opium was lax. At that time many in my old village planted opium. Because of this most of the sons of rich families and unemployed hoodlums smoked opium. Our family had a tenant, Dr. Li, whose wife was an opium smoker, and many of the unemployed hoodlums would come there to smoke. Thus I was familiar with the opium situation from my youth. The opium flower is indeed beautiful and attractive, but looking at the haggard and lazy smokers, who could not understand the dangers of opium?

As I grew older I noticed that of the village's opium smokers, all degenerate men from well-off families, none came to a good end. From this I understood the harm caused by opium. Once I entered school and started reading books and being instructed by my teachers and gained more experience of society I came to understand that opium's dangers were as great as the dangers of floods and wild beasts. Because of this I started crying out against it. In the home, in school, in society all must cry out. It must be at the tip of everyone's tongue and pen so that public opinion can be mobilized to sweep away the opium plague.

Before 1930 I knew the dangers of opium, but only its dangers to the individual and the family. I did not understand how it could harm the nation, the race, the economy, the government, world morality, and the popular will. Thus I paid little attention to the opium problem. After 1930 I began to travel widely because of a change in my circumstances, and I came to a deeper understanding of the problem and began to study it attentively. I read newspapers from all over, read books, and talked with friends from different places, leaving no stone unturned. After two or three years of work my mind was startled and astounded and my heart hurt and angry. Because opium cannot only harm the individual and the family but also the nation, race, economy, government, world morality, and popular will, and because of my fear for the fate of the Chinese race and fear for the success of our party's revolution due to the opium problem, I decided to put the results of my research in a book and distribute it around the world that we might avoid the destruction of the race and the nation.

Most comrades know that imperialism, feudalism, and warlordism threaten to destroy China, that politicians, bureaucrats, corrupt officials, local bullies and evil gentry, lackeys of foreigners and compradores are all traitors, and the Communists and Red Bandits are the enemies of the revolution. We cry out to defeat them and dedicate lives to purifying the nation but do not know that opium is an enemy of the revolution! Consider imperialism. It is a threat to destroy China, and it is clearly related to opium, but imperialism by itself can only destroy the nation, it cannot extinguish the race. Opium can destroy both the nation and the race, reducing both to a point where they will never recover.

NOTE

Mei Gongren, *Wangguo miezhong de yapianyan huo* (The opium destruction of the nation and the race) (Beijing: Minyoushudian, 1935).

The Guomindang and Opium, 1927

The Guangxi Clique was not the only political group in China trying to increase its control over opium. Almost all Chinese governments tried to extend their control over the opium trade, partially for the revenue and partially to deny this revenue to rivals. Regional governments, such as the Guangxi Clique, could do what they wanted about opium without much fear of criticism. They could not openly admit to selling opium for the purpose of making a profit, but even a fairly transparent claim that their opium control system was aimed at eventually suppressing the trade was enough to provide cover, as regional governments were not held to very high standards. The situation of the Nationalist government in Nanjing, heir to the principles of Sun Yat-sen, was quite different. Chiang Kai-shek's national government was successor to China's responsibility to eliminate opium trafficking under the 1912 treaties of the Hague, as well as claimant to the position of leaders of the Chinese people. Chiang's government was centered on the Lower Yangzi Delta, the richest area in China but also the center of China's new urban elite, the modern publishing industry, and the modern public sphere in general. Given the potential for criticism it was not possible for the Nanjing government to be as open about its involvement with opium as the Guangxi Clique could. The Nationalists also had a disadvantage in that the area they controlled produced little opium, and therefore they had to focus on the innately more public and more difficult process of controlling the retail distribution of the drug.

The following readings, taken from the British Foreign Ministry archives, discuss the failure of the Nationalists' first opium control efforts in 1927. At this point Zhejiang and Jiangsu were the most important provinces thoroughly under Nationalist control and thus were the center of the attempts to control opium sales. Each province already had many people who were involved in opium sales, of course, and the Nationalists attempted to co-opt rather than eliminate these people.

※　　※　　※

WITH reference to paragraph 12 of the Shanghai intelligence report for the half year ending the 30th September, 1927, I now have the honor to report on the measures taken by the Nationalist Government to bring under control the opium traffic in the area within their jurisdiction, and particularly in the Provinces of Jiangsu and Zhejiang.

2. The object of these measures is, as explained by the representatives of the Government, twofold: first, to eliminate the opium trade by degrees, immediate elimination having proved impossible; and secondly, to divert the enormous revenue, which at present flows into the pockets of militarists and smugglers, into the Government Treasury.

3. There is some difficulty in giving an exact description of the steps which have been taken, as the original mandate and the opium suppression regulations issued by the Government do not appear to have been published, and I have been unable to obtain copies. But the three officially inspired Nationalist news agency reports, dated the 23rd July, the 30th July, and the 11th August, copies of which are attached, give a reasonably clear picture of the measures which have been adopted.

4. The substance of these three reports is as follows.

The Nationalist Government and the Central Guomindang Headquarters, having decided to bring about the total prohibition of the opium trade within a period of three years, proposed to institute a Government monopoly of the trade. An Opium Suppression Bureau had therefore been created and attached to a Ministry of Finance. All cultivation of opium was prohibited forthwith. The import of, and wholesale traffic in, the drug was placed in the hands of the Opium Suppression Bureau, which would resell to the opium dealers, who, in turn, would retail to the public. All dealers and smokers would be licensed, and no license would be granted to any person under the age of 25 years. The amount of opium shipped, sold, and consumed annually was to be estimated at the end of the present year, 1927, and an annual reduction of one-third of that quantity was to be effected so that the trade should be exterminated at the end of 1930. A stamp tax, equivalent to 70 percent of the value of the opium, was to be levied during the first year, this tax being increased to 100 percent for the second and 200 percent for the third year, in the intention of making opium smoking so expensive as to be prohibitive. Dealers' licenses would cost 3,000 dollars, 1,000 dollars, or 500 dollars, according to the class, plus 10 percent of the above sum per menses as tax. Smokers' licenses would vary from 12 dollars to 36 dollars per month. With regard to the Provinces of Jiangsu and Zhejiang, the Government proposed to farm out the monopoly while retaining complete control over the traffic.

5. There was considerable competition for the monopolies for Jiangsu and Zhejiang, which was eventually granted to the Xinyuan Gongsi for the sum of 15,400,000 dollars for one year. A preparatory period was allowed during which no demands were to be made, and thereafter installments were to be paid to the Government as follows:

(a) One million dollars monthly for the first and second months after completion of preparations.
(b) 1,100,000 dollars monthly for the third and fourth months.
(c) 1,200,000 dollars monthly for the fifth and sixth months.
(d) 1,300,000 dollars monthly for the seventh and eighth months.
(e) 1,400,000 dollars for the ninth month.
(f) 1,500,000 dollars for the tenth month.
(g) 1,600,000 dollars for the eleventh month.
(h) 1,700,000 dollars for the twelfth month.

Cash security in the amount of 1 million dollars was to be deposited. The terms of the Monopoly Agreement are attached (annex 4). Subsequently, the contract for Zhejiang Province was sublet by the Xinyuan Gongsi to the Zhongxing Gongsi, which company then came under the direct control of the Opium Suppression Bureau, on the same footing as the Xinyuan Gongsi.

6. A special branch of the Opium Suppression Bureau was established in Shanghai, which is of course the most important center of the trade, and commenced to function on the 20th August, 1927. The division of functions between the "Monopoly Bureau" (i.e., the contractor) and the Opium Suppression Bureau was rather obscure, and both bureaus commenced to issue sets of regulations, translations of some of which are enclosed herewith. Annex 5, being the rules and regulations of the Monopoly Bureau regarding the establishment of branches, shows that the object of the Monopoly Bureau and the advertised object of the Opium Suppression Bureau were much at variance, for whereas the advertised intention of the Government was to suppress the opium trade, the Monopoly Bureau required that their own agents should undertake to sell as much as possible (Article 2, Subsection 2), and a rebate was granted to agents who managed to sell a quantity of opium in excess of the agreed quantity (Article 4). Annexes 6, 7, 8, and 9 contain certain regulations and notifications issued by the Opium Suppression Bureau.

7. As may be surmised, it was not long before difficulties arose in connection with the monopoly. The Shanghai opium trade has for a long time been under the control of the naval and military authorities, whose main source of revenue it has been, and they were not likely to allow the enormous profits

from the trade to be wrested from them by the civil authorities. The bulk of the trade is carried on in the French concession by a well-known trinity of scoundrels named Zhang Xiaolin, Du Yuesheng, and Sang Qingyuan, who operate as the "Da Gongsi" (Great Company) and enjoy the value received, the protection both of the French concession authorities and of the Chinese, civil and military. These three men were among the original promoters of the Xinyuan Gongsi, but all resigned from the latter company, owing, no doubt, to the fact that as long as they were permitted to run the Da Gongsi in the French concession and thus have a monopoly without the supervision of the National- ist Government, it was against their interests to press the claim of the Xinyuan Company.

8. But as long as the Da Gongsi maintained their business with the power- ful support of the Chinese naval and military authorities, it was clear that the Xinyuan Gongsi's business was not likely to prove remunerative. The latter company made frantic efforts to induce the proprietors of the opium shops in the French concession to remove into the Chinese city. These efforts were a complete failure, and the Xinyuan Gongsi had to set about establishing a new sales organization of its own. This it did by subcontracting to a company known as Dazheng the right to establish 100 opium shops in Shanghai and dis- trict at a fee of 200,000 dollars per annum. Some fifteen or twenty shops in the city had been fitted up and were prepared to open as retailers of opium under the direct control of the Dazheng Company, when suddenly, on the 18th Octo- ber, the Ministry of Finance canceled the monopolies granted both to the Xinyuan and Zhongxing companies. Translations of the ministerial orders are appended (annexes 10 and 11). From this it will be seen that the offenses charged against the companies were, firstly, that they sought to push the opium trade with a view to their own profit without considering that it was the object of the Government to put an end to the trade; secondly, that they were behind with their payments to the Government; and thirdly, that they had bribed—or attempted to bribe—the chief of the Opium Suppression Bureau. Another and utterly frivolous charge of selling pure opium in place of anti-opium medicines was made. This will be further referred to below. From the facts given in the lat- ter part of paragraph 6 of this report there is every reason to suppose that the first ground of complaint was well founded, but it is difficult to understand what different result the government can have anticipated from granting a monopoly of this character.

9. The company, however, contend that the government, in the first place, failed to respect the Monopoly Agreement, inasmuch as a considerable quan- tity of opium has been sent into the French concession without passing through the hands of the company. One consignment of 502 cases of Persian

opium was, on or about the 16th November, located on the Huangpu by agents of the company, who ascertained that it had been conveyed to Shanghai on a Chinese man-of-war. The agents of the company seized the opium, but the Da Gongsi prevailed upon General Bai Zongxi to release the drug seized, which was subsequently landed on the French band and delivered to the order of the Da Gongsi. The Xinyuan Company further declare that the Minister of Finance is deliberately trying to put the company in a false position in order to cancel the monopoly, owing to the fact that a certain Cantonese has offered to pay the Ministry 18 million dollars a year for the monopoly, as against the 15,400,000 dollars payable by the Xinyuan Company under its agreement. The company does not deny offering a bribe to the chief of the Opium Suppression Bureau, alleging as its excuse the fear of losing the monopoly.

10. I have referred above in paragraph 8 to a charge by the Finance Ministry against the monopolists that they were selling pure opium in place of anti-opium medicines, and I have called this charge utterly frivolous. An examination of the annexes to this report will reveal the fact that, as far as possible, references to the opium monopoly and the Government trading in the drug are avoided and some such expression as "anti-opium medicine monopoly" is substituted. This is possibly done with one eye on Geneva or merely because the Government is ashamed; but the result is extremely confusing, and a certain amount of ambiguity is thereby introduced into the regulations. At the same time, the periphrasis would not deceive a child, for it takes but a superficial examination of the documents to make it clear that what is referred to as "anti-opium medicine" is, in fact, opium. It is sufficient merely to call attention to annex 8, where a shop dealing in "anti-opium medicines" would have to pay 3,000 dollars down and 300 dollars a month for the privilege of selling anti-opium pills! It is possibly this same sense of shame which makes it so difficult to obtain copies of the original mandate and opium suppression regulations.

11. The public reaction to the proposed Government opium monopoly is interesting. The Chinese press has published numerous protests from different organizations against the public sale of opium, and under the auspices of the Anti-Opium League a meeting of representatives of various local organizations was held on the 18th November for the purpose of registering a protest on the same subject, when the following resolutions were passed:

(i) That the cultivation, consumption, and all other narcotics should be totally prohibited at one and the same time, and that no compromise in any form should be allowed.

(ii) That any income received from opium suppression should be used wholly for establishing anti-opium hospitals and expanding anti-opium education.

(iii) That since the purpose of opium suppression was not the collection of revenue, the Opium Suppression Bureau should be attached to the Ministry of the Interior and not to that of Finance.

(iv) That foreign narcotics, being more noxious than opium, should be simultaneously prohibited.

(v) That officers under the Nationalist Government, whether civil or military, who were found to be connected in any [way] with the trade in opium or other narcotics should receive the death penalty.

12. The Government, having canceled the monopoly to the Xinyuan and Zhongxing companies, proposes to conduct the monopoly itself. It remains to be seen whether it will prove any more successful than before in preventing the abuses of which it complains. It seems unlikely, in any event, that protests from public bodies will affect its determination to tap a source of revenue of such a profitable character.

I have, &etc. BARTON

Rules and Regulations of the "Anti-Opium Medicine Monopoly Bureau of Kiangsu and Chekiang," Which Aim at the Establishment of Branches in Various Districts

ARTICLE 1. This bureau, with the permission of the Government, has acquired the right of monopoly of anti-opium medicine in Zhejiang and Jiangsu and has been authorized to invite tenders for the establishment of branches of this bureau in certain districts in the above-mentioned two provinces.

ARTICLE 2. Merchants willing to undertake to act in certain districts in the two provinces on behalf of the bureau will be responsible for the collection of special permission charges, &c. They should have the following qualifications:

1. They must be reliable and familiar with the conditions of the district concerned.
2. They must promise to sell as much as possible.

Each applicant should first of all submit an application to this bureau. When the application has been approved and a letter of attorney issued to him by the bureau, he is considered to be a qualified applicant. The bureau retains the right of choice of applicants.

ARTICLE 3. According to the plan, a branch of this bureau will be established in every district of the provinces in question, and the branch may establish suboffices in the district concerned.

ARTICLE 4. Any merchant appointed as the sole agent in a district has to pay in advance a sum equivalent to 90 percent of the value of medicine which he has agreed to sell. However, he has to pay only 85 percent instead of 90 percent in case he is selling in excess of the quantity agreed upon. This condition is subject to alteration after having been tried for three months. The agreed sum should be paid at the end of every month. This rule applies also in case he may not have sold the whole quantity of this medicine which he has agreed to sell during the month.

ARTICLE 5. Any merchant who is found guilty of smuggling opium secretly and making pills himself will be severely dealt with.

ARTICLE 6. Merchants are not allowed to mix the medicines supplied by the bureau with some other cheaper ingredients and thereby to effect a profit, nor to increase the prices. They are permitted, however, to increase the price by a small percentage to cover the cost of transportation, &c.

ARTICLE 7. The period of trial is to be counted from the date on which the application is approved. Any merchant who does not fulfill the agreement satisfactorily during the probation period forfeits all his privileges, and his agreement will be canceled. This bureau has the right then to appoint another merchant in his place.

ARTICLE 8. Any merchant who wishes to undertake the establishment of a branch in a certain district has to submit to the bureau an application, in which he should state the quantity of medicines he agrees to sell monthly, and has to pay a certain sum of cash security to the bureau on the date on which his application is approved. A receipt will be issued by the bureau for the cash security, and this will be considered as a part of his last installment he has to pay to the bureau.

ARTICLE 9. Any branch of this bureau, before applying for medicines, should submit a written application, in which should be stated the quantity and the kinds of medicines and the value of the stamp duty required. The amount in payment of goods ordered should be sent in with the application together with a reliable officer to the bureau. The bureau then will get the medicines ready and send them to the branch under the escort of a special corps.

ARTICLE 10. Medicines will be supplied twice monthly, but merchants may apply for them any time during the month. Those who fail to apply for medicines in time will be dealt with in accordance with Articles 4 and 7.

ARTICLE 11. Except for grave reasons, no merchant is allowed to demand the reduction of the amount of medicines specified in the agreement, nor to withdraw the tender before the expiration of the agreement. During the term of the agreement all matters should be executed in conformity with the anti-opium regulations.

ARTICLE 12. The branches of this bureau are permitted to establish suboffices at important places in their districts, and these suboffices should function under the direction and supervision of the branch which has to take full responsibility for the working of the suboffices in accordance with the regulations.

ARTICLE 13. The branch is authorized to investigate and arrest anyone found smuggling opium in the district. This work should be carried out by the officers of the branch in company with two or four representatives from the bureau. The total expenses thus incurred should be defrayed by the branch. Any person found guilty of smuggling should be sent to the Opium Suppression Bureau to be dealt with, and the goods are to be confiscated. Fifty percent of the goods thus confiscated should be sent to the bureau, and the branch may keep the balance as compensation.

ARTICLE 14. The fees charged on special permits issued to opium smokers should be collected by the branches every ten days and the sum collected subsequently remitted to the bureau. The branch should deduct from this money 10 percent in lieu of the expenses incurred. The special permits can be obtained only at the bureau, and the branch should not attempt to imitate them.

ARTICLE 15. Besides receiving these medicines direct from the bureau, the branches can purchase medicines from other sources on the following conditions:

(a) Before the arrival of medicines ordered, the merchants should report to the bureau the quantity and the nature of the medicines imported, and the bureau will dispatch representatives to take charge of the transportation and the custodianship of these goods. These services will be rendered free of charge by the bureau.
(b) A stamp tax equivalent to 70 percent of the total value of the goods imported will be levied.
(c) After the price has been fixed by the merchants concerned, the sate of these goods should be placed at the disposal of the bureau.
(d) The merchants concerned have to pay only 85 percent of the value of the goods which they are willing to sell in excess of the quantity agreed upon.

ARTICLE 16. At the end of every month the branch should report to the bureau the quantity of anti-opium medicines sold during the month and should be kind and gentle in their dealings with opium smokers and with those who apply for smoking permits.

ARTICLE 17. The branch is permitted to fix the number of the employees, but it has to pay their salaries from the income of the branch.

ARTICLE 18. These regulations will hold good as such as our company and the bureau have been established and are subject to revision at any time.

Order of the Ministry of Finance Regarding the Zhongxing Gongsi

Mr. Mei Guangbei, director of the Opium Suppression Bureau attached to this Ministry, reports as follows:

> Having received your instructions to the effect that, as the Zhejiang Provincial Government had telegraphed requesting the cancellation of the contract granted to the Zhongxing Gongsi for the monopoly of the sale of anti-opium medicines for the Province of Zhejiang in order to put a stop to abuses, I had to proceed immediately to Hangzhoou to investigate and report. I reached Hangzhou on the 9th instant and conferred with the members of the Provincial Government and also collected the views of all classes of society. All agreed that the present anti-opium medicines monopoly, as directed by the farmers thereof, was replete with abuses, of which the most glaring were (1) that the monopolists kept as their main object the pushing of the trade, losing entirely from view the fact that the Government's intention was to use regulations as a means of prohibition, and (2) that, although the monopolists were nominally selling anti-opium medicines, what they were actually doing was to cook the medicines in spite of the regulations and to sell pure opium, so that persons buying and smoking it had not the slightest chance of gradually breaking off the habit. It is essential, therefore, that the Ministry should directly dispatch officers to deal with the matter according to regulations, in order that the purposes of the Government to suppress opium may be fulfilled. After careful examination I find that the facts are as stated, and I therefore have the honor to report and request instructions that a decision may be taken as to the manner in which the case is to be handled.

While the Ministry was considering this matter, the company in question sent delegates to the Minister with two banknotes to a value of 12,000 dollars, so it is obvious that, fearing punishment for their offenses, they desire to buy themselves off with a bribe. The Minister being of upright and honorable character was deeply distressed at this crooked proceeding, The merchants in question cannot but be dealt with most severely for such wicked behavior as an example to other ill-doers, and, therefore, as from today, their former monopoly contract is canceled, and the monopoly will be transferred to a department which will be established by this Ministry for its operation. Further, the security money which has already been paid over by the merchants amounting to 420,000 dollars is confiscated, while the merchants must still pay in full the balance of salaries, &c., that are still outstanding. As to whether or not there are any other irregularities, an officer will be sent later to investigate, and suitable punishment will be inflicted.

NOTE

The Opium Trade (Wilmington, DE: Scholarly Resources, 1974), 25:6–18.

The Yangzi
Opium Trade

In addition to being the home of the Chen family opium den Yichang was an important Yangzi River port and thus an important place for governments to try and tax the opium moving down the Yangzi River. Eventually, Chiang Kai-shek would take control of the Yangzi River trade from Hankou. At this point, however, the trade was still open. This reading, from the British diplomatic archives, describes the Yichang opium trade in 1930.

Yichang, June 14, 1930

Consul Fitzmaurice to Sir M. Lampson

Sir,

I have the honor to furnish the following report on the opium situation in this consular district.

2. Cultivation is not extensive in southwest Hubei, and the only opium-producing area is the Shinan district, in the extreme southwest corner of the province, lying between Hunan and Sichuan. This district is mountainous and comparatively difficult of access; it is overrun with local bandits and constantly threatened by Communist armies from Hunan, and the Chinese authorities, far from being able to take any effective steps to suppress the cultivation of the poppy, or otherwise control the doings of the inhabitants, seem satisfied with a mere semblance of official control. Shinan is, moreover, not far from some of the opium-producing districts of Sichuan, and any rigid

enforcement of suppression on the Hubei border might be bad policy until the National or Provincial Government can speak with greater authority than is at present the case. The opium produced in the Shinan district, which is insignificant in comparison with the quantity produced in Sichuan, is exported for the most part by way of Idu and pays the Hubei opium taxes at a branch office there of the Yichang Opium Prohibition Bureau.

3. Some opium-producing provinces, such as Sichuan, are to all intents and proposes independent of the National Government. Elsewhere military commanders have not infrequently promoted the cultivation of the poppy in order to raise funds for the support of troops who would not otherwise be paid. Where, however, the National Government—as distinct from their nominal representatives—is in effective control, cultivation seems to have been suppressed, and in those areas under their control, the most effective of the feasible methods of reducing consumption, if this were their sole interest in the question, might well be to raise the price by taxation. Apart from their need of the opium revenues, any attempt on the part of the National Government to exclude Sichuanese opium forcibly from the rest of China seems impracticable, as it would probably throw the military leaders of that province into the arms of the Government's opponents. The opium revenues of Yichang constitute its greatest importance in the eyes of the Chinese authorities, and any weakening of the control of the National Government is invariably followed by an increase of the interest of the Hubei Provincial Government in matters relating to opium.

4. The importance of Yichang in connection with opium traffic lies in the convenience of its situation at the lower end of the Yangzi Gorges both for purposes of taxation and as a meeting place for the producers of Sichuan and the downriver dealers and their respective agents.

5. Estimates vary as to the amount of the Yichang opium revenues, but my inquiries go to show that, while the monthly figures have risen as high as 4 or 5 million dollars, the monthly average is probably 3 million dollars or a trifle less. The revenue is misleading as an indication of the volume of the trade, as, apart from the amount of opium smuggled, shipments owned by the military are often passed tax-free or taxed at a reduced rate. Probably, also, such military protection and favored treatment are often obtained for a consideration by opium dealers. On the 2nd November last the local

vernacular press gave details of what was considered the remarkable quantity of opium arriving in Yichang during October. The total amounted to 3,841 cases, or approximately 7 million oz.; and the article concluded by saying that taxes had been paid on only about a half of this quantity and that these figures did not include smuggled goods. On this occasion a special Deputy had been sent from Nanjing to urge the opium dealers to expedite their shipments on account of the urgent need of the National Government for funds to meet expenses of military disbandment. The large proportion of untaxed opium seems to have been due to the transfer of Guo Rutong and his troops from Sichuan to Hubei.

6. Last spring negotiations were carried on between Chiang Kai-shek and Liu Xiang for several weeks through a Mr. Chen regarding the collection of opium taxes. I am informed that Liu Xiang offered to pay 5 million dollars monthly for the sole right to tax Sichuan opium but that the scheme came to nothing in consequence of the opposition of parties whose interests would have suffered if the taxes had all been collected in Sichuan.

7. There seems little doubt that the arms and ammunition supplied recently by the National Government to Liu Xiang were largely paid for with opium. The steamship *Jingzheng,* which was bought by Lu Xiang at Chongqing in the middle of last year, lay at that port until the end of January. She then passed through Yichang bound for downriver, fully loaded with "presents," the nature of which was not specified, and the search party, on attempting to board her in the usual way, were turned off very summarily.

8. The searching of British ships for untaxed opium has caused much trouble in the past, but informal arrangements with the Opium Prohibition Bureau have led to a better understanding, and there have been no recent complaints against the search parties. This is no doubt largely due to an increase of authority of the bureau, since much of the difficulty arose from a multiplicity of competing search parties. Probably there are few ships from the Upper River on which no opium at all is smuggled; and this seems to be recognized by the officials of the bureau, one of whom told me regretfully some days ago that the only arrests that they made were of the "small fry" whom they did not particularly want, while the big operators, amply provided with funds, found means of escaping the net. The tactics adopted by the smugglers vary from time to time. Thus, it was a common practice last year to land opium from downward bound vessels into sampans some miles above Yichang, to conceal it until some suitable time, and

then to run the blockade of searchers on a dark night in fast sampans near the far banks of the river. This led to much wild shooting in the harbor and to considerable danger at times to boats engaged on their lawful business. More recently, packages have been thrown into the water by previous arrangement with sampan men in the vicinity, a short distance above the port. The largest recent seizure of smuggled opium, of which I have a note, was made on the American steamship *Yiling* on the 6th July last year, when 64 piculs (nearly 2 tons) were found.

9. As instances of large shipments of taxed opium, there may be mentioned the departure of the steamship *Fuyuan* for Hankou on the 8th April, 1929, with nearly 100 tons and the arrival of the steamship *Yujiang* from the Upper River on the 21 October, 1929, with about 61 tons.

10. For purposes of rough calculations, the cost of opium in Sichuan is generally taken as 500 dollars per 1,000 oz. On arrival at Yichang, opium is taken to the Opium Prohibition Bureau's godowns, where it remains until the taxes are paid. If intended for local consumption, it is released. If destined for Hankou or below, and the quantity is considerable, the opium is usually carried on one of two small steamers chartered by the bureau for the purpose. These vessels carry armed guards, and shippers are assured of immunity from interference by other Government Departments; a transportation fee is charged of 35 dollars per case of about 1,800 oz. from Yichang to Hankou.

11. Prior to the 1st November, 1928, the rates of tax levied at Yichang were comparatively low. A new scheme for raising revenue, and for reducing consumption by increasing the price, was then introduced. From that date the Yichang opium tax was 350 dollars per 1,000 oz., an additional 15 percent surtax, and a fee of 15 dollars per 1,000 oz. for warehousing at Yichang and Hankou. These taxes proved so successful that they were soon increased from time to time, until in May 1929 they were said to amount to as much as 1,200 dollars per 1,000 oz. Then the trade began to fall off somewhat. Probably larger quantities of opium were smuggled or were carried overland via Laohekou and the Han River. The Yichang taxes were therefore reduced and, since the summer of last year, have amounted to between 700 dollars and 800 dollars, inclusive of surtaxes for each 1,000 oz. The present charges at Yichang, exclusive of the transportation fee mentioned in the preceding paragraph, are as follows:

TABLE 16.1.

	Dollars per Picul (1,000 oz.)
Opium tax	600
Police and education local surtax	60
Dike surtax	60
Military disbandment surtax	30
Warehousing fee	15
Stamp surtax	5
Public welfare surtax (militia, road repairs, etc.)	5
Total	775

12. The above figures represent the Hubei taxes only. The Sichuan Opium Bureau now have a branch office in Yichang, and, if any opium should be detected at this port not covered by a Sichuan receipt, the Sichuan tax—which now amounts, so I am informed, to 400 dollars per 1,000 oz.—is also collected here, the proceeds, however, being remitted to Chongqing. . . .

14. The Opium Prohibition Bureau conduct their operations quite openly, their headquarters being in the Bank of China building. For the sake of appearances, however, the words "Opium Prohibition" are not used, and the bureau is known as the "Special Tax Office"—so called not because the taxes are special in any way but because they are levied on "special goods," the official designation of opium, &c. Since the National Government is ostensibly committed to a policy of opium suppression, it also becomes necessary for the Special Tax Office to report from time to time that the "special merchants" still have considerable stocks of "special goods" which have not been disposed of and to obtain authority from Chiang Kai-shek through the Ministry of Finance to continue their special tax operations for a further period of a few months.

15. Consumption is very extensive, but by no means general. In Chongqing one cannot fail to be impressed by the appalling proportion of opium addicts among all classes met in the streets. In Yichang the percentage is not nearly so high. Public opinion has never, so it would seem, contributed seriously to reducing consumption in Sichuan, as it has done elsewhere; but the question of price is probably a still more important factor. Although opium is cheap in Yichang, the cost has been raised by taxation to two or three times the Sichuan figure; and the consequent diminution of

consumption seems to furnish considerable justification for the Government's policy of opium taxation.

16. Even so, however, judged by any other than Sichuan standards, the extent to which opium is smoked is astounding. Not long ago the police contemplated a monthly tax of 3 dollars on every opium lamp in a private residence, but they were obliged by the strength of the opposition, and their official influence, to abandon the scheme. A monthly tax of 60 cents is, however, collected by the police on every lamp in use in an opium den or similar establishment, and this tax brings in a sum of between 2,200 dollars and 2,500 dollars per month. There would thus seem to be about 4,000 public lamps paying the police tax in Yichang, and each lamp may supply several pipes in the course of a day.

17. Another source of revenue exploited by the police for a time was the sale of smoking permits. Proprietors of opium dens were only allowed to carry on their trade if they purchased every day at least fifty such permits costing 20 cents each—in other words, a tax of 10 dollars or more per opium den per diem. The collection of this tax has, however, been discontinued; and on payment of the "Opium Lamp Tax" referred to in the preceding paragraph, opium dens are permitted to carry on business without any attempt at concealment. They are, in fact, indicated by inscriptions on red lamps hung at the doors, advertising their wares. Private individuals who wished to indulge in opium smoking were also required for a while to register their names and to obtain permits; and in the autumn of 1928 I was informed that over 800 such names had been registered. Influential opposition has also been responsible for the cessation of this measure, and there are no longer any restrictions on opium smoking in private residences. Apart from such private consumption, many visitors and others avail themselves of permission to enjoy a pipe in semiprivacy at a hotel, official requirements being satisfied by a "medical certificate" costing 20 cents.

18. Opium is also taxed in other ways. When the campaign of opium suppression and taxation was launched at Yichang in the autumn of 1928, every opium shop was required to deposit 5,000 dollars with the Opium Prohibition Bureau and to pay 500 dollars monthly for a license. In spite of the volume and value of the local opium trade, the effect of the collection of these deposits and license fees from the opium shops was to reduce their number from twenty-eight or twenty-nine to ten; and the number at the present time is only nine. The explanation of the falling-off was that in the vast majority of

cases the so-called opium shop was merely a rendezvous for buyers and sellers, with accommodation similar to a hotel, the shopkeeper, in return for a commission, attending to the payment of taxes and shipment. He was, in fact, more often a broker than a dealer, and, his capital being small, the introduction of these levies compelled most of the shops to suspend business. During the spring of 1929 the Guangxi generals appropriated the deposits of 5,000 dollars which had been collected from each of the opium shops; and when the Guangxi faction disappeared and the authority of the National Government was restored, a further deposit of 1,250 dollars was required from every shop. In the autumn of last year the opium shops were informed that these deposits were to be treated as registration fees and would consequently never be refunded; and the "special merchants" were also called upon, in spite of protests of poverty, to pay further registration fees until, so I understand, a total of 10,000 dollars was reached in each case.

19. A new feature of the opium question at Yichang is the appearance of morphia. This, so I am informed, is manufactured for the most part at Chongqing but also at Wanxian. The parties principally interested in its manufacture are said to be some of Liu Xiang's generals, and there are also unconfirmed reports of the engagement of Japanese experts as advisers. There is no local demand for morphia, on account of the cheapness of opium, but the drug dealers find it very much more convenient to smuggle downriver. Opium is comparatively bulky, and the search parties now seem to do their work very thoroughly. No provision has apparently yet been made for the taxation of morphia, so that it cannot be carried legitimately and is liable to seizure if detected. I have heard of more than one case of seizure recently; the morphia in one case being so packed as to pass for preserved ducks was wrapped in clay; but it would appear that a considerable amount must escape detection, since the price of Chongqing morphia in Yichang is said to be only about 12 dollars per oz.

I have, &c.

N. FITZMAURICE.

NOTE

The Opium Trade (Wilmington, DE: Scholarly Resources, 1974), 28:89.

The Six-Year Plan
to Eliminate Opium, 1936

After the failure of attempts to set up a national opium monopoly in 1928 and 1931 the Nationalists concentrated on controlling the less public wholesale trade, with which they had growing success. In 1935 Chiang Kai-shek announced the Six-Year Plan to Eliminate Opium. This plan involved setting up national monopolies for the production, distribution, and sale of opium. Opium smokers were to be registered and allowed to smoke limited amounts of opium until they could be processed in one of the new anti-opium clinics that were to be established.

Although none of this was new, the plan did have considerable success, in part because it built on the considerable success the government had in controlling the wholesale trade and in part because the Nationalists were able to explain the plan in such a way as to deflect possible criticism, both foreign and domestic. The National Anti-Opium Association was not entirely happy with the plan but felt that their only recourse was to disband themselves, which they did in 1937. This document, originally published in English, is aimed partially at foreign public opinion. In addition to the usual desire to avoid the embarrassment of having China's opium situation criticized by the League of Nations, Nanjing was also working to turn foreign opinion against the Japanese, who were smuggling great amounts of opium and refined drugs into North China.

Opium Suppression in China

Opium was first imported into China by the Arabs in the eighth century, but it was then restricted to medicinal uses, and the habit of smoking was not known until the end of the eighteenth century. One of the early edicts prohibiting opium smoking was issued by the Chinese Emperor in 1796, and the importation of opium from foreign countries was forbidden in 1800. After the Opium War (1840–42), the importation of opium was forced upon China. By the Treaty of Tianjin of 1858, the opium trade was legalized. The evil of opium smoking became so great that it threatened to ruin a large section of the Chinese people. An agreement was concluded between China and Great Britain in 1907 whereby imports of opium from India were to be reduced by 10 percent each year provided that China should reduce home production proportionately. By another agreement in 1911 imports from India were to cease altogether in 1917. China was able to carry out her obligations under the agreement of 1911, and the evil of opium officially came to an end in 1917.

In 1909, the International Opium Commission met in Shanghai at the initiative of President Roosevelt. The conference resulted in no more than an exchange of views between various governments concerned, but its resolutions served as the bases for The Hague Convention and The Hague Opium Conference of 1911. Two successive conferences were held at The Hague in 1913 and 1914.

Article 295 of the Treaty of Versailles was intended to secure the ratification of The Hague Convention by all signatory states. By virtue of Article 23 of the Covenant, the League of Nations took over from the government of Netherlands the responsibility over the execution of The Hague Convention of 1912. The Advisory Committee on the Traffic in Opium and Other Dangerous Drugs was established in 1921. The failure of the Geneva Opium Conference of 1925 was largely due to the reluctance on the part of some of the Great Powers to stop the legalized trade and the use of prepared opium in their territories or possessions.[1] The Convention for Limiting the Manufacture and Regulating the Distribution of Narcotic Drugs was concluded at Geneva in 1931. The campaign against opium and its derivative drugs has therefore passed through many stages.

Ever since the establishment of the National Government in Nanjing, opium suppression has been one of its irrevocable policies. In accordance with the teachings of the late Dr. Sun Yat-sen, the Government has determined to remove the humiliation inflicted upon the Chinese people during the last hundred years. General Chiang Kai-shek since the very beginning of his advent into power has decided to fight against the twin foes: opium and narcotic drugs. Since his appointment to the responsible position of Superintendent-General of the Opium Suppression Commission by the Central Political Council, General Chiang has tackled the problem with an uncompromising attitude. Under suppression measures, China has therefore banned by law the production, sale, transportation, and consumption of opium. The program of opium suppression as promulgated by the Government aims at the eradication of opium and narcotic drugs in six years as from 1935.

Up to date, the cultivation of poppy has been suppressed in twelve provinces, namely Jiangsu, Zhejiang, Fujian, Anhui, Jiangxi, Hunan, Hubei, Henan, Shandong, Hebei, Shanxi, and Chahar. Before the National Government unified the country, poppy cultivation was fostered by corrupt military authorities, and farmers in many districts were forced to grow poppy. But the situation has been changed. Now that the Government has achieved a certain measure of centralization opium suppression has also become more effective. According to the National Opium Suppression Commission, the program of the Government in connection with opium suppression is as follows. [The author describes the schedule for gradual suppression by which opium growing was to be eliminated in the provinces of Sichuan, Yunnan, Guizhou, Shaanxi, Gansu, Ningxia, and Suiyuan by 1940.]

This program aims at the entire prohibition of opium in 1940. In this connection, it may be noted that it will not be advisable to halt poppy cultivation all over the country at the same time while there is still a demand for production. Under suppression measures, addicts are required to register and to pledge to eradicate the habit eventually, though they may still smoke a limited quantity of opium within a stipulated period. The demand and the supply of opium, however, will be placed entirely in the hands of the Government. To stop production when there is still consumption is merely to create an incentive to greater importation of opium from abroad, and therefore the prohibition of poppy cultivation by stages is necessary during the transitional period.

Regarding opium consumption, addicts are required to register with the authorities, but the number of licenses issued is to be reduced annually.

1st period: 1936, Addicts shall be reduced by one-fifth.
2nd period: 1937, one-fourth.
3rd period: 1938, one-third.
4th period: 1939, one-half
5th period: 1940, All addicts shall be entirely rid of their habit.

Special treatment is accorded to the poor people. The experience of the first year is so promising that more than one and a half million addicts have applied for registration. They also pledged to eradicate this habit under Government supervision.

Though opium smoking is an expensive habit, its practice is not confined to rich people alone. Among 30,833 registered addicts in Shanghai, 17,995 belong to the poorer classes. Also, the fact that opium addicts are found among both young and old people shows that age is not an important criterion. The following second table shows the distribution by age of addicts in Shanghai.

TABLE 17.1. Number of Registered Opium Smokers in Different Provinces and Municipalities on Dec. 31, 1935

Name of the Place	Number of the Registered
Anhui	104,050
Jiangsu	303,546
Sichuan	139,361
Henan	92,675
Hebei	114,557
Hunan	136,119
Fujian	81,384
Jiangxi	99,508
Yunnan	54,585
Shanxi	208,451
Gansu	95,206
Shaanxi	60,891
Suiyuan	42,259
Qinghai	1,271
Shanghai	30,844
Beiping	4,953
Tianjin	145
Total	1,569,805

TABLE 17.2.

Age	Number of Addicts
Under 20	17
21–30	2,248
31–40	9,468
41–50	9,437
51–60	6,628
61–70	2,698
71–80	351
81–90	22

The figures illustrate clearly that the age of the majority of addicts is between 30 and 50. In other words, people are being ruined in the prime of life. For the sake of national reconstruction, it is necessary to turn those miserable and unproductive people into useful and industrious citizens of the country. Out of the total population of 2,028,814 in Shanghai, there are 30,833 registered opium smokers, the ratio being 1:51. This percentage, however, by no means reveals the true state of affairs, since a large number of addicts naturally are unwilling to undergo the humiliating experience of being registered.

In order to assist those addicts who really desire to have their smoking habits cured, many hospitals for this purpose have been established during recent years. These hospitals, it will be remembered, are doing a thriving business, and their usefulness cannot be underestimated. The following table may be of interest.

TABLE 17.3. Number of Hospitals for the Treatment of Opium and Narcotic Addicts Established in Different Provinces and Municipalities

Name of the Place	Hospitals for the Treatment of Opium Addicts	Special Hospitals for the Treatment of Opium and Narcotic Addicts	General Hospitals Where Medical Treatment May Be Secured by Opium Smokers	Total Number
Shangha	3	1	17	21
Nanjing	2			2
Beiping	1	1		2
Qingdao		1	1	2
Tianjin		1	1	2
Jiangsu	1	60		61
Zhejiang		51	22	73
Hebei		80	28	108
Weihaiwei		2		2
Henan		30	14	44
Shaanxi	9	58		67
Shanxi		106		106
Hubei		35		35
Hunan		53		53
Chahar		11	2	13
Shandong		82	7	89
Jiangxi	1	105		106
Fujian		2		68
Gansu		1		1
Ningxia		10		10
Qinghai		5		5
Total	17	695	98	810

Under the present suppression measures, opium has been placed under government control; private sale and transportation are strictly forbidden. Customs, railway, and postal authorities have been instructed to watch against the traffic in opium and narcotic drugs by individuals or shipped in parcels.

That opium has undermined the vitality, decreased the efficiency, and weakened the moral perception of the people has long been realized by the general public. Various means have been devised, therefore, to combat the evil of opium addiction. One of these measures, for instance, is to infuse the knowledge into the people regarding the necessity of the suppression campaign. China, it may be recalled, has begun work on a six-year program. In order to

TABLE 17.4. Statistics Showing the Quantity of Opium and Narcotic Drugs Confiscated during 1935

Category	Authority	Quantity in Ounces	Total
Opium	Customs	33,598.04	
	Posts	8,910.77	
	Railways	29,519.99	
	OSO[a]	519,613.99	591,660.94
Derivatives	Customs	1,696.35	
		34,142.18	35,838.53
Raw morphine	Customs	47.25	
	OSO	59.89	107.14
Morphine	Customs	192.62	
	Posts	60.03	
	Railways	156.97	
	OSO	29.37	438.99
Heroin	Customs	925.14	
	Posts	405.14	
	Railways	429.90	1,760.18
Codeine	Customs	27.22	
	Posts	27.18	54.50
Cocaine	Customs	52.23	52.23
Heroin pills	Customs	228.80	
	OSO	554.27	784.07
Narcotic pills	Customs	1,346.83	
	Posts	3,017.48	
	OSO	1,050.00	5,414.31
Cocaine powder	Posts	4.00	
	Railways	562.83	566.83
Poisonous drugs	Customs	1,302.45	1,302.45
Raw materials	Posts	3,286.99	3,286.99

[a]Opium Suppression Offices

further the success of this campaign, mass meetings were held, slogans were posted, pamphlets were distributed, lectures were broadcast, and special supplements were published by the newspapers so as to arouse the moral consciousness of the people. The Anti-Opium Week, in commemoration of China's first determined effort to suppress opium, was conducted on a nationwide scale. It is interesting to note that opium is now regarded as a social enemy, and everywhere you go you will meet people denouncing it in the strongest of terms.

Together with the Anti-Opium Week, opium suppression conferences were convened by the authorities in different provinces. The conference in Jiangsu that began on April 20, 1936, was attended by about seventy district opium suppression inspectors as well as delegates from various public and private institutions. Mr. Zhen Gefu, chairman of the Jiangsu Provincial Government, speaking before the conference, admitted that more than 300,000 addicts were registered during last year, about a third of whom having been restored to normal health. There is every hope for the rest of the addicts to become once more useful members of society. Meanwhile, of about 20,000 persons prosecuted under the opium suppression laws, 339 were opium traffickers, 11,967 smokers, 1,074 opium den owners, 3,261 addicts who took up smoking a second time after being freed from the habit, 38 accomplices in smoking, and 1,588 found guilty of other miscellaneous violations of law. Emphasis was laid upon the necessity of social sanctions that ought to be raised to assist the Government in enforcing suppression measures.

General Chiang Kai-shek, in his capacity as the Superintendent-General of the Opium Suppression Commission, has issued from time to time instructions to local authorities that suppression measures should be strictly enforced. All addicts should be registered, and no poppy cultivation would be allowed except in a few districts outlined in the six years' program. Special opium suppression commissioners and inspectors were sent to different provinces and municipalities to investigate the actual situation and see if the law has been effectively carried out. Investigation is, however, of high importance, as China is a vast country and conditions in distant provinces are very complicated.

Military officers, soldiers, civil servants, school teachers, and students will be given heavier punishment should they be found smoking opium. From the social point of view, it is a very important distinction, as civil servants are persons who administer the law, while school teachers and students are members of the intelligentsia, and they should act as model citizens of the country. Moreover, soldiers and military officers, in view of their strenuous work, need to have a strong physique. However, opium smoking among these classes of people is, one is happy to note, not general.

That the National Government has set upon a determined course of opium suppression with a view to stamping out the evil in its entirety is well evidenced by the strict laws dealing with habitual opium addicts and traffickers. There is probably no other country which has made the violation of anti-opium laws a capital punishment. The existing practice in China to submit anti-opium law violators to such severe sentences is, therefore, worth mentioning. The following table shows the number of death sentences passed in 1935.

Despite the determination of the Government to exterminate the evil, the task is complicated by the existence in different parts of China of foreign concessions and settlements where Chinese opium suppression laws are not capable of being strictly enforced, with the consequence that the illicit traffic continues to flourish. The failure of effective suppression in such areas naturally creates a serious obstacle to the operation of the policy in other parts of the

TABLE 17.5.   Number of Death Sentences
Passed upon Opium and Narcotic Convicts
during 1935

Place of Execution	Number of Convictions
Jiangsu	31
Zhejiang	119
Anhui	12
Jiangxi	8
Henan	112
Hubei	16
Beiping	5
Nanjing	51
Shanghai	5
Fujian	4
Shandong	485
Shanxi	106
Shaanxi	12
Total	964

country. Owing to the existence of extraterritoriality in these concessions and settlements, Chinese authorities are powerless in dealing with cases which took place outside of their jurisdiction. Vested interests, Chinese as well as foreign, have been most stubborn in resisting any suppression measures the Government may take, as their own profits are based on the continuance of the evil. A certain foreign concession in Tianjin, for example, is well known as the home of the illicit trade in opium and narcotic drugs in North China.[2]

The following table shows the annual importation of opium into Tianjin.

TABLE 17.6.

District of Production	Quantity in Ounces	Number of Importers
Ganzhou	2,600,000	over 20
Liangzhou	9,100,000	50
Ningxia	2,600,000	20
Chahar	100,000	7
Suiyuan	200,000	10
Shaanxi	700,000	6
Jehol	600,000	1

The annual import of opium into Tianjin from Gansu, Ningxia, and Shaanxi amounts to more than 5,600,000 ounces. The quality of opium produced in these districts is of a much lower grade, and nearly all of the imports were sold to manufacturers of narcotic drugs in the Japanese Concession in Tianjin. One of the well-known manufacturers is named Wang Ding Sing. While the import from Liangzhou, Jehol, Chahar, and Suiyuan amounts to more than 7,000,000 ounces, 50 percent of which is sold in Tianjin, 20 percent in Shandong, 10 percent in Chefoo (Yantai), 10 percent in Qingdao, and 10 percent in Shanghai.

There are about 42 illicit opium firms and 160 opium dens in the Japanese concession in Tianjin which are not capable of being reached by Chinese law. Meanwhile, conditions in North China are getting from bad to worse. In an article [that] appeared in the *China Weekly Review* on February 8, 1936, entitled "Manchurian Opium and Heroin Monopoly Expands into North China," it was shown that opium suppression in foreign concessions is a failure. While the Chinese authorities are directing all efforts in fighting against the drug evil, transactions have been going on openly between the nationals of a certain friendly nation on the one hand and Chinese opium traffickers on the other. During the period from January 1, 1933, to February 16, 1935, the Chinese authorities in Beiping dealt with 206 cases in which foreigners were found concerned in drug smuggling, 205 of whom were Japanese and Koreans. Drug smuggling conducted by Japanese subjects is not, however, confined to North China. In Shanghai, according to the *Sin-Wen-Pao* of February 23, 1936, "Five Koreans were arrested by the police of the French Concession for selling morphine to Chinese and Europeans." But that was not the only case. A casual perusal of the day's news any day will reveal similar violations perpetrated by persons who either enjoy extraterritorial privileges or are residents in this or that foreign concession.

In this connection, it might be said that the opium suppression campaign under the present six-year program has been a success insofar as Chinese efforts [are] concerned but a failure where extraterritoriality and foreign vested interests are involved. So it is necessary to have the support from the friendly powers in order to put an end to this most inhuman and disgraceful crime through united action.

This point has further been expounded by General Chiang Kai-shek, Superintendent-General of the National Opium Suppression Commission, who, in a recent speech on June 3rd in commemoration of the National Opium Suppression Day, attributed the partial failure of the suppression campaign to three reasons: lack of confidence among the people in the Government's suppression work, lack of persistence among the officials in enforcing anti-opium laws, and the absence of any concerted action and organized campaign among the various component elements in society. Continuing, General Chiang declared, "If foreign opium continues to pour into China unabated, all her (China's) efforts and all her sacrifices would have been made and sustained in vain, and it is hoped that the friendly Powers would not revert to a policy of poisoning China and thus further enhancing the causes of mutual misunderstanding." The motive behind the national opium suppression as a whole is to increase national productivity, by preventing national wastes in unproductive expenditures, aside from the vital question of public health. Taking the long view, the foreign Powers should derive much comfort in seeing the purchasing power of the Chinese people for foreign goods raised, which can only come about through increasing their productive capacity. "The present difficulties confronting China's opium suppression authorities are unparalleled elsewhere in the world. The conditions in China are such that illicit establishments engaged in the trafficking and manufacturing of opium and drugs can exist in China and defy the powers of the Chinese authorities to suppress them. Cognizance of this fact by the Powers is therefore necessary, in order to lend every support and cooperation to the Chinese Government to stamp out the drug evil."

International efforts at opium and drug suppression by the League of Nations are worthy of notice. According to the annual report of the Advisory Committee on Traffic in Opium of the League of Nations the three International Conventions relating to opium have the largest numbers of members taking part, showing the success of international coordination, for which the League was established. Although China did not participate in the Geneva Convention of 1925, she is a member of the Convention of The Hague of 1912 and of the Convention on Limitation of 1931. Subsequent to the three Conventions there were the Agreement concerning the suppression of the Manufacture of, internal trade in, and use of prepared opium, signed at Geneva on February 11, 1925, which was ratified (in 1928) by all countries party to the Geneva Convention, and the Agreement for the Suppression of Opium-Smoking, signed at Bangkok on November 27, 1931, which has been ratified by five countries.

The Chinese Government has always been disposed to cooperate with the treaty powers and responsible authorities of all other countries through the League of Nations for the suppression of opium traffic and the manufacture of allied drugs. To facilitate the work of coordination, reports on opium and drug conditions are submitted to the League of Nations for reference by accredited delegates of the respective countries. In a recent report, the Chinese delegate took pain to explain the earnest effort of the Chinese Government to exterminate opium in the country by citing laws and regulations governing the smoking and traffic in opium. Immediate suppression, according to the report, is difficult, especially in the frontier provinces where the population is so steeped in the evil that only a gradual course is advisable. In these localities officers are appointed during sowing and harvesting seasons to supervise production, so that there will be no increase, but a gradual decrease of acreage under poppy. The final termination of all poppy cultivation is expected within a six years' period. Difficulties to carry out Chinese Government measures in foreign-controlled areas have also been communicated to the League, and the cooperation of the interested powers is sought.

Apropos of these difficulties it is interesting to read reports submitted by the Shanghai International Settlement and the French Concession and concessions under Japan and Italy in other ports. Nearly all reports make mention of the legitimate import, export, and transit of narcotic drugs, over which the Municipal authorities seemed to have no control. Such legalized importation into the treaty ports is supposed to be subject to the control of the Chinese Maritime Customs, for which an import certificate is required. The drugs thus imported are only for medical and chemical purposes. From the reports it would seem that constructive cooperation is being given by some concessions where Chinese Government measures are encouraged if not actually enforced. But, in other concessions, especially in North China, the evil of narcotic drugs has been used as a weapon to make room for territorial aggressions.

While the evil of opium smoking still constitutes a vital problem awaiting solution, it is nevertheless true that a definite beginning has been made to have the situation under control. The strengthening of the power of the National Government, under the guidance of General Chiang Kai-shek and other leaders, has no doubt meant a happy augury for the facilitation and eventual achievement of the task of opium suppression. Also, China has recently demonstrated her sincerity not merely by verbal promises but by joining hands with other nations of the world in combating this great evil against humanity. Dr. Victor Hoo, Chinese Delegate to the League, it may be recalled, has recently affixed his signature on behalf of the National Government to the Opium and Narcotics Convention drawn up at Geneva. In a report submitted to the National Government, Dr. Hoo expressed the view that the enforcement of this Convention will greatly facilitate the task of opium suppression in China. It is therefore earnestly hoped that, with the close cooperation of all the nations signatory to this Convention, a more auspicious international situation will prevail wherein China's efforts at suppressing the evil of opium will be met with fewer and less strong obstructions now obtaining on account of the attitude of certain of the Great Powers and the existence of extraterritoriality, foreign concessions, and foreign settlements.

NOTES

Kuo Tse-Hsiung, "Opium Suppression in China," *Information Bulletin* 1 (9 August 1936) (Published in English for the Council of International Affairs, Nanjing).

1. The Geneva Opium Conference was not a complete failure. It was intended to improve control over the international flow of opium and resulted in the Geneva Treaty of 1925. The Chinese and the Americans walked out of the conference because of the unwillingness of the other nations to agree to the elimination of their colonial opium monopolies.

2. The reference is to the Japanese.

Opium Control
in Manchuguo

Manchuguo was the puppet state set up by the Japanese after their takeover of Manchuria in 1931. It was never recognized by any of the foreign powers and ceased to exist in 1945. Manchuguo also got little financial help from Japan, and its government was forced to rely on the money it could generate internally. This, of course, meant opium, and Manchuguo received a substantial portion of its revenue from opium in its early years. This was the same policy that the Japanese had pursued in Taiwan in the early years of its occupation and the same policy that the Japanese army would use in China after 1937. Like the government of Taiwan, the government of Manchuguo began with a simple system of what could be called "opium farming" and then moved on to a more sophisticated control system. Also like Taiwan, the Manchuguo government claimed that these control methods were not aimed at increased revenue but at the eventual elimination of the trade. This document, originally published in English, was intended as a justification of Japan's policy to the international community.

Manchoukuo's Opium-Smoking Eradication Policy

Ever since 1932, due to the activities of certain foreign publicity organs attempting to conceal the shameful conditions existing within their own countries or for some political reason through willful exaggeration and misrepresentation of the actual conditions in this country, Manchoukuo's opium policy and conditions have been made the target of numerous groundless charges. The serious efforts made by the Manchoukuo authorities in reducing the traffic in, and the accompanying evils of, opium with the object of their eventual elimination have been given little publicity or have been deliberately ignored by Western countries.

Among the outstanding reasons for this situation may be counted: (1) because of her geographical position, the general conditions of Manchoukuo have been little known abroad; (2) facts have been willfully twisted or misrepresented; (3) the Manchoukuo government has not been given sufficient time to carry out its policy in full; and (4) Manchoukuo is always looked upon with some suspicion and prejudice.

Manchoukuo has just completed the first five-year experimental stage, true, with many shortcomings but definitely with a bright outlook for the future. With five years' experience the Government will, beginning 1938, launch upon a new ten-year program with renewed vigor in an effort to eradicate completely by the end of 1948 all opium smoking and narcotic uses, except for medicinal purposes.

In the following pages will be found essential facts relating to the policy and the efforts of the Government to date and their results, together with an explanation of the ten-year program.

Before proceeding in an explanation of the policy of Manchoukuo with regard to the prevention of opium smoking, it should be noted that some circles hold that the opium question would be easily solved if only the Government immediately prohibited the cultivation of poppy and undertook thoroughgoing measures to suppress the transport, sale, and consumption of this drug.

It would be indeed fortunate if the question could be solved in such a simple manner. But, unfortunately, the problem is of such a nature as to defy a real solution through the mere issuance of State decrees or the meting out of punishment. It invariably involves a number of problems that are closely related to politics, economic, public welfare, and international affairs.

It is not out of place to survey the opium situation existing in China during the latter decades of the old Qing Dynasty and subsequent to the establishment of the Republic of China. True, the Chinese Government promulgated many laws rigidly banning opium smoking and providing capital punishment and mercilessly heavy penalties for violators, but in reality, very little was accomplished towards the ultimate settlement of the question. One should not, however, rush to the conclusion that all these government measures possessed inherent defects. The determination of the Chinese Government to suppress opium smoking was quite firm at times, but all their efforts proved well nigh futile.

One of the chief reasons for this failure lay in the chaotic condition of the Chinese administrative structure. National prestige, strength, and unity were lacking. Different militarist cliques, politicians, and privileged classes held their own ground, all indulging in an orgy of corruption.

The second reason lay in the fact that the country was not strong enough to take any coercive and drastic actions against the importation of opium from abroad, while the existence of secret opium rings was a deep-rooted, irremediable will in the economic structure of the country.

The third lay in the opium-smoking habit among the people. A great number of people in China were confirmed opium addicts, deprived of the power of judgment and reasoning and thus unable to realize the harms of opium smoking. Even among high government officials, there were many addicted to the drug. Under such circumstances, it was no wonder that the habit should become popular among the people.

Inconveniences in communications and the preservation of peace and order, the defective structure of society and the corruption of family life are other reasons which cannot be overlooked. Under such unfavorable conditions the suppression of opium smoking could not have been accomplished with success, no matter how many State decrees and laws might have been promulgated, no matter what sums of money might have been spent, and even with the sacrifice of many human lives.

A closer study of the causes for the failure of the efforts of the Chinese Government to suppress the opium-smoking habit will enable us to ascertain the prospects of the Manchoukuo Government's policy with regard to eradication of opium smoking.

1. Opium Smoking in Former Days

Never in the past has the Chinese Government really unified the whole nation. Only through the medium of local regimes was some semblance of unity established. But the government was unable to extend its rule into every nook and corner of the country. Even if the government resolved to suppress the taking of dope, their efforts were always brought to naught by the selfishness of military cliques, corrupt politicians, and petty local factions.

One salient social characteristic in China prevented the carrying out of the Government's intention more than any other thing. And that is, individuals of high social standing or with public influence felt that it was a great shame to acquiesce to the dictates of the rulers. By refusing to obey orders from the government or by violating publicly laws and regulations, they, oddly enough, felt a sense of self-pride in their own power. And, the government authorities could do nothing against the defiance of these persons of great social influence. Typical men of this type were Dang Yulin and Wu Zhunsheng, the "Big Two" under the now ousted Northeastern Regime in former Manchuria.

Those who dared to commit illegal acts in defiance of the government were restricted not merely to these influential figures outside of the government service but also included their following and relatives, immune to punishment as long as they were under the aegis of their master's protection. No matter how rigidly opium smoking was prohibited by law, only the general masses observed the government decrees. In the final analysis the innocent farmers were the ones to be actually punished by the law.

Out of the necessity of maintaining its prestige, even outwardly, the Government shut its eyes to the fact that corrupt individuals of the privileged class were engaging in the clandestine production, transport, and sale of opium and other narcotics, in order to extend their spheres of influence and power both in the social and economic fields. At the same time the majority of these men were inveterate addicts themselves, who, knowing the harms inherent in the drug habit, were unable to break themselves from the evil clutches of opium. On the other hand, the general masses were warned of the dangerous effects of opium smoking and severely punished for any violation of the law.

Together with the great influence exerted by men of social prominence indulging in the habit, the totally inadequate medical facilities to cope with the situation made measures for the control and suppression of the widespread vogue practically useless.

Needless to say, there were other contributing factors in the failure of the efforts of the Chinese authorities. Thus, the Manchoukuo Government early saw that, in order to halt the spread of the drug habit and to root out the evil, it would have to take into consideration the actual conditions which had made earlier efforts futile. In formulating her anti-opium policy and in adopting appropriate measures, the Manchoukuo Government, therefore, first made a thorough study of the difficulties which it would have to overcome in order to gain success. Close attention was especially paid as to what extent and to what degree of strictness the new measures should go.

It was only after this preliminary study and investigation that the Manchoukuo Government promulgated the Opium Law and established an opium monopoly for the control of the production and distribution of opium and other narcotics. In this way it planned the eventual eradication of the noxious habit permeating the whole of society.

The evils concomitant with the prevalence of the drug habit had woven itself intimately into the fabric of society. Secret organizations and narcotic rings had attached themselves like parasitic leaches to the social structure. Before any success in the establishment of opium control could be hoped for these illegal organizations had to be wiped out.

Thus, the Manchoukuo Government began a campaign to purge society of these criminals, continually sucking the vitality of the people. At the same time, it began the limitation of the area used in the cultivation of poppy, subject to increase or reduction as the circumstances demanded. A nationwide census of opium addicts was undertaken, in order to place them under medical care and control. In a few years, the basic measures taken by the Manchoukuo Government for the suppression of the opium habit were crowned with success.

The success of the efforts made by the Government to stamp out the habit was only made possible by the modernization of the new State. Peace and order, which Manchuria had scarcely known before, were established, military cliques and corrupt bureaucrats were eliminated, and crime, rampant in the old days, was curbed together with narcotic rings and underground networks of illicit traffickers.

With the remarkable progress of communications throughout the country, administrative changes, the abolition of Japanese extraterritoriality, and the transfer of Japan's administrative rights within the S.M.R. Railway Zone, the unification of Manchoukuo was finally achieved. Together with these rapid advances, the opium situation improved by leaps and bounds.

Today, government supervision of the opium habit is moving in smooth grooves, and the whole system of control has been adjusted and perfected to the minutest detail. But, responding to the ardent desires of the public, the Manchoukuo Government is redoubling its efforts, in particular since 1938, in order to achieve its ultimate aims. A new outlook has been adopted by the general masses. Those who had indulged in the habit because it was fashionable and because it was an earmark of the leisured class now regard the smoking of opium in its true light. In keeping with the tempo of the times, occasional users of the drug have abandoned their intermittent indulgences, and the populace in general have come to abide faithfully by the instructions of the Manchoukuo Government.

For confirmed addicts, the Government measures proved the shortest and only way out of self-destruction. The Government treatment, it must be remembered, was not limited merely to those in the service of the Manchoukuo Government but extended to every individual citizen. In fact, the efforts of the government was in line with its policy to construct a new and rejuvenated order in East Asia.

With the rapid progress made in the preliminary steps in the eradication of opium smoking, the Government of Manchoukuo is now ready to embark on the final step of its program, in an undertaking long considered as extremely difficult.

In view of the fact that the world situation is becoming more and more strained as all nations bend themselves feverishly to the task of increasing their manpower, productive capacities, and development of natural resources, Manchoukuo cannot afford to lag behind. She must surge ahead without slackening her efforts in order to enhance her national position and to fulfill the great mission that she has taken upon herself. Thus, it is that she is putting forward greater efforts to attain the solution to the troublesome opium question, which bears, to a greater or less degree, upon all phases of administration, general national mobilization, as well as industrial development and economic reconstruction.

II. Opium Smoking in Relation to National Problems

In spite of its determination to dispose of the opium question in as short a period of time as possible, the Manchoukuo Government is faced with certain problems, a knowledge of which is essential to the understanding of its policy with regard to the eradication of the opium habit. In the following paragraphs a close study will be made of the urgent problems related to the whole opium question.

1. Government Finance

According to figures for the past several years, the profit derived from the opium monopoly by the Manchoukuo Government amounted to the sum of ten million yuan for one of the record years. On the surface, this may seem a profitable source of state revenue. But close scrutiny reveals that this sum is not a profit in the real sense of the word. In the first place, Manchoukuo consumes annually some 180 million yuan worth of opium. In the second place, the opium habit not only demoralizes the addicts spiritually but also weakens them physically. Together with the decline in their utility comes proportionate lessening of the productivity of the country. It appears that addicts consume more resources than the average individual, at the same time producing much less. As a proverbial Chinese adage says, they are "fond of eating but dislike work." If this extra consumption and the subsequent loss in national productivity are computed in terms of money, it is estimated that Manchoukuo loses 150 million yuan annually.

Worse still, the criminal rate increases in direct ratio to the number of addicts, putting an extra burden on the policing and administrative costs to the State. Taking into consideration these various facts, the elimination of the opium habit from Manchoukuo would mean approximate savings every year to the State of over 300 million yuan, conservatively estimated.

The net saving of this huge sum, directed into usual channels, would mean a corresponding increase in the consuming power in the country, providing a potential incentive to the general economic prosperity and well-being of Manchoukuo. It is also evident that, as a result of the increase of economic activity, the state revenue from taxes would more than offset the rather dubious gains to be gotten from the enforcement of the opium monopoly.

The relatively small profit accruing incidentally from the opium monopoly may arouse some suspicion on the part of foreign public opinion as well as misunderstandings. But an examination of the actual situation leaves no room for such doubts or cynicism.

True, there are difficulties and obstacles to be overcome in any undertaking. But in connection with the opium problem, the Manchoukuo government is firmly determined to hurdle any and all obstacles to the achievement of ultimate success.

2. Politics

Conscientiousness and a sense of responsibility on the part of government officials are prerequisites in the proper functioning of the general political organization of a country. During the period preceding the advent of Manchoukuo, many government authorities were slaves to the drug habit. The higher, the more common the habit. But it was not restricted merely to the upper group; the whole body of public servants, in fact, seemed to be devotees of Morpheus.

Such a situation naturally resulted in the utter demoralization and the corruption of the State machinery. Petty officials found that in satisfying their cravings they could not live within their earned incomes. Thus they were forced to seek other sources of revenue. High Government officials found their rank and elation a distinct advantage in gaining illegal funds. Soon the whole political structure became honeycombed with graft, bribery, extortion, and underhand connivance. State policies failed to be carried out, peace and order changed to chaos and insecurity. The example of the rulers of the State served to influence the public mind to a tremendous extent. Opium smokers arose, some in sheer imitation of the life led by the higher officials. Culture, national pride, and spirit all deteriorated.

Furthermore, addicts increased in number daily and monthly. Crime rose in direct proportion. Eventually the proud Chinese race which from time immemorial had vaunted to the world of its traditions of humanity, justice, and morals, its code of Sankang Wuchang,[1] degenerated to a mere ghost of its former material and spiritual splendor.

A study of the situation prevailing throughout Manchoukuo under the now ousted military regime impresses one with the extent of the havoc wrought by that archenemy of mankind, opium, in all phases of national activity. Only with the radical elimination of opium smoking could government officials be hoped to act according to the dictates of their conscience and their responsibilities. Only in this way could national unity be achieved and national prestige enhanced.

3. State Economy

Already, the economy of Manchoukuo has developed from a primitive to a new, systematic form, in spite of the lapse of a short time since the new State was brought into being. In surveying the general tendency of our capitalists possessing fortunes of several million yuan, it is to be noted that many of them lack a spirit of progressiveness, soundness of health and body, or are managing indirectly their own enterprises by entrusting their businesses to third persons. In the case of those who directly manage enterprises of their own, many seem to be too eager to seek selfish profits. The opium-smoking habit is responsible for this to a large extent.

No matter how the State may control the nation's economy, the economic activity of an individual affects not only his immediate family or public organization but the whole State and race. Hence, the harmful habit of opium smoking even among individual persons cannot be overlooked. It is from this point of view that Manchoukuo, now bent upon economic construction, must keep its economy free from all the destructive effects of opium smoking.

4. People's Welfare

The greatest achievement of the Oriental races is its spiritual culture of many centuries standing. As a matter of fact, Oriental culture forms a vital and brilliant part of world civilization. Thus, our race is ruled by a morality inherent in the Oriental races, in addition to modern laws. Humanity is nothing but moral virtues. Even in present society, featured by a materialistic civilization, the real value of these Oriental morals can never be diminished.

In this sense, our daily life of necessity is being influenced by our spiritual civilization. Our family system and State structure also have in this civilization their common origin, so is the case with our manners and customs. In a nutshell, moral virtues are the mother of all these.

Unfortunately, however, the importation of foreign opium after the now famous Opium War had a serious effect upon the health standard of the nation and destroyed, though gradually, these traditional moral virtues, with the consequence that the race finally fell into the state of inactivity such as existed at the time when the ousted militarist clique was still in power.

Addicts, when well-off, may not do any wrongs, but once they have been confronted with the danger of bankruptcy, then, bereft of reason and their sense of honor, they will only seek for selfish profits and finally go the length of committing unlawful acts. This renders the preservation of social order difficult as well as affecting public health and sanitation.

5. Industry

One of the primary objectives of the Manchoukuo Government's administration policy is the development of industry, for the attainment of which certain ideal conditions are necessary.

Of these conditions natural resources, capital, labor, and production technique are the four most important ones. In labor and production technique, Manchoukuo suffers a certain shortage. But it is believed that this question will solve itself when the dope habit has been completely stamped out in the country.

The huge sum of roughly 300 million yuan spent yearly in the consumption of opium and other narcotics could then be shifted to be used usefully in the industrial development of Manchoukuo.

Among addicts are to be found intellectual individuals. But since falling prey to the opium-smoking habit, they have been unable to utilize to the fullest extent their knowledge and abilities, besides losing the courage to cope with life in general. Should these addicts be cured, their knowledge and abilities could be put to useful purposes.

There is a shortage of labor, notwithstanding the fact that between 80 and 90 percent of the whole population of the country is engaged in agriculture and industrial enterprises. The opium habit has much to do with this situation. Individuals falling into the habit do not lose the whole of their labor capacity in a short time, but it is needless to point out that their labor capacity is considerably lowered.

The habit, however, rapidly becomes chronic. Investigation shows that only two or three percent of the addicts can withstand some sustained labor. Thus if opium smoking were completely suppressed, the labor of several hundred thousand men could be available to offset the shortage of labor needed in the exploitation of the industrial resources in the country. In this way is the opium question closely related to public health, politics, and national policy.

6. International Situation

Although it is not long since Manchoukuo was established, a number of countries have already extended their formal recognition to the new State. Despite the fact that there still are foreign Powers who have not recognized Manchoukuo, Manchoukuo has made herself into the modern State that she is at present, thanks to the untiring, united efforts of her Government and the people.

Seeing Manchoukuo steadily consolidating her national foundations, these third Powers must sooner or later discard their prejudiced and biased attitude toward her and accept her in the family of nations.

In view of the fact that the opium question is one of great concern to the whole world, and that all Powers have been interested more or less in this question and have felt great apprehension over the harmful effects of opium smoking, should Manchoukuo settle the opium problem that has defied a satisfactory solution for the past several decades and that has had unwholesome effects upon all mankind, the world would then speedily realize the fundamental national policy of Manchoukuo and come to recognize her worth.

7. Racial Unity

Racial unity is the sole objective which Manchoukuo has had in view ever since her foundation. On this principle are based all the foundations of her political system and institutions. For the purpose of bringing about this racial unity, the Manchoukuo Government has established what is now known as the Hsieh Ho Hui (the Concordia Association) as a fabric of state structure. This organ of the Government is charged with the task of exalting Manchoukuo's national spirit of racial unity and harmony.

It means, in a nutshell, the perfect unification of all the different races residing in Manchoukuo so that they may be able to forge ahead together in attaining the great common ideal, namely, the creation of a land of peace founded on "Wang Taoism" (the Kingly Way).

Everyone may fully understand this spirit theoretically and act loyally to the State in line with this principle. But in the efforts expended towards establishing this racial unity, everyone in the country should be not mere theorists, but men of action and practice. Only when the whole nation acts positively and faithfully in accordance with the spirit can real racial unity be brought about.

With the Manchu and Mongol races opium smoking is, so to speak, a historically hereditary disease. Although a heroic combat has been continued for many years by them against this disease, the battle has not as yet been won.

The harms of opium smoking have permeated so deeply into the fabric of Manchoukuo society and every phase of the daily life of her people that young and old, men and women, have come to regard the habit as a great national agony and to dread it as such. Even addicts, themselves, knew fully the dreadful harms of the habit. Once they fell into its clutches, their willpower gradually weakened and their spirit of self-recovery became completely lost. Thus, the opium habit developed into a national calamity.

Opium smoking cannot be eliminated unless proper collective counter-measures are taken by a group of different but harmonious races. If the

Manchurian race, long a slave to opium smoking, can free itself from its shackles with the assistance and cooperation of the Japanese race, unfurling as it does the banner of racial harmony, then the Manchus would naturally appreciate and feel grateful for the efforts of the Japanese made in the spirit of racial unity.

Since her foundation, Manchoukuo has accomplished various things meriting admiration in the administrative field, too numerous to enumerate here. In those undertakings which so far have relatively failed to show tangible results, the fullest cooperation of the general public has not been forthcoming. But as far as the opium question is concerned, the whole nation fully realizes its dangers and is cooperating in the successful suppression of this habit. The successful termination of this campaign will be an accomplishment of historical significance and of great credit to the Manchoukuo Government. Undoubtedly it will have a profound effect upon the promotion of understanding on the part of foreign Powers of Manchoukuo.

The nation as a whole will also come to realize the sound administrative policy of the Government and form a better understanding of its efforts, thereby promoting harmony between the Government and the governed. The secret of racial unity lies in the sharing by different races of their respective difficulties and pains. The suppression of the opium-smoking habit which calls for the highest form of sharing can be regarded therefore as the first step taken towards the establishment of real racial unity.

Fundamentally, a government by virtue of laws can guide its nation and regulate its activity. But the Manchoukuo Hsieh Ho Hui (the Concordia Association), it should be noted, is an organization which, from a moral standpoint, affords spiritual guidance to the nation and puts into practice various state programs based upon the Wang Tao principle.

For example, with regard to the opium question the Hsieh Ho Hui was asked to play the main role in disseminating necessary information for the subjugation of opium smoking when the Government had decided upon its anti-opium program. Thus, the organization has been carrying on various activities for the suppression of this habit, rousing public attention to its danger, trying to prevent the birth of new addicts by means of social sanctions and administering speedy medical treatment to confirmed drug fiends.

At the same time the Hsieh Ho Hui has constantly and steadfastly exerted every effort, out of its spirit of mutual assistance, to help and to encourage addicts both directly and indirectly to recover their self-respect without disappointing or disheartening them in face of innumerable difficulties.

The Hsieh Ho Hui is continuing its movement for the creation of a richer and stronger State. In accordance with its principle of national guidance sorely needed at this crucial moment, curtailment of material consumption, encouragement of productivity and money savings, utilization of waste goods, exaltation of the national spirit of loyalty, and the encouragement of voluntary labor service to the State are the ideals that guide this movement.

At present, there are still about a million addicts in this country. Several hundred million yuan is expended in the consumption of opium and other narcotics while the number of persons succumbing to the harmful effects of opium smoking is estimated at several tens of thousands. These facts show the serious harms which narcotics affect the physical strength, manners, and customs of the whole nation. Unless the consumption of dangerous drugs is speedily suppressed, the encouragement of productivity and money savings and the exaltation of the popular mind will be nigh impossible.

III. Conclusion

Already, more than a year and a half have passed since the Government first adopted its positive policy of suppressing the drug habit. During this span of time, the Government has left nothing undone in its efforts to find a speedy solution to the various problems that are related to the policy. Taking into consideration the failure of past attempts in this direction and the necessity of meeting the exacting requirements of the current situation in the country, the anti-opium campaign has been divided into several different stages.

The first stage, completed by the end of July 1937, was occupied with the registration of all old addicts. The second stage, which was started immediately after that date, covered the perfecting of medical facilities to be placed at the disposal of the addicts. The third included the institution of stringent laws to prevent the rise of new addicts. This was started the very day the registration of the addicts was finished. But its enforcement was not to begin until after the completion of the second stage. Accordingly, individuals not duly registered found smoking opium and those found profiteering from the narcotic traffic have been severely punished and will be punished with equal severity in the future.

Beginning with 1939, moreover, addicts in government service or in the employ of special corporations will not be tolerated. From every angle, efforts are being made to eliminate smokers once and for all, no matter what difficulties may crop up in the way. It should also be pointed out that the year 1936 was the time limit allowed for the reformation of such addicts. Thus if any addicts are found among public servants or employees of special corporations, there should, of course, be no room for any sympathetic considerations.

The opium laws mentioned above are applicable according to the social position or occupation of the addict. Besides, age restrictions are in force, in accordance with which all addicts aged under 30 are required to cure themselves voluntarily from the evil habit by the end of this year. In case any such addicts are found after that date, they are to be indicted and subjected to forcible remedial treatment.

The original policy for the suppression of the drug habit was to be spread over a maximum period of ten years. But the Government intends to complete the policy within the shortest possible period. With respect to some narcotics, the Government, seeing that they were several times more poisonous than opium, adopted a policy of immediate suppression at the very outset.

In spite of this policy, some supply of these narcotics is still permitted. This is for no other reason than the prevention of their illegal traffic which otherwise would be impossible. After the perfection in the future of necessary medical facilities, the addicts will preferentially be taken into infirmaries and other institutions. All addicts and illegal drug traffickers when found even after that will be severely dealt with.

An Outline of the Opium Administration

Preface

For the purpose of carrying out the principles for the prevention of opium smoking that were formally adopted and announced in October 1937, Imperial Ordinance No. 487 was promulgated on December 27 of the same year, to be effective on and after January 1, 1935, and providing for revisions of the Opium Law. Accordingly, regulations governing the enforcement of the revised Opium Law, the procedure relating thereto and the control of addicts, and other supplementary regulations and official instructions were issued, along with the progress of various other necessary arrangements. With the executive organs concerned fully posted about the matter, every effort was made to leave nothing undone to ensure a satisfactory enforcement of the revised Opium Law. By the revised law, narcotics other than opium were affected as well.

1. State Retail Sale System

The old private retail sale system left room for undue profiteering and therefore was incompatible with the object of prohibiting opium smoking. Taking stock of this fact, it was decided to transfer opium retail sales to municipalities, counties, and banners by the end of the year 1940, with the view of properly regulating the use of opium and other narcotics, rationalizing their distribution, curbing their misuse through illicit transfers, and preventing the appearance of new addicts. The State retail sale system is also intended as a means of exercising better control over the old addicts.

Before the enforcement of the state sale system, all necessary investigations and arrangements had been made in accordance with what was stipulated in Decree No. 72 of November 1, 1937, issued by the Department of People's Welfare. At the same time, a conference of the provincial government officials in charge of the matter was convoked, at which the Central Government policy was clarified and discussed. With all these investigations and preparations completed by the end of that year, the business of old private retailers, along with their buildings, various establishments, and employees, was taken over most smoothly by the State without any trouble or friction. The State opium sales system thus enforced from January 1, 1938, is now being observed in a total of 17 cities, 134 counties, and 18 banners, representing slightly upward of 90 percent of the whole territory of the country. The State sale system has yet to be enforced in a small number of counties in Jehol and Hsingan Provinces where the situation with regard to the maintenance of peace and order is still somewhat unsatisfactory or in some other counties where specific local conditions prevail.

The total amount of money expended for buying up establishments of the old private opium retailers aggregated M¥ 904, 659. In the provinces of Lungkiang, Tunghua, Mutankiang, East Hsingan, and North Hsingan and in the special Hsinking Municipality, the needed money was met by advances from the budgets for general accounts, to the extent of M¥ 333,941. In all the other provinces necessary sums were raised by flotation of bonds which totaled roughly M¥ 571,700.

For the State retail sale of opium, opium sale control offices were created against private retailers. The total number of private opium retailers officially designated before the enforcement of the State sale system was 2,139 throughout the country. Simultaneously, however, with the enforcement of the system, private retail shops were either merged together or abolished. At present, 1,363 State-managed opium sale control offices are operating, whereas the number of private retailers stands at only 272, indicating a startling decline of 504. These State-managed opium sale control offices, in principle, are attached to State opium-smoking houses, and in each city or county, one to three of them are being maintained.

The management of the State opium-smoking houses, generally speaking, is satisfactory. In surveying the budgetary estimates for the 1935 fiscal year of the various provinces, it is noted that net profits from the public sale of opium aggregated M¥ 9,000,000, of which M¥ 2,600,000 were to be offered as dues to the provincial coffers. Relatively large though this amount of profits may appear, it is thought that even if these profits are forthcoming at their present rate, it may require at least three years before the projects enumerated below, which have a direct bearing upon the absolute prohibition of opium smoking, can be completed, whilst considerable State subsidies are needed in Jehol, Sankaing, Tunghua, and Hsingan Provinces, where the State opium sale system has not yet been enforced or where the system, though already adopted, has proved unsatisfactory thus far:

    a. Redemption of bonds and loans floated for enforcing the state opium sale system
    b. Improvement of state opium-smoking houses (repairing and perfection of sanitary and other facilities)
    c. Qualitative improvement and better treatment of employees of State-managed opium sale control offices
    d. Construction of opium-addict infirmaries
    e. Management of opium-addict infirmaries
    f. Establishment of facilities necessary for the guidance of addicts
    g. Anti-opium propaganda and social education
    h. Simple remedial hospitals and other medical institutions
    i. Distribution of relief medicines.

2. Registration of Opium and Narcotic Addicts

To ascertain the precise number of addicts was the basic and most important conditions for the execution of all programs and measures aimed at the eradication of drug taking. Naturally, the Central Government took every opportunity to give instructions and encouragements to local authorities with regard to the registration of addicts, in the hope that all addicts might be registered before the end of July 1938, the time limit set for registration.

But some addicts in those districts where the preservation of peace and order was unsatisfactory or in other areas shocked by the intensity of the anti-drug movement launched immediately after the announcement of the Government's policy misconstrued this registration system as presaging the imposition of a tax or compulsory labor.

For these and other reasons, only slightly more than 200,000 addicts had been registered after a lapse of four months since the registration system was started, according to official reports received from the various provincial governments by the end of May. Thus, the results of the registration were far from satisfactory.

In order to cope with this situation, the Central Anti-Opium Encouragement Committee dispatched parties of officials to local districts to expedite the registration of addicts. For about one month, these parties acted positively upon the various organs concerned in the principal cities of the country, thus dispelling groundless rumors of an extension of the time limit for registration. At the same time the local authorities concerned were better informed in order to understand the real objective of the registration system and to make positive efforts towards accelerating the registration task. Quite fruitful, indeed, was the dispatch of these parties. Thus, the registration of addicts throughout the country had nearly been completed by the end of July, save for some districts in Sankiang, Tunghua, and Jehol Province and Huatien-hsien, Kirin Province, where specific conditions prevailed.

3. Relief of Opium and Other Narcotic Addicts

As remedial institutions for the benefit of opium and other narcotic addicts, ten State infirmaries have been established, in addition to 36 county-managed infirmaries created with the proceeds from the public sale of opium. Thus, there are altogether 46 infirmaries in operation at present. Frankly, however, most of these infirmaries are far from satisfactory in point of scale and equipment; some of them even have the appearance of establishments for sheltering indigents.

Further, no active endeavors have been exerted to accommodate many addicts into these infirmaries. Due also to the failure of these establishments to institute any positive remedial measures for the addicts taken in, seven out of the ten persons treated at the infirmaries again become addicts after retiring from the institutions. This fact has given rise to the occurrence of the opinion that the curing of the addicts is impossible.

In the firm conviction, however, that, if such remedial facilities are substantially improved better guidance is given to the addicts and thoroughgoing control is exercised, the undertaking can progress successfully, the Government decided to erect a total of 200 more infirmaries in different provinces during the three years of 1938, 1939, and 1940 and has mapped out a 10-year program under which all addicts (estimated at 900,000, including young

TABLE 18.1.

Population	Opium Addicts Registered	Percentage of Opium Addicts	Other Addicts
34,882,461	587,907	1.7	17,808

Source: The Department of People's Welfare, July 1938. (This data was presented both as the total figure presented here and divided into the seventeen provinces that Manchuguo was divided into by the new government.)

addicts or legal minors) [are] to be taken under remedial treatment during the period of 10 years.[2] . . . The period of accommodation for each addict is 50 days. Estimating the total number of addicts in 1938 at 900,000, of whom about 50,000 will be cured or will die during the 10-year period over which this program spreads, it is indicated that there will be no addicts left by the end of 1947 (the 14th year of Kangte).

4. Control of Addicts and Illicit Drug Traffic

a. During the period of registration, the entry of persons into opium-smoking houses and other affairs were controlled rather moderately in order not to cause excessive apprehension among the addicts, but after the lapse of this period, strict control began to be exercised over such affairs.

Since the lapse of the period of registration, only those addicts bearing official certificates have been permitted to enter smoking houses, and the entry of any other person has strictly been prevented with the view of checking the spread of this evil practice and prohibiting illicit traffic in drugs.

b. The supply of opium to registered addicts is being made most strictly without any excessive quantity being granted. Also, the distribution of raw opium to cities, counties, and banners is undertaken on the basis of the exact number of registered addicts.

c. With regard to the control of drug smuggling and illicit traffic and of the cultivation of poppy, efforts are being made to leave no room for such activities by rounding up all persons engaging therein as was done in 1937. In connection with the control of poppy cultivation, the police organs in the various provinces in cooperation with the other authorities concerned have been assigned to the task, following the abolition of local peace preservation societies at the end of March 1938. Necessary instructions in this connection have already been given as regards the manner of control.

d. It will be well nigh impossible to carry out satisfactorily the opium-smoking prohibition policy only by reliance upon the powers of existing police. Hence, the appointment of a greater number of opium monopoly supervision officials has long been desired by the various provincial governments. As a temporary measure, 227 of the supervision officials of the Opium Monopoly Bureau have been transferred to police organs with the view of establishing unification of control.

In reality, however, this measure involved the transfer of one-half of the old number of these supervision officials and the discharge of the other half. So, it may be said that this entailed a decline in the force of control.

With regard to the disposition of these supervision officials, the main emphasis was laid upon urban districts. In frontier districts, the control of illicit drug traffic in the past has been entrusted almost exclusively to supervision officials of the Monopoly Bureau. But this has had to be discontinued, and at present, the local police authorities are requested positively to take up this task as incumbent upon themselves. In order, however, that the 10-year anti-drug program may be carried out successfully, there is a need of keeping at each police station one or two officials in charge of this matter for the purpose of preventing the illicit ingress of private drugs and of attending to all other affairs relating to the eventual prohibition of opium and narcotic taking.

NOTES

"Manchoukuo's Policy for the Eradication of Opium Smoking," *Manchuria Daily News,* 1939.
   1. *Sankang* means "the way of Heaven, Earth, and Man"; *Wuchang* means "loyalty, filial piety, fraternal love, conjugal affection, and friendship."
   2. In 1938 there were forty-six infirmaries.

Opium Suppression under the Communists

This article is an account of opium suppression under the Communists in Yanhe, a county in northeastern Guizhou, now the Yanhe Tujia Autonomous County. The Communists, like all other governments in China, had profited from the opium trade in the years before 1949, and like other governments they had publicly committed themselves to the eventual elimination of the opium trade. Although many of the specific techniques they used were similar to those of the Nationalists, the Communist anti-opium campaigns were carried out in the context of the successful effort to use mass campaigns to bring all aspects of local life under control, and thus the Communists were considerably more successful than were the Nationalists. Opium and drug use would not be a problem again in China until the post-Mao era.

Before Liberation Yanhe was one of the counties that suffered the most from opium, and I was one of those who suffered from the evil that opium fomented in society. After liberation I participated in the anti-opium struggle, and all this is still clear in my memory. This account is based on what I saw and heard, as well as on relevant archival sources.

1.

Opium is a poison from the bulb of the poppy plant. It induces sleep and cures illness and medicinally is used to make narcotics. If a person uses it too long, however, they become addicted, harming their body, mind, and constitution. In former years British imperialists sold much opium in China, making great profits while harming many people. The Japanese during their military invasion, feudal forces, and bureaucratic and capitalist groups all profited from control of the opium trade, causing opium to swiftly engulf all the towns and counties of our country. It is not recorded when opium first came to Yanhe, but it was already being grown in the county by the 1920s. In the 1930s, when I was a young boy, I remember seeing our neighbors growing opium. Many people smoked it as well, and the village had three opium dens, full of smoke day and night. The Nationalist government issued proclamations against opium and started the so-called New Life Movement. I remember a song I learned in school in the 1940s. "Opium is the king of harm, when you are not sick it makes you stay in bed. If you take it you will not be able to hide. It makes you sell your fields, land, and wife; Only those with no conscience harm people by opening an opium den or growing opium. They will be caught and taken to the execution ground and with the bang of a gun sent to see the Yama King."

There were many calls for opium prohibition, and legally it could lead to death, but it was a case of lots of thunder and little rain. Opium suppression got some results in the central areas, but in the borderlands it was entirely different, and opium was still openly grown, sold, and smoked. Prior to the collapse of the Nationalist government, the governor of Guizhou, Su Zhenglun, collected fines on "special goods," and on shipping it out of the province, and also taxed the people of Yanhe who planted it. In 1948 and 1949 not only did the outlying areas of the county produce a lot of opium, the fields near the county seat, where it had not been seen before, were full of poppies. In the towns of the county there were hundreds of opium dens, and in the rural districts opium dens were often open day and night. A group of opium- and salt-smuggling officials and gentry made a lot of money from opium in this period. The officials would confiscate opium from the farmers, and it would then be exchanged for weapons, increasing their military power. One subcounty official, Zhang Jiayen, accumulated over 100 guns this way between 1946 and 1947 and was able to completely dominate the people because of this. The officials also encouraged addicts to gamble. Once they were high they would rob people, kill, set fires, loot stores, and molest women. The people called officials and gentry, opium addicts, gambling, and bandits the four evils. On the Yunnan-Guizhou border one household out of a hundred could expect to be attacked by opium bandits every three years. I myself saw people lose their family property, sink into banditry, and die in a ditch. Husbands and wives were driven to suicide, a thing horrible to mention and unbearable to see. The masses suffered greatly from opium. It was said that "before Liberation the Southwest led the nation in the amount of opium grown and the number of smokers. The extent of its problem was beyond the power of words to describe." Yanhe, near the boundaries of Sichuan and Guizhou, was obviously part of this.

2.

In December 1949 the people of Yanhe achieved Liberation, and in February of 1950 the people's government was established. After this, under the leadership of the party and the army, plans were made to eliminate opium, beginning with those who had become addicts under the old regime. In February of 1950 Premier Zhou Enlai issued an order against opium, as did the county and provincial governments. Opium suppression was just getting started, but in April it was ordered to be suspended temporarily.

In October, after the bandit suppression troops returned to Yanhe, the county head made opium suppression, bandit suppression, and grain production his chief priorities. All local governments and anti-bandit troops were ordered to participate in the struggle, closing opium dens, punishing opium sellers, and uprooting poppy plants. To ensure that opium suppression penetrated deeply into the Yanhe county, the Anti-Opium Commission was established on November 19th. The county magistrate, Bai Yuren, was chair, and the heads of the civil affairs, public security, education, finance-and-food, and public health departments were also members. It set up a secretariat, an investigative branch, a propaganda office, a security bureau, and an opium clinic, thus really initiating the anti-opium movement in Yanhe.[1] On November 26 the first Yanhe All-Classes Assembly debated and passed the regulations for opium suppression.

The key parts of opium suppression at this point were 1. Deep and broad propaganda about the dangers of opium, encouraging the masses to participate in opium suppression. 2. Prohibiting poppy growing. The local cadres, anti-bandit troops, and leaders of mass organizations were to carry out inspections and encourage peasants who raised poppy to uproot it themselves. Those who refused were to be dealt with by the Public Security Bureau. 3. To prohibit opium shipment, manufacture, and sales. These things are entirely evil, and those who dared to challenge the law would be punished. Those who produced opium had to give up their equipment to be destroyed by the masses.[2] Even those who turned in their tools voluntarily and switched to another profession were to be investigated. 4. Prohibiting opium smoking. As opium had been poisoning the county for a long time there were many opium addicts, with the greatest numbers being among the workers and peasants, and it was important to educate them so that they could cure themselves. Those who were deeply addicted and found it hard to quit could be registered and receive anti-opium pills from the Public Health Bureau. Those who, in the end, could not be cured, besides undergoing forced labor, would not be eligible to receive the fruits of the struggle with feudalism. Those addicts whose lives were fairly acceptable would, on being exposed by the mobilized masses, undergo criticism and have their opium and pipes confiscated. Under these orders the local governments soon arrested many opium criminals and confiscated much opium and many pipes. In Qianguang village, a major opium town, one Zhang XX, on the excuse of "checking on the cows," went out to smoke some opium in a grass hut. He was revealed by a grazing calf and arrested by the Liberation Army. Some old opium smokers from the Farmers Association, and some people from the Sisters Association and the Youth Association, went down to find opium and pipes. By December the county had confiscated 1663.3 ounces of opium and 274 pipes. Leaving out the bandits, 15 opium addicts were purified. At that time of year it was very hard to tell poppy sprouts from other sprouts, and so only 6 *mu* of poppy were discovered.

At this time the struggle between opium suppression and those who opposed it was very fierce. The rumor was that anyone who had ever smoked opium would be executed, and many opium addicts were deeply concerned and used any method they could to hide their habit, burning their opium pipes or throwing them in the latrine. Some brazenly lied and claimed that they had not used opium for years, and others sent their wives or children to the Peasants Association to lie and make false declarations (on their behalf) or contrived other schemes. Some of the activists were also afraid of being exposed and asked their friends and relatives to keep quite about their opium use. There were about 10 villages where opium suppression was particularly arduous.

In January of 1951 the county Anti-Opium Commission drew up new plans in response to a directive from the provincial government to deal with the minority of intellectually backward people who were still growing opium. First came uprooting the poppies. Inspections had to penetrate deep into the mountains to keep the poppies from being planted and to uproot those that had been. Any opium or pipes that were discovered were to be destroyed by the masses as a sign of the government's determination. The inspectors were from the county and district governments and were empowered to punish cadres who concealed opium addicts, opium, or pipes. This would show the basic-level cadres and the masses that the government was determined and that it had effective measures to deal with the problem, which would remove doubts and encourage action. In Jiashi subcounty some 10 *mu* of poppy were found growing in the mountains, which was uprooted. In Xinmin village 10 *jin* of opium hidden by the evil landlord Xiao Xiaofeng were found, and some crafty opium smugglers were found out, and various opium pipe makers had their tools confiscated. In Qitan subcounty, cadre Yang Shenghai was out for a stroll after dinner one evening when he saw Liu Shaozhou carrying a bundle of cloth around to various shops to sell it. The bundle seemed a little thick, so he investigated and found 10 ounces of opium. The people's soldiers were sent to examine the other bundles in the shops and found more opium. The county government publicized this case and ordered the localities to be vigilant, and opium was found inside merchants' bamboo hats, under their chickens, and in their underwear and shoes. The ordinary opium addicts underwent education and forced cure and then were set on the path of reform through labor. There was a small group of hard-core addicts who, after their pipes were taken, made new ones, using spoons for opium lamps, eggshells for the bowl, and the stems of writing brushes for the shaft of the pipe. They were found out by the Sisters, Youth, and Mothers Associations. Opium addicts and smugglers were entirely under the eyes of the masses, and there was no hole for them to hide in. Opium smokers had no choice but to endure the aches and pains of withdrawing from opium.

In May of 1951 the county Anti-Opium Commission decided to add another method, in addition to the supervision of the masses. 1. Those who had been opium-free for less than three years were to be registered by the district or city police and pledge not to smoke again. 2. Addicts who were unable to quit were to be sent to the county anti-opium clinic. 3. Those for whom coming to the clinic in town would be a difficulty were to be given anti-opium pills, which they would take under the supervision of local cadres. 4. Subcounties and villages were to establish anti-opium pacts, which everyone would be required to join. 5. The anti-opium propaganda and education movement was to be revived. Lower- and middle-school students gave speeches in public places, put up posters, and gave dramatic performances. On June 2 an anti-opium exhibition was put up in front of the county cultural office. 6. The tax and salt offices and the police set up an anti-opium organization. 7. At the "7.7" commemorative rally, the resist Japan and America rallies, and the aid Korea rallies, opium was criticized, there were public arrests, and there was a public burning of opium and pipes.[3]

On July 7 the day was clear. The leaders of the people's government, the anti-bandit forces, and the People's Liberation Army assembled in the county seat. The police had assembled 1248.3 ounces of opium and six pipes to be burned. Five recalcitrant opium addicts were arrested, and there was a march through some of the districts that had been slow in opium suppression.

During 1951, 6,171 *mu* of poppies were uprooted, and 147,385.3 ounces of opium and 272 pipes confiscated. Thirty-six opium criminals were sentenced to periods from four months to two and a half years. The anti-opium struggle ended in victory. In 1952, during the 3 and 5 Anti Campaigns and land reform, investigators found some opium, returning like a poisonous snake, but it was again struck down.

3.

It used to be said that "ridding Yanhe of opium is as hard as ascending to heaven," but with the combined efforts of the party and the people it vanished like a puff of smoke in two years. It showed to the people that "when the party says they will do something, they do it. In two years they eliminated a poison that had lasted through many dynasties. They are indeed the common people's lucky star." One opium addict, after being cured, found that his strength had returned and that he could work and support himself. He said to his mother, "The Communists turn opium devils into people. Their virtue is unending, and they are worthy of being remembered to the last generation." The two most popular songs in the area, which people sang without stop, were "Without the Communist Party There Would Be No New China" and "The Sky in the Liberated Areas is Bright and Clear."

NOTES

Chao Zhongli, "Yanhe jinjue yapainyan du de huigu" (Looking back on the elimination of opium smoking in Yanhe), *Guizhou wenshi ziliao* 2 (1990): 87–93.

1. This commission is very similar to the organization of local anti-opium efforts under the Nationalists.

2. Presumably the reference is to those who boiled opium down to prepare it for smoking.

3. "7.7" commemorates the Marco Polo Bridge Incident and the beginning of the Resistance War.

Glossary

tutu	viceroy or governor-general
daotai	intendent supervising a circuit of counties
yamen	an official's residence and headquarters

Weights and Measures

Although they varied from time to time and place to place, these values should provide a comparison.

picul (*dan*)	133 pounds or 100 catties
catty (*jin*)	1 1/3 pounds
mace	1/10 *liang*
candareen	1/100 *liang*
tael	a unit of money, referring to one ounce of silver
mu	0.16 acre

Suggested Readings

Bakalar, James, and Lester Grinspoon. *Drug Control in a Free Society*. Cambridge: Cambridge University Press, 1984.

Berridge, Virginia, and Griffith Edwards. *Opium and the People: Opiate Use in Nineteenth-Century England*. New Haven, CT: Yale University Press, 1987.

Brook, Timothy, and Bob Wakabayashi, eds. *Opium Regimes: China, Britain, and Japan*. Berkeley: University of California Press, 2000.

Chen Yung-fa. "The Blooming Poppy under the Red Sun: The Yan'an Way and the Opium Trade." In Tony Saich and Hans van de Ven, eds., *New Perspectives on the Chinese Communist Revolution*. Armonk, NY: M. E. Sharpe, 1995.

Hall, J. C. S. *The Yunnan Provincial Faction, 1927–1937*. Canberra: Australian National University, 1976.

Hao Yen-P'ing. *The Commercial Revolution in Nineteenth-Century China: The Rise of Sino-Western Mercantile Capitalism*. Berkeley: University of California Press, 1986.

Hattox, Ralph H. *Coffee and Coffee Houses: The Origins of a Social Beverage in the Medieval Near East*. Seattle: University of Washington Press, 1985.

Jennings, John. *The Opium Empire: Japanese Imperialism and Drug Trafficking in Asia, 1895–1945*. Westport, CT: Praeger, 1997.

League of Nations. "Minutes of the Meetings and Documents Submitted to the Conference on the Suppression of Opium-Smoking." Bangkok: League of Nations, 1931.

Lodwick, Kathleen. *Crusaders against Opium: Protestant Missionaries in China, 1874–1917*. Lexington: University of Kentucky Press, 1996.

Madancy, Joyce. "Revolution, Religion, and the Poppy: Opium and the Rebellion of the 'Sixteenth Emperor' in Early Republican Fujian." *Republican China* 21, no. 1 (November 1995): 1–42.

Marshal, Jonathan. "Opium, Tungsten, and the Search for National Security, 1940–52." *Journal of Policy History* 3, no. 4 (1991): 440–67.

Martin, Brian G. *The Shanghai Green Gang: Politics and Organized Crime, 1919–1937*. Berkeley: University of California Press, 1996.

Matthee, Rudi. "Exotic Substances: The Introduction and Global Spread of Tobacco, Coffee, Cocoa, Tea, and Distilled Liquor, Sixteenth to Eighteenth Centuries." In Roy Porter and Mikulas Teich, eds., *Drugs and Narcotics in History*. Cambridge: Cambridge University Press, 1995.

May, Herbert L. *Survey of Smoking Opium Conditions in the Far East*. New York: Foreign Policy Association, 1927.

McCoy, Alfred W. *The Politics of Heroin: CIA Complicity in the Global Heroin Trade.* Brooklyn, NY: Lawrence Hill, 1991.

Merlin, Mark David. *On the Trail of the Ancient Opium Poppy.* London: Fairleigh Dickinson University Press, 1984.

Merrill, Frederick T. *Japan and the Opium Menace.* New York: Institute of Pacific Relations, 1942.

Mintz, Sidney W. *Sweetness and Power: The Place of Sugar in Modern History.* New York: Viking Penguin, 1985.

Musto, David F. *The American Disease: Origins of Narcotics Control.* Expanded ed. Oxford: Oxford University Press, 1987. Original ed., 1973.

Newman, R. K. "Opium Smoking in Late Imperial China: A Reconsideration." *Modern Asian Studies* 29, no. 4 (1995): 765–94.

Opium: A World Problem (English Journal of the National Anti-Opium Association of China). Various issues, 1927–31.

The Opium Trade. 5 vols. Wilmington, DE: Scholarly Resources, 1974.

Ours, Jan C. van. "The Price Elasticity of Hard Drugs: The Case of Opium in the Dutch East Indies, 1923–1938." *Journal of Political Economy* 103, no. 2 (1995): 261–79.

Renborg, Bertil. *International Drug Control: A Study of International Administration by and through the League of Nations.* Washington, DC: Carnegie Endowment for International Peace, 1947.

Riens, Thomas D. "Reform, Nationalism, and Internationalism: The Opium Suppression Movement in China and the Anglo-American Influence, 1900–1908." *Modern Asian Studies* 25, no. 1 (1991): 101–42.

Spence, Jonathan. "Opium Smoking in Ch'ing China." In Frederic Wakeman and Carolyn Grant, eds., *Conflict and Control in Late Imperial China,* pp. 143–73. Berkeley: University of California Press, 1975.

Taylor, Arnold H. *American Diplomacy and the Narcotics Traffic, 1900–1939.* Durham, NC: Duke University Press, 1969.

Traver, Harold. "Opium to Heroin: Restrictive Opium Legislation and the Rise of Heroin Consumption in Hong Kong." *Journal of Policy History* 4, no. 3 (1992): 307–24.

Trocki, Carl. *Opium and Empire: Chinese Society in Colonial Singapore, 1800–1910.* Ithaca, NY: Cornell University Press, 1990.

———. *Opium, Empire, and the Global Political Economy: A Study of the Asian Opium Trade, 1750–1950.* London: Routledge, 1999.

Wakeman, Frederic. *Policing Shanghai, 1927–1937.* Berkeley: University of California Press, 1995.

Walker, William. *Opium and Foreign Policy: The Anglo-American Search for Order in Asia, 1912–1954.* Chapel Hill: University of North Carolina Press, 1991.

———, ed. *Drugs in the Western Hemisphere: An Odyssey of Cultures in Conflict.* Wilmington, DE: Scholarly Resources, 1996.

Westermeyer, Joseph. *Poppies, Pipes, and People: Opium and Its Use in Laos.* Berkeley: University of California Press, 1982.

Willoughby, W. W. *Opium as an International Problem: The Geneva Conferences.* Baltimore, MD: Johns Hopkins University Press, 1925.

Zhou Yongming. *Anti-Drug Crusades in Twentieth-Century China: Nationalism, History, and State Building.* Lanham, MD: Rowman and Littlefield, 1999.